Children and Social Competence

Children and Social Competence:
Arenas of Action

Edited by

Ian Hutchby and Jo Moran-Ellis

Foreword by

Allison James

 The Falmer Press

(A member of the Taylor & Francis Group)
London • Washington, D.C.

UK   The Falmer Press, 1 Gunpowder Square, London, EC4A 3DE
USA   The Falmer Press, Taylor & Francis Inc., 1900 Frost Road, Suite 101, Bristol, PA 19007

First published in 1998

A catalogue record for this book is available from the British Library

Library of Congress Cataloging-in-Publication Data are available on request

ISBN 0 7507 0650 3 cased
ISBN 0 7507 0651 1 paper

Jacket design by Caroline Archer

Typeset in 10/12 pt Times by
Graphicraft Typesetters Ltd., Hong Kong

Printed in Great Britain by Biddles Ltd., Guildford and King's Lynn on paper which has a specified pH value on final paper manufacture of not less than 7.5 and is therefore 'acid free'.

Every effort has been made to contact copyright holders for their permission to reprint material in this book. The publishers would be grateful to hear from any copyright holder who is not here acknowledged and will undertake to rectify any errors or omissions in future editions of this book.

Contents

Contents

Foreword

Allison James

That a book which raises questions about children's social competence and their arenas of action should be written at the end of the twentieth century gives pause for reflection on the tremendous changes which have occurred not only in children's everyday lives worldwide, but also in attitudes towards childhood itself. Why is the question of children's competence a pressing issue of our time? What has prompted this concern? Whose concern is it? Not just rhetorical devices, these questions are, I think, very pertinent to the topic: they force us to confront the fact that children's social experiences and everyday lives are not only shaped by their engagement with childhood as a social institution but that children's own actions can work to shape the changing face of childhood itself.

By way of illustrating the changes which have occurred with respect to children's status in society, we can look to Britain at the beginning of the twentieth century. Perhaps for the first time, all children, and not just those of the upper and middle classes, were at last united under the umbrella institution of 'childhood'. Child protection legislation, which had been drafted towards the end of the nineteenth century, had begun to filter into both the home and the workplace to touch the lives of all children by sharpening up the distinctions between adults' and children's activities which are the mark of childhood (Archard, 1993). This could be seen in the introduction of universal compulsory schooling, the exclusion of children from full-time work and placing of the duty of care and responsibility for children's well-being firmly in the hands of adults in their roles as parents, teachers or guardians. Justifications for this divide, argued with increasing certainty and vehemence, charted the progress of the century and drew upon older and more enduring images and mythologies of the child: they recalled the innocence espoused by Rousseau and later the Romantics; they pointed to the child's need for correction, training and restraint which had been the hallmark of seventeenth century Puritan attitudes; and they drew strength from the scientific framing of the process of children's maturation offered by the rapidly expanding discipline of developmental psychology. It seemed that we were becoming increasingly sure of what children needed, precisely because they were children.

Taking stock at the end of the twentieth century, however, these certitudes seem less so. The spotlight has fallen upon the child to illuminate an increasing diversity, rather than uniformity, in children's experiences, rendering any notion of 'childhood' as a singular phenomenon now obsolete. The sources of this doubting are manifold. Rapid changes in family form and composition within the United States and Western Europe have called into question the extent to which familial socialization plays a determining role in children's social maturation (Brannen and O'Brien, 1996); the apparent increase in child sexual abuse has ruptured notions of the 'family' as a safe haven for children and, in turn, raised questions about children's own sexuality and rights to sexual knowledge (Kitzinger, 1990; Jenks, 1994). The exposition of child labour worldwide and atrocities towards children have not only led to calls for increasingly tighter controls on children's activities and the assertion of children's rights vis-à-vis those of adults but, at the same time, drawn attention to the work that children can do and the wider contributions they make as citizens (Boyden, 1997). Brutalities perpetrated against children have revealed their powerlessness in relationships with adults, while the public exposure of child bullies and child murderers have demonstrated children's power over one another and thrown into disarray any notions of an all-embracing childish innocence (James and Jenks, 1996). That children can act as child soldiers and as carers for their parents we know for sure (Stephens, 1995). This makes any claims to a naturalized incompetence increasingly difficult to sustain and, in Britain, the Children Act (1989) has put this issue firmly on the statute book (Alderson, 1993). To ask questions about children's participation in society, as the chapters in this volume seek to do, is therefore not only necessary but, it would seem, most timely indeed.

This questioning is, however, neither singular in its purpose nor in its framing. Nor does it simply lie within the domain of 'public interest', brought to our attention and for comment through the media and changes in policy legislation. Within what has come to be called the new social studies of childhood researchers are embracing these questions from a variety of different approaches and from within a number of disciplinary traditions. Sociologists, anthropologists, historians, social geographers, demographers and socio-legal experts have joined together to ask about the constitution of childhood in society (James, Jenks and Prout, 1997). These researchers explore, from different perspectives, both the ways in which childhood as a social institution constructs spheres of action for children and how children themselves engage with, and participate in, that process. And central to each of these perspectives are differing views both of children's abilities to participate in the social world and the extent to which the social institution of childhood draws on and shapes their social competence. However, these differences do not stem simply, if at all, from the manifestation of different disciplinary research traditions but reflect, rather more complexly, a different positioning of the child in relation to the adult world. And it is these varied points of departure which, in turn, permit different kinds of question to be asked.

For those researchers for whom exploring children's roles as social actors constitutes a central concern, children's competence is taken-for-granted. The question they pose, instead, is how that competence is acknowledged and expressed or disguised and controlled in and through children's everyday relationships. For some, it is only by looking inside the social worlds of children that their competence can be discovered and explicated. In this view, the institution of childhood separates children off from adults in such a way as to disguise their competencies. These are to be revealed by exploring the ways in which children's own social relationships construct a child's world, distinctive and unique in its form and content (Hardman, 1973). For others, by contrast, their interest is in championing children as social actors in an adult world, where they can be revealed to be demonstrating a shared human competence, rather than a child-specific set of abilities which are of and about the concerns of children. In such research children take on the characteristics of a minority group vis-à-vis the adult population (Mayall, 1995).

The other main focus for research within the new social studies of childhood is that which, rather than exploring children's agency, concentrates much more on questions of how childhood is structured for and by children. Within this kind of research again two main approaches can be identified. The first looks at the ways in which a social space for childhood is marked out in different societies and points to the particular competencies, or their lack, which are signalled for the occupants of that space. Through thus denying that the universality of the 'child' can be plotted through a naturalized set of competencies, such approaches are diametrically opposed to the model of growth and maturation offered from within developmental psychology (Stainton-Rogers and Stainton-Rogers, 1992). Instead, their intention is to explore the ways in which the life course is differentially classified across time and space and to demonstrate the extensive range within which notions of children's social competence can be situated. From this view there is no constancy in what constitutes the 'child'. A second strand, though also concerned with the social space of childhood, argues in contrast for the universality of the child. It begins, however, from the assumption that the ways in which childhood is structured in any society are expressive of a particular view of children's competence and ability. It is in this sense that the institution of childhood is a truly social phenomenon (Qvortrup et al., 1994).

These four models are, of course, ideal types and there is, in practice, a great deal of overlap between them. As this volume clearly demonstrates, researchers may at different times and for different purposes choose to thread their way between these approaches and may not pin their colours to any particular mast. However, what is I think significant about the models, as ideal types, is the questions they raise about the twin themes that are central to this volume: social competence and arenas of action. The models underline, first, the need for reflexivity on the part of researchers concerning their assumptions about 'what children are', for these may implicitly shape the process and progress of research. Second, they raise an awareness of the variety of ways in which 'the child' has been and can be constituted in society. In the chapters presented in this volume it is the focus on social competence which brings both these issues immediately to the fore. Thus, variously, the chapters ask questions about the social relations children have with adults and point to the tensions that can arise, tensions often centred on what children can or cannot do; they explore children's relationships with one another, revealing a sophistication of social interaction not widely remarked, let alone accounted for; they demonstrate children's facility with the material and technological world and raise awkward questions as to why this competence has long been unacknowledged; they tackle head-on the assumed sequential progression which takes a child from incompetence to competence as he/she moves towards adulthood.

But more than this, the chapters collectively signal the massive strides which have been made in our understanding of children and childhood and the increasing sophistication with which researchers are addressing children as research subjects. The interdisciplinary nature of the new social studies of childhood, so clearly represented in this volume, signals that, although we may no longer be able to cling with any certainty to a fixed idea about what childhood is, we may move into the next millennium confident that, at the very least, we have the reflexive awareness of how best to proceed.

References

ALDERSON, P. (1993) *Children's Consent to Surgery*, Buckingham: Open University Press.

ARCHARD, R. (1993) *Children: Rights and Childhood*, London: Routledge.

BOYDEN, J. (1997) Postscript to 'Childhood and the policy makers: A comparative perspective on the globalisation of childhood', in JAMES, A. and PROUT, A. (eds) *Constructing and Reconstructing Childhood*, Second Edition, London: Falmer Press.

BRANNEN, J. and O'BRIEN, M. (1996) *Children in Families: Research and Policy*, London: Falmer Press.

HARDMAN, C. (1973) 'Can there be an anthropology of children?', *Journal of the Anthropology Society of Oxford*, **4**, pp. 85–99.

JAMES, A. and JENKS, C. (1996) 'Public perceptions of childhood criminality', *British Journal of Sociology*, **47**, pp. 315–31.

JAMES, A., JENKS, C. and PROUT, A. (1997) *Theorising Childhood*, Cambridge: Polity Press.

JENKS, C. (1994) 'Child abuse in the postmodern context: An issue of social identity', *Childhood*, **2**, pp. 111–21.

KITZINGER, J. (1990) 'Who are you kidding? Children, power and the struggle against sexual abuse', in JAMES, A. and PROUT, A. (eds) *Constructing and Reconstructing Childhood*, London: Falmer Press.

MAYALL, B. (1995) 'Children as a minority group: Issues and prospects', paper presented at the Seminar on Childhood and Society, Institute of Education, London.

QVORTRUP, J., BARDY, M., SGRITTA, G. and WINTERSBERGER, H. (1994) *Childhood Matters*, Aldershot: Avebury.

STAINTON-ROGERS, R. and STAINTON-ROGERS, W. (1992) *Stories of Childhood: Shifting Agendas of Child Concern*, Hemel Hempstead: Harvester Wheatsheaf.

STEPHENS, S. (1995) *Children and the Politics of Culture*, Princeton, NJ: Princeton University Press.

Acknowledgments

This volume has its starting point in a conference on 'Children and Social Competence' which we organized at the University of Surrey in July 1995. Most of the chapters contained herein were originally presented as contributions to that conference; some additional chapters were commissioned subsequently. The editors would like to thank all those who took part in the conference, and all at the University of Surrey who helped in its administration, organization and running. We are especially grateful to Linda Bates for her tireless work in coordinating the event.

With special thanks to Allison James for framing the volume in such an elegant manner, and to Anna Clarkson at Falmer Press for her enthusiasm and patience.

Ian Hutchby
Jo Moran-Ellis

Introduction

Ian Hutchby and Jo Moran-Ellis

Challenges to the traditional socialization and developmental models of childhood are currently being made from within a variety of disciplines. Increasingly, children are being seen as competent social agents in their own right, rather than as apprentice versions of adults. These challenges pose critical questions for how we understand the social worlds of children and their relationships with each other, as well as with adults. This volume explores those questions from a variety of theoretical and methodological standpoints, through the use of a wide range of empirical data.

Within this expanding field, the present volume is distinctive on both methodological and thematic dimensions. In terms of methodology, the chapters contained in the book range across disciplinary boundaries and demonstrate the fruitfulness of varying methodologies. Contributions from well-established perspectives in sociology and anthropology are included alongside chapters using newer methodologies such as discourse analysis and conversation analysis. This interdisciplinary approach enables us to provide a multifaceted account of the social competencies of children, and is cemented in the opening chapter, in which we discuss the disciplinary as well as historical matrix in which the book is situated, and stress how approaches such as sociology, anthropology, discourse analysis and conversation analysis have addressed issues of childhood in the past and how such approaches, particularly the latter two, inform us about the specific topic areas covered in the book.

On the thematic level, the emphasis of the chapters is on thinking through the social competence of children in practical, empirical terms, by focusing on the arenas of social action in which children routinely engage with each other and with adults. Contributors address children's social competence as an achievement, but one which is bounded by structural features of the milieux in which children live their lives. These include the priorities of politics and policy-making which structure the institutionalized worlds of childhood, and the nature of children's relationships with adults, both within and outside the family. However, one upshot of those discussions is that the notion of social competence is not treated unproblematically. Rather, the overall effect of the chapters is to interrogate that notion itself. Authors ask, not only to what degree can children be viewed as socially competent within their own social worlds, but also, to what extent are children allowed to be competent, and indeed forced into special kinds of competence, through their relations with adults?

The chapters in Part I of the book focus on children in various forms of family order, and show how children can use the resources afforded by family frameworks as opportunities to develop and display increasingly sophisticated social competencies. Whether in single parent families (Alanen), in situations of parental separation (Barrett), or even as 'runaways' detaching themselves from the family framework (Baker), children respond competently to the situation, and use that situation to increase their relevant social competencies.

Leena Alanen focuses on the lives of children in one parent families in four Scandinavian countries. Asserting that she takes for granted the fact that children are socially competent, what she is interested in is exploring the range of possibilities for competent participation in social life that are afforded by this particular form of family order. But she recognizes that such participation is not just enabled but also constrained by various constructions of childhood, in which children themselves as well as their parents play a key role.

Yet although Alanen does not set out to focus directly on children's competence but on the structuring practices surrounding children's social participation, a particular conception of social competence emerges from her discussion. One of the ways that children are categorized in her study is in terms of how far they or their mothers (all the parents in the study are single mothers) control and organize the child's everyday life. This conception centres around material and cultural resources which provide the means by which children can be socially competent, and the ways in which social competence as a process can contribute to the very availability and creation of those resources.

Picking up on this aspect of competence as the management of material and cultural resources in everyday life, Rachel Baker focuses on children who have more or less purposely placed themselves *outside* family structures. Her Nepalese ethnography found that children as young as ten years detach themselves from their families and take up an existence as 'street children', but that this is within the context of their families already viewing them as having the potential, even the responsibility, to be competent contributors to the family economy. On the street, however, the children differ in their ability to be socially competent street children, and are also concerned to negotiate competent identities between various settings: home, street and social aid projects.

In another setting where children are dislocated from their families, Helen Barrett shows, through her reanalysis of archival material of children's reactions to leaving their primary caregiver, that children in fact display a range of behaviours that allow them to manage their experiences and which can be seen to constitute displays of social competence even at very young ages. Barrett uses this reanalysis to take issue with the 'protest-despair-detachment' model of the stages in children's reactions to parental separation that has acquired the status of a truism in psychology textbooks. Barrett remodels the empirical evidence on which the original research was based to show that many children in fact deployed a battery of social competencies in their efforts to manage the situation. In particular, instead of an initial reaction of protest followed rapidly by increasing withdrawal from social contact, children are seen to work hard to contain their anxieties, often by maintaining an exaggerated level of sociability for some time.

Part II of the book focuses on an area which has so far been little researched within the sociology of childhood, though as we show in Chapter 1, there is a long tradition of research in interactional sociolinguistics: the forms of competence displayed by children in discourse and interaction.

Robert Sanders and Kurt Freeman focus on what they call 'neo-rhetorical participation' in peer interactions between children of 6 to 7 years. Neo-rhetorical participation in interaction involves the fashioning of turns so as to influence the course of the current interaction, regarding what it includes and/or how it concludes, according to the child's goal(s). Using discourse analysis based on video-recordings of children at play in a cooperative task environment, they describe the skills and strategies deployed by young children in this form of participation.

Sanders and Freeman argue that children's neo-rhetorical participation in interaction involves something more than has been considered in much of the previous work on children's communicative competence. It is not simply a matter of acquiring specific interaction techniques such as how to manage conflict (Sheldon, 1990), make mitigated requests (DeHart, 1996), and so on. Sanders and Freeman's interest is in the children's adaptation or innovation in the local moment of their expressive resources, in speech and behaviour alike, to be not only responsive to their playmate, but anticipatory of what difference it would make to the future course of the interaction how they fashioned their speech and behaviour in the current turn. This brings to the fore what children actively do in peer interactions to exert influence over what happens between them.

In a similar methodological vein, Hilary Gardner's chapter uses conversation analysis (Hutchby and Wooffitt, 1998) to look at interaction between speech-impaired children and their therapists in the speech therapy clinic. Arguing that social competence has as great a role to play in determining success in therapy as does linguistic ability, Gardner shows in intricate detail how 4-year-old children use interactional skills already displayed in mundane talk to tackle the more stylised talk of speech therapy. In her data, one of the goals of therapists is that children should make phonetic self-repairs of speech-sound errors following understanding checks. Gardner finds that this phonetic goal of the therapist is not shared by the children. She explores reasons for this, and for the occurrence of alternative strategies that put the onus on the adult to provide further information necessary for the appropriate completion of a repair. Gardner's analysis begins to show the value of a methodology involving close attention to the details of verbal (and non-verbal) interaction in revealing the levels of competence displayed by children in the utterance-by-utterance unfolding of conversations.

Joanna Thornborrow places the emphasis squarely on how children's participation in discourse and interaction can be severely constrained by adults in the scene. She does this by looking at a specific context: children's participation in the discourse of television programmes expressly designed for, and often directly involving, children. Although as Thornborrow discusses, there is a body of work within media studies which addresses the relationship between children and television, none of this work deals specifically with the language of children's television as a form of 'public' discourse, produced within a broadcast context for a viewing audience; while work in the field of language and the media has been mainly concerned with analysing broadcast talk that is produced by adults for an adult audience (Scannell, 1991; Thornborrow, 1997). Thornborrow's analysis here addresses questions concerning the nature of children's participation in the discourse of children's television compared with other forms of talk. Looking first at the various ways in which adult presenters provide highly circumscribed spaces for child participants, Thornborrow then looks at a programme in which children themselves are the presenters. In either case, analysis of the talk that is produced raises the issue of how far children have the possibility to be competent participants in the production of mediated discourse.

Part III of the book takes as its theme what we describe as 'institutional knowledge'. This refers to two things. First, to the ways in which the adult-defined discourses of social institutions may function to constrain and construct children in institutional terms; and second, to the types of alternative and possibly oppositional knowledge deployed by children in articulating the cultural spaces of social institutions with their own, more or less autonomous spaces for action.

Susan Danby and Carolyn Baker explore a particular issue here: the ways in which teachers and children in a kindergarten have different ways of dealing with the emergence of conflict between children in play situations. Using a conversation analytic methodology they show how the teacher's interventions are underpinned by a quite different rationale from that informing behaviour in the children's own world. Drawing on professional notions of conflict as a 'bad thing', the teacher's actions come in response to a crying child, and involve identifying the 'cause' of the crying (i.e., another child) and requiring the perpetrator to comfort the one who is 'sad'. Once this has been accomplished, the teacher sees the conflict episode as resolved and leaves the scene. What Danby and Baker show, however, is the quite different moral structure that underpins the children's world, which is revealed once the teacher is out of the picture. Here, children mobilize their own ways of dealing with the crying child, ways which reestablish their own cultural order in contrast to that imposed by the adult. Significant gender differences emerge here, with boys' groups departing much more radically from the adult-defined discourse of conciliation than girls' groups.

Pia Christensen adopts ethnographic techniques to examine similar kinds of issues in the setting of the family home. Her subject is the family practices surrounding knowledge about, and administration of, medicines for children. Drawing on a range of interviews with Danish families about pharmaceutical use, Christensen explores the practices through which adults' and children's competencies are constructed as similar or different in this arena. Making some intriguing comments about the fluidity of the cultural categories of 'child' and 'adult' and their normative relation with 'incompetence' and 'competence', Christensen shows how the different knowledges about pharmaceutical use that can be mobilized by children and adults represent sites for the situated negotiation of competence.

4

In another sense of 'institutional' knowledge, Gerald de Montigny explores the responses of children in the care of a Children's Aid Society to what Habermas (1987) has called the 'colonization of the lifeworld by the system'. His focus is on tracking the practical devices used by children to make sense of and negotiate the intersections of their everyday lived worlds with the powers and authorities of child welfare systems. While children in care are often treated as the objects of child welfare processes, through involuntary apprehension from their families of origin, and as subjected to a variety of professional treatments and interventions, only rarely are they regarded or treated as active subjects.

De Montigny examines audio and video tapes of interviews and group sessions conducted by social workers with children in care, between the ages of 6 to 16, that addressed the processes of coming into and being in care. The analysis identifies the practical manoeuvres children employed to recover and to construct a working sensibility from such situations. One of his primary concerns is to explicate how the occasion was socially accomplished as such, marked as it is by differential repertoires of power: primary, professional, generational and organizational. The chapter shows how children appropriate and play with the structures of professionally organized occasions such that these work not only for social work purposes, but for the children themselves.

In the final chapter, David Silverman, Carolyn Baker and Jayne Keogh raise a similar kind of issue about the participation of children and adolescents in institutionalized interactions. Using a conversation analytic perspective they compare interactions recorded in parent–teacher meetings and hospital clinics run for adolescents. Their analysis addresses a social problem well known to both professionals and parents: the non-response of adolescents when told what to do or asked questions by adults. However, the authors are not concerned so much with *explaining* this phenomenon as with locating its interactional achievement. In order to do this, they engage in a detailed analysis of the design of individual utterances by teachers and doctors, and reveal a systematic ambivalence in terms of who might be heard as the 'proper' recipient of such utterances: the child or their co-present parents?

Silverman et al.'s analysis suggests that children in these settings can use silence or non-response (or at least no verbal response) as a competent strategy for dealing with the somewhat loaded ambivalence built into both the design of teachers' questions and that of parents' responses. They conclude that such non-response is a way of avoiding implication in the collaboratively accomplished moral universe of the adults. Thus, we see that while institutional discourses can be used by adults to frame and constrain the social competencies of children, children in turn may use aspects of those institutional discourses to 'protect' their status as competent actors outside the frameworks or parameters of adult discourse.

We believe that, collectively, these chapters make a substantial contribution to the consolidation of what Alan Prout and Allison James described in 1990 as 'an emergent paradigm' in the social study of childhood (Prout and James, 1990). In that chapter, Prout and James outlined the emergence of what in Chapter 1 of this volume we label the 'competence paradigm' in broadly theoretical terms, placing special emphasis on its radical break with accepted wisdoms in developmental psychology and socialization theory, and on its key claim that 'childhood' is not a natural phenomenon or stage of life but a historically and culturally variable social construction. Much of the subsequent work in this emergent paradigm has similarly had what Mayall (1994, p. 2) describes as an 'essentially political' purpose. The aim has been to establish, theoretically and, to a lesser extent, empirically, the status of children as competent social agents and of childhood as a constructed arena of action both enabling and constraining the exercise of that agency.

As Leena Alanen begins by asserting in Chapter 2, it is now possible for researchers to 'take for granted that children are competent social actors'. What remains to be done is to establish in close empirical detail the properties of children's social competence and the relations between competence and the arenas of social action in which it is situated. The chapters in this book are all primarily empirical studies which begin from a standpoint within the competence paradigm and use broadly ethnographic and conversation analytic techniques to bring back news of the real-world, real-life dimensions of children's social competence.

References

DeHART, G.B. (1996) 'Gender and mitigation in 4-year-olds' pretend play talk with siblings', *Research on Language and Social Interaction*, **29**, pp. 81–96.

HABERMAS, J. (1987) *The Theory of Communicative Action: Lifeworld and System*, Boston, MA: Beacon Press.

HUTCHBY, I. and WOOFFITT, R. (1998) *Conversation Analysis: Principles, Practices and Applications*, Cambridge: Polity Press.

MAYALL, B. (1994) 'Introduction', in MAYALL, B. (ed.) *Children's Childhoods: Observed and Experienced*, London: Falmer Press.

PROUT, A. and JAMES, A. (1990) 'A new paradigm for the sociology of childhood? Provenance, promise and problems', in JAMES, A. and PROUT, A. (eds) *Constructing and Reconstructing Childhood*, London: Falmer Press.

SCANNELL, P. (1991) *Broadcast Talk*, London: Sage.

SHELDON, A. (1990) 'Pickle fights: Gendered talk in preschool disputes', *Discourse Processes*, **13**, pp. 5–31.

THORNBORROW, J. (1997) Special Edition: Broadcast Talk, *Text*, **17**.

Chapter 1

Situating Children's Social Competence

Ian Hutchby and Jo Moran-Ellis

In the summer of 1996, when this volume was in preparation, one of the biggest news stories in the UK was the crisis in the British beef industry caused by bovine spongiform encephalopathy (BSE). During this crisis, European nations banned the importation of British beef and associated products. The British government struggled to get the ban lifted, but for a long time its only success came in the form of small concessions. The first of these related to one of the 'associated products': the lifting of the ban on importation of bulls' semen. Hearing this story reported on the morning news, one of the authors (IH) and his partner, struck by its bizarrerie, treated it as the occasion for an exchange of jokes about possible reasons for importing bulls' semen. When their 8-year-old child came in wondering what the laughter was about, their response was to stop laughing, say that nothing was going on, and claim that she was too young to understand what they had been talking about. Although the child demanded, increasingly angrily, that the adults 'just tell her' what the joke was, it was some time before her mother gave her a somewhat diluted description of the cause of the laughter: 'It was just a story on the news.' 'What about?' 'About bulls' semen being sent to other countries.' After one or two further aggrieved questions as to why that should be amusing, the child went back to her previous activities.

This seemingly trivial story illustrates some very significant points about the relations between children and adults in contemporary Western culture. Primarily, it indexes the extent to which, and the ease with which, adults construct children as essentially non-competent, or at least, as competent only in specific ways and within certain parameters. In our story, the adults elected to treat the child as not in possession of the competence to understand their joke. More significantly, they situated the child within a certain definition of 'childhood', particularly in relation to the subject matter of the joke with its sexual, or at least reproductive, connotations. The lack of competence accorded the child in that moment was not so much a cognitive competence — the issue was not whether the child was able to understand the humour, even if it might have to be explained to her. Rather, the child was constructed as non-competent in the *normative* light of a particular conception of childhood as a time of 'innocence': in this case, a conception evidently underpinning a view that children of 8 should not be exposed to jokes which implicate such matters as sex and reproduction.

However, the story also illustrates how the child herself is concerned to *contest* her construction as an innocent, non-competent party to this overheard exchange. There are good reasons why she might want to do this. Consider that overheard laughter can represent something intrinsically interesting, and also potentially threatening. We are apt to wonder why people are laughing, and depending on the context, we may be under the impression that we ourselves are the butt of some joke. There is thus a strong tendency for humans to try to discover the cause of overheard laughter. Yet in our story, having exercised that curiosity the child in response is treated 'like a child' and told that it is beyond her understanding. Thus, her competence is denied in two ways: first in regard to her ability to find out the cause of some overheard laughter; and second in regard to her ability to understand that laughter. The significant thing is, of course, that this child actively refuses to be so treated and demands to be accorded competence.

In microcosm, we find here the twin dynamics that are at the heart of what has come to be called the new social studies of childhood. On the one hand, the dynamic of children's social competence: children are neither as innocent nor as non-competent as common-sense ideologies of childhood often make them out to be, but active agents who possess and can assert complex social competencies in their own right. On the other hand, the dynamic of social enablement and constraint: children's competencies are situated within concrete social contexts in which there may be differently structured and variably enforced efforts to constrain, as well as enable, the competencies that children are allowed or encouraged to manifest.

Over recent years, what can be described as a 'competence paradigm' in the sociology of childhood has emerged in a number of key publications (James and Prout, 1990a; Waksler, 1991; Mayall, 1994a; Qvortrup et al., 1994). The main thrust of this research is to take issue with the perspective on children and childhood propounded by developmental psychology, and by socialization theory in mainstream sociology, in which children are seen as the objects of overarching social processes by which they move from being non-adults to being adults. Without denying that human beings develop over time and in describable ways, nor that appropriate social behaviours are learned and not natural, the competence paradigm seeks to take children seriously as social agents in their own right; to examine how social constructions of 'childhood' not only structure their lives but also are structured by the activities of children themselves; and to explicate the social competencies which children manifest in the course of their everyday lives *as* children, with other children and with adults, in peer groups and in families, as well as the manifold other arenas of social action.

As Allison James points out in her 'Foreword' to this volume, there are many different ways in which the dynamics of children's social competence have been subject to analysis in this research. Drawing from disciplines as diverse as sociology, sociolinguistics, policy studies, law, anthropology and social geography, researchers have sought to redraw our ways of conceptualizing the 'child' and the parameters of 'childhood'. Among the central questions that are addressed in this research are the extent to which children can be said to possess social competencies that are somehow unique and specific to the peer cultures of childhood; or alternatively, whether the social competence manifested by children is better seen as essentially the same, or of the same order, as that possessed by adults. In either case, explicating the nature and uses of those competencies reveals to us a picture of childhood as a dynamic arena of social activity involving struggles for power, contested meanings and negotiated relationships, rather than the linear picture of development and maturation made popular by traditional sociology and developmental psychology.

The latter picture, the genesis of which can be traced back to the early years of the twentieth century, has infiltrated common-sense in numerous ways in contemporary capitalist societies. Although the family is by no means any longer a straightforward, unitary phenomenon, the idea that children 'belong' in family frameworks is still an immensely powerful and pervasive one. Underlying this belief is the notion that children are socialized in important ways by the family, as well as by the education system and other ideological systems often seen as more harmful, such as the mass media. This view was made famous by Talcott Parsons in one of the seminal texts of functionalist sociology, *The Social System* (1951). Parsons' writings drew rather uncritically on what were by then well-established tenets of developmental psychology (see Prout and James, 1990). In a version of what Giddens (1976) describes as the 'double hermeneutic' — the process by which the accounts of social theorists both draw on and subsequently influence common-sense ideas in everyday life — these theories about socialization, like Piaget's earlier theories about developmental stages in childhood (1926), have become part of ordinary thinking about the role of the family in children's social development.

As Thorne (1993) remarks:

> 'socialisation' and 'development' [are] perspectives that many parents, teachers, and other adults *bring* to their interactions with children. As mothers and teachers of young children, women, in particular, are charged with the work of 'developing the child'. But children don't necessarily see themselves 'being socialised' or 'developing', and their interactions with one another, and with adults, extend far beyond these models. (p. 13)

At the same time, 'asking how children are socialised into adult ways, or how their experiences fit into linear stages of individual development, deflects attention from their present, lived, and collective experiences' (*ibid.*).

It is precisely this attention to the present, lived and collective experiences of children that the competence paradigm seeks to prioritize. Prout and James (1990, pp. 8–9) listed a number of key features of this paradigm. Primary among them were: (a) that 'children's social relationships and cultures are worthy of study in their own right, independent of the perspective and concerns of adults'; (b) that childhood itself is a social construction, neither a natural nor a universal feature of human groups; (c) that childhood is therefore historically and cross-culturally variable and can 'never be entirely divorced from other variables such as class, gender or ethnicity'; (d) that 'children are and must be seen as active in the construction and determination of their own social lives, the lives of those around them and of the societies in which they live'; (e) that qualitative methods represent the most appropriate means for conducting research on children and childhood.

To this list, we would add the following points. First, that empirical research should be primary: the idea that children are competent social agents requires that researchers *situate* the study of those competencies in the empirical circumstances of children's real, ordinary, everyday lives. Second, that those empirical circumstances, or 'arenas of action', can be both enabling and constraining in terms of children's capacity to display social competencies. Third, that in order to understand adequately the properties of children's social competence in the arenas in which it is situated, it is necessary to attempt to view the relevant social action 'from within', that is, as far as possible, to reveal the procedures by which the participants themselves organize and make sense of their activities in a given social context.

Each of these points throws up particular problematic issues for research. For instance, what methodologies are most appropriate for the aim to reveal the social organization of children's worlds 'from within'? Secondly, what are the most appropriate ways of conceptualizing 'competence' or 'social competence' in such research? And third, what are the best means by which to think through the relationship between children's social competence and the arenas of action in which social agency is situated? In this chapter, our aim is to explore each of these issues in turn, and suggest some of the ways in which the chapters that follow present a particular set of responses to them.

Methodologies of Competence

Among the questions we are faced with in attempting to explicate children's social competencies empirically is that of how the researcher gains access to the child's perspective. This is not an issue which is confined to research on childhood. There is a long-standing tradition of interpretive or phenomenological methodology which has grappled with the problem of how the researcher can come to 'see' the world from the point of view of the researched. The foremost response in the sociology of childhood has been to adopt ethnographic approaches such as participant observation, interviews, and the analysis of children's documentary accounts of their lives (James and Prout, 1990a; Waksler, 1991; Thorne, 1993; Mayall, 1994a). James and Prout (1990b, p. 5) state that ethnography 'allows children a more direct voice in the production of sociological data than is usually possible through experimental or survey styles of research' (though see Qvortrup et al., 1994, for an attempt to give children a voice in survey research).

Nonetheless, some of the techniques of ethnographic research are highly problematic when employed with children. For instance, to what extent is it possible for an adult researcher to 'participate' in children's social worlds? Certainly, some inventive attempts have been made. Mandell (1991) advocates what she calls the 'least-adult' role in studying young children. Mandell outlines three types of observer role that may be adopted by ethnographers of childhood: the detached observer, a role which recognizes an absolute distinction between the social, intellectual and cultural worlds of children and adults; the marginal semi-participatory role, which does not go so far as to recognize an absolute distinction but asserts that the age-based power relation between children and adults can never be transcended; and the least-adult role which claims that 'all aspects of adult superiority except physical differences can be cast aside, allowing the researcher entree to the children's world as an active, fully participating member' (p. 39).

Mandell found adopting this role in her research to be extremely difficult, although she also found that indeed it appears to be possible for an adult researcher to be accepted by children as a participant on their own terms. The insights this method allows are exquisitely demonstrated in David Goode's phenomenologically oriented research into the experiential world of deaf-blind children (Goode, 1991). Goode describes how such children were seen as virtually feral by the medical staff who looked after them in the clinic where they lived, and were treated as being almost entirely incompetent. Yet by adopting a least-adult role with one child he was able to begin to 'see' the world from her perspective and to understand her apparently chaotic behaviours as highly competent strategies for managing the contingencies of that world. The least-adult role in this case involved particularly stringent demands: Goode refers to one 'thirty-six hour period during which I remained by [Christina's] side' (*ibid.*, p. 153). His aim throughout the research period was to use:

> a strategy of 'passive obedience' in which I physically allowed her to take the lead in structuring our interaction. This proved a most beneficial (though difficult to arrive at) stance. Once Chris knew that I was cooperative to this degree, she initiated a huge variety of activities and exchanges *in her terms*. (*ibid.*, p. 156, original emphasis)

This suggests that it is possible to gain important insights into the organization of children's social and experiential worlds by means of a particular version of participant observation. However, it should be borne in mind that the least-adult role is not to be seen as producing 'authentic' or 'true' accounts of children's worlds. The search for authenticity has been a feature that has characterized a great deal of ethnographic research, but as Silverman (1993) argues this search is misguided. All that ethnography, and social research in general, can accomplish is to explicate what people appear to be doing and how they appear to be doing it, while bearing in mind that the researcher is an active participant in the production of research itself, and that the research process is reflexively related to its own subject matter: the social process (see Hammersley and Atkinson, 1983).

This does not invalidate ethnography. As Prout and James (1990) ask, 'is it not possible for ethnography to make a claim to a weaker sense of authenticity in which previously unexplored or unreported aspects of childhood are made available and previously mute children empowered to speak?' (p. 27). In the present volume, while none of the authors go so far as to use the least-adult technique, ethnographic methods inform us of a wide variety of ways in which children's social competencies interrelate with the interactional, situational and social structural features of such settings as the family, the street, and the institutions in which some children are forced to live their lives (see Alanen, Baker, Christensen and de Montigny in this volume).

However, in their advocation of ethnography as the most suitable method for the new social studies of childhood, Prout and James (1990) explicitly contrast ethnography with survey and experimental research, as if these are the only alternatives. As many of the chapters in this volume demonstrate, other methodologies which focus closely on the organization of children's verbal and non-verbal interactions both among themselves and with adults can reveal a depth and range of interactional competence that has so far been little remarked in the sociology of childhood. Primary among these approaches is conversation analysis (Hutchby and Wooffitt, 1998), a sociological approach to the study of language use which views ordinary talk as a highly organized medium of social action. The main claim of conversation analysis is that we can gain access to the ways in which participants make sense of one another's actions, and so establish mutual and collaborative courses of social activity, by studying the construction of, and relationships between, utterances in 'talk-in-interaction' (Schegloff, 1982, 1990 and 1992).

There is a good deal of research in conversation analysis which is relevant to the question of how talk and other interactional activities represent resources through which children, as social participants or 'members' (Garfinkel and Sacks, 1970), can display their social competence, both in interaction among themselves and in dealing with adults in their lives. Probably the finest example of this can be found in Marjorie Goodwin's book on 'talk as social organisation' among children in a Black urban neighbourhood of Philadelphia (Goodwin, 1990).

Goodwin used the standard conversation analytic technique of tape-recording the talk of the children in a natural setting: that of play on the streets near their homes. The recordings are then transcribed and analysis is performed through listening to the tapes and reading the transcripts to discover structured and patterned ways in which social activities are accomplished in and through the talk (see Hutchby and Wooffitt, 1997). This is explicitly contrasted both to experimental methods in which subjects are selected and then required to engage in researcher-controlled (as opposed to naturally-occurring) activities (see Hopper, 1989), and to ethnographic interviewing which relies on the gleaning of information by the researcher from 'trusted' informants (Sacks, 1992, vol. 1, pp. 26–31).

As Goodwin (1990) shows, this method has a number of benefits. First, by focusing on talk, Goodwin is able to demonstrate in close empirical detail the ways in which the children in her study use language actively to create social organization among themselves. For example, in a highly complex analysis of a dispute format used among girls, called 'he-said-she-said', Goodwin reveals the competent construction of a whole set of situated, contingent social identities among the disputants and their audience(s):

> within the he-said-she-said confrontation, a field of negotiated action, complete with its own relevant history, is invoked through the structure of an . . . accusation . . . ; a single utterance creates a complex past history of events, providing operative identity relationships for participants. (p. 286)

The complexity of the work done within a single utterance in these cases is more than matched by the intricate social shaping of identities, relationships and participation structures created in the sequences of talk examined elsewhere in the study.

One thing Goodwin emphasizes is the contribution such an analysis makes to research on gender differences in talk. As she notes (see also Sheldon, 1996a), there is a strong tendency, following work such as that by Lakoff (1975) and Gilligan (1982), to view male and female patterns of speech as essentially different: male talk is thought to be characterized by competitiveness and hierarchy whereas female speech is characterized by cooperation and supportiveness. However, while Goodwin indeed reveals differences between the girls' and boys' groups in her study, the differences do not support such a dichotomy. For instance, girls may display just as much adeptness at competition and hierarchy as boys; indeed, close analysis of talk shows that 'cooperation and competition are not mutually exclusive agendas and often coexist within the same speech activities' (Goodwin, 1990, p. 284).[1]

A further relevance of this approach is that talk is thus viewed not as a means of obtaining information *about* social organization and competence, but as a medium of action in its own right: the focus is on 'how competent members use talk socially to act out the ordinary scenes of their everyday life' (*ibid.*, p. 286). This takes us beyond the limitations of standard ethnographic techniques in our attempt to view the social world of children 'from within'. As Goodwin argues:

> By making use of the techniques of conversation analysis and the documentation of the sequential organisation of indigenous events, we can avoid the pitfalls of 'interpretive anthropology', which tends to focus its attention on ethnographer/ informant dialogue rather than interaction *between participants*. This will enable us to move . . . towards an 'anthropology of experience' concentrating on how people themselves actually perform activities . . . (*ibid.*, p. 287)

In other words, by recording naturally occurring activities and attempting dispassionately to elucidate how the participants engage in those activities and how they make sense of one another's actions in the setting, we can locate another way, in many respects a more powerful way than the least-adult technique discussed above, of coming to 'see' the world from the perspective of the children.

This approach is not only informative about the social worlds of children in their peer groups. As Thornborrow (this volume) and Gardner (this volume) among others show, it is also possible to use such a technique to reveal aspects of how children and adults make sense of each other. For instance, Gardner examines how children with speech impairments verbally interact with their (adult) speech therapists. Through an analysis of the relationships between therapists' utterances, which attempt to get the child to self-correct their 'faulty' verbalizations, and the children's responses, she shows how children and therapists can be seen to be working with quite different conceptualizations of the purpose of the therapists' actions. Lying behind the therapists' talk is a clinical conception of the child's 'problem': they are attempting to get the child to speak 'properly' within an adult-defined institution of correct pronunciation.[2] But the children can be seen to be orienting to an alternative, and altogether more pervasive institution: the framework of everyday, mundane conversation. The point here is that without paying close attention to the organization of talk in the therapy session, within an overarching conception of children as competent actors, we may well end up colluding in an adult-centred, clinical definition of such children as incompetent language users, rather than reaching a child-centred understanding of their competent manipulation of conversational resources.[3]

But like Goodwin's (1990) study, Gardner's chapter also highlights the importance of combining ethnographic sensibilities, and ethnographic data, with the study of talk-in-interaction (see also Moerman, 1988). Without ethnographic information about the ostensible purposes behind speech therapy sessions, and more specifically, knowledge about the clinical models that therapists' practice relies upon, Gardner would not have been able to develop the kind of analysis she presents, since such information is not available simply from the raw data presented in the tape-recording (see Mehan, 1991).

In sum, then, we are suggesting that despite the problems attending the attempt to view children's social competence 'from within', various methods enable researchers to go a significantly long way towards accomplishing that task. Ethnography is useful in allowing children more of a voice in social scientific accounts of their lives, and can provide much needed ways of linking the micro-level details of agency to the macro-level constraints of social structure (see Alanen, this volume). Conversation analysis, on the other hand, provides a means by which we can see into the details of children's social worlds in situ, as they are being negotiated and constructed. Together with suitable ethnographic data, this represents the closest we can yet come to viewing how children themselves competently organize their lives and accomplish the activities involved in 'doing' childhood.

Conceptualizing Competence

A second issue that emerges with the competence paradigm is that of precisely how best to conceptualize competence in the social study of childhood. In the chapters that follow, the unifying notion is that the social competence of children is to be seen as a *practical achievement*: that is, it is not something which is accorded to children by adults, like a right, and can thus be redefined or removed. Rather, social competence is seen as something children work at possessing in their own right, the display of which is an active, agentic achievement. But it is an achievement that is bounded by structural features of the milieux in which children live their lives. These 'arenas of action' include the priorities of politics and policy-making themselves, which structure the institutionalized worlds of childhood; but they also include the nature of children's relationships with each other and with adults, both inside and outside families and peer groups. In thinking about children as competent social agents, therefore, it is necessary to link the social competencies integral to children's real-world activities with the structural and interactional frameworks of everyday life in modern societies: we need to 'account for children as both constrained by structure and as agents acting in and upon structure' (Prout and James, 1990, p. 28).

But before coming to this issue, a number of prior questions need to be addressed. For instance, how straightforwardly is it possible for us to conceptualize children as competent social agents? And what are the implications of such a shift in the mode of social scientific theorizing about children and childhood? Underlying a good deal of research in the new social studies of childhood, as well as recent legislation such as the 1989 Children Act in the UK, is what we might describe as an 'incremental' view that children should be accorded more social competence and allowed to possess greater reflexivity about their own circumstances and actions. Thus, ethnographic research has sought to give children more of an authorial presence in social scientific accounts of their lives (James, 1993); survey research has aimed to give children more autonomy by enabling them to act as respondents in their own right instead of relying on the accounts of parents and caregivers (Qvortrup, 1990); and legislation has provided new opportunities for children to bring complaints, initiate legal action in relation to where they live and over issues of parental access, and brought extensions to the requirements to seek children's consent to certain medical procedures (Alderson, 1993).

But while this incremental, and essentially moral, idea that children should be accorded more scope for exercising competence in social arenas also underpins many of the studies in the present volume, each of the contributors is intensely aware that, analytically speaking, 'social competence' is not a simple property of childhood which we can straightforwardly place at centre stage. Children's competence may be taken-for-granted for most researchers in the new social studies of childhood. But that is so only in the sense that the basic case no longer needs to be established. What children's competence actually consists of, the forms that it takes and the relational parameters within which it is enabled or constrained, still need to be ascertained on an empirical level. What research at that empirical level shows is that children's social competence is a constantly negotiated dynamic, a phenomenon which is stabilized, to greater or lesser degrees, in and through the interactions between human actors and the material and cultural resources which are available, and which can be recruited to play a part in the constitution of specific, situated activities. In short, empirical work needs not only to conceptualize children as competent but to establish the *ways* in which children display, can be required to display, and are policed in their displays of social competence.

All this only serves to emphasize the importance of *situating* children's social competence empirically in the arenas in which children act, and of bringing into play the material and cultural resources with which children are required to engage in order to operate within those arenas. This in turn leads to a particular perspective on social competence. One way of viewing competence is as the mastery of some task-domain: for instance, children may be 'competent' in dressing themselves at some stage in their life; or they may attain 'competence' at various levels of language use. But these kinds of usages imply a developmental perspective that sees children essentially as learning to be competent in adult terms. Other senses of 'competence' to be found in the English dictionary include efficiency, capacity, and legal power, and this sense of competence as adequate membership, especially in the legal sense, has as we have said underpinned a number of the claims about children's social status that have emerged from previous research. However, much of the discourse on children's social membership tends to adopt the stance of viewing childhood 'downward' from the perspective of adults: whether policy-makers, caregivers or social researchers (see Oakley, 1994).

By contrast, we would argue that competence has more to do with children's ability to manage their social surroundings, to engage in meaningful social action within given interactional contexts. Thus, we should ask how children competently manipulate material and cultural resources in order to engage in contextually appropriate behaviours: behaviours that are appropriate at the level of the participants themselves, whether other children, adults, or some combination of both. By material and cultural resources we mean here simply the resources for social action that are to hand in any given context. These may be such things as toys (Sanders and Freeman, this volume), participation rights in games (Sheldon, 1996b), imaginary roles or even imaginary physical spaces (Danby and Baker, this volume); access to adult-controlled resources such as money or parents' friendship networks (Alanen, this volume); the range of resources afforded by specialized settings such as television studios (Thornborrow, this volume), therapists' surgeries (Gardner, this volume), or parent-teacher interviews (Silverman et al., this volume); or on a wider level, the resources of language and interaction generally (Cook-Gumperz et al., 1986; Goodwin, 1990).

Observing children's manipulation of the array of these resources allows us to see two things. First, that social competence is not a unitary phenomenon; nor is its 'possession' something that can be traced in a linear, developmental fashion. Rather, the possession, or display, of competence is something that is established in situ, for this particular here-and-now occasion; and competence, its possession or the lack of it, is something that children themselves negotiate, argue about and struggle over in local occasions of activity, rather than being a function of the attainment of some specific stage of development.

The second thing we see is that social competence is therefore an intrinsically contextual matter. Competence cannot be separated from the structural contexts in which it is displayed or negotiated. Neither can social competence ultimately be understood simply as a property of individuals: whether it is with other children or with adults, in everyday situations of peer group play or in more formal, adult-framed settings, children's manipulation of culturally available resources to manage the trajectories of interaction, as well as the social impact of others' actions in the setting, represents the true grounding for claims about children's social competence.

Arenas of Action

Earlier we noted that studying children as competent social agents reveals a picture of childhood as a dynamic arena of social activity involving struggles for power, contested meanings and negotiated relationships, rather than the linear developmental picture of children progressing through various stages of apprenticeship on their way to adulthood. In the developmental paradigm, there is an implicit notion that full membership of society only comes with the attainment of 'adulthood'; children are 'immature, irrational, incompetent, asocial' while adults are 'mature, rational, competent, social' (MacKay, 1973, p. 28). For the competence paradigm, of course, this dichotomy does not exist. Children, considered *as* children rather than as apprentice adults, are just as mature, rational, competent and social as adults.

However, it is clear that there are radical differences between the rationalities and competencies of children and those of adults. Although the competence paradigm recognizes that 'children' and 'childhood' are not natural categories but historically and culturally variable social constructions, we have to take care to avoid the kind of relativism which would deny the essential difference of childhood as opposed to adulthood and thus risk failing to see the often very real consequences of the power relationship between adults and children (see Kitzinger, 1990; Alderson, 1994). At the same time, we need to avoid the alternative extreme of viewing 'childhood' as essentially 'other'. As Prout and James (1990) point out, this was the fate of one of the most pioneering early works in the competence paradigm, Iona and Peter Opie's *The Lore and Language of Schoolchildren* (1969):

> [D]espite the richness of the ethnographic archive which they assembled, [they] present a picture of childhood as a world apart. It is linked to the dominant adult culture only as a sort of anachronistic attic containing the abandoned lumber of previous times. (Prout and James, 1990, p. 28)

The alternative, Prout and James argue, is to 'elucidate the links between given (and largely adult defined) social institutions and the cultures which children construct for and between themselves' (*ibid.*).

One place in which these links may be explored is in the family, understood here not merely as a biologically-based relational unit, whether 'nuclear' or 'extended', but as a set of ideologies making up what Alanen (this volume) calls the family order. Recent years have seen rapid changes in family form and composition, in both Western and non-Western contexts. Correspondingly there has been a proliferation of different relational structures which define themselves as 'families'. Indeed these social developments have led to serious debates on what the defining characteristics of 'a family' might be. Whereas traditionally, it may have been unproblematic to say that the family was a biological as well as social unit consisting of married adults and their offspring (a definition which held for the extended as well as the nuclear family), now there are competing definitions which focus more on the child's involvement in stable patterns of relationships enabling a secure sense of self than on the centrality of legal marriage and biological procreation.

But however families are defined and whatever forms they take, for most children they still represent significant social units in which competencies of various kinds are learned and utilized. For instance, families are the initial, and one of the most temporally enduring, arenas in which children are subject to prohibitive rules.

As we began this chapter by illustrating, the parents or guardians of children take it as one of their main tasks to establish boundaries around the forms of knowledge and the types of activity to which children have access.

Yet families are also arenas in which children learn and can exercise a vast range of social competencies. Some of these are 'subversive': for instance, Sacks (1978) discusses why the punchline of a particular dirty joke, which involves allusions to oral sex, is amusing for 12-year-old girls. Primarily, he suggests, it is not because of the sexual content of the joke but precisely because the punchline, 'You told me not to talk with my mouth full', appropriates a parents' prohibitive rule and redefines it in a context which allows a parent's complaint to be effectively 'squelched'.[4] As Sacks (1992) says in a more extended treatment of this joke:

> one characteristic way that parents do . . . correcting is to juxtapose some rules: 'You applied rule X here, but rule X doesn't apply here, rule Y applies here'. . . . And the question then, in part, is learning which rules apply in any given scene; a problem which seemingly has to be handled empirically. In evolving ways of dealing with that problem, a special skill is to be learned which involves mobilising multiplicities of rules to be juxtaposed against each other in handling circumstances. So, as adults characteristically use a rule to correct a child's intendedly rule-governed activity, one thing that can and does occur is the child using a rule to counterpose a proposed violation. (Vol. 2, p. 492)

Intriguingly, then, the rules by which adults may attempt to constrain the activities of children, and through which it might be thought a form of power is exercised, themselves provide for their own appropriation in the light of children's own agendas, and represent ways in which children can 'turn the tables' and exercise a form of power over adults.

This appropriation of family rules can also be seen on those occasions where children play at families among themselves; here, the game, and the roles and rules that children associate with family life, can be the occasion for the working out of power relations between children. Walkerdine (1984) shows how a game of doctors and patients in which the Wendy House in a nursery represented the hospital was transformed by one participant into a game of families, in which the Wendy House represented 'home', such that the female participant could use her power in the 'mother' role to subordinate the boy who, as 'doctor', had been constructing a position of power over her. Sheldon (1996b) discusses a girls' game in which two participants are trying to close off access to their game for a third girl. The way they do this is by allowing the girl to play, but only in the role of a baby who has not been born yet, and who therefore cannot actually participate in the discourse of the game.

The structures and organization of family life, then, present children with manifold resources by which to develop and display social competencies of varying sorts. Children are not simply 'socialized' by their involvement in family rules and structures: the family order is an arena of action whose rules and structures themselves represent resources which children competently manipulate in dealing with others' agendas and working out their own.

Another significant arena of action is the peer group. Research in both ethnography and interactional sociolinguistics has shown that children generate and operate within relational structures and power dynamics in their own right, independently of the adult-centred arena of the family order.[5] In their classic study on children's peer cultures, the Opies (1969) showed that in such routine peer group contexts as the school playground, children could be observed defining, using, defending and reproducing specific cultural practices independently of adult intervention. Primary among these cultural practices were rhymes, jokes, games and other pieces of what could be called 'childlore', which circulated among children apparently without knowledge or assistance from adults. Moreover, new components of this childlore appeared to crop up in different geographical locations at more or less the same time, without any clear evidence of having been physically transmitted there. This prompted the suggestion that aspects of the peer culture of children are not only autonomous from the surrounding adult culture, but are somehow generically specific to childhood.

Other research has sought to determine the specific competencies displayed by children in deploying linguistic resources and managing interaction. Sociolinguistics in general has had a longstanding interest in how children acquire linguistic competence. Much of this work has been path-breaking in terms of situating children as competent manipulators of complex verbal and interactional resources (Garvey, 1984; Ochs, 1988; Ochs and Schieffelin, 1979 and 1983; Schieffelin, 1990). However, as Thornborrow (this volume) observes, most of it is still couched within a developmental framework, in which children are seen as passing through stages marked by factors such as the increasing sophistication of sentence structures and the growing ability to engage in more complex interactional sequences.

Goodwin (1990) is critical of the way that a great deal of the sociolinguistic research on children's communicative competence has restricted itself to studying children in interaction with adults: either in the nursery, the classroom or the family setting. Goodwin's work was among the first to concentrate specifically on children talking among themselves, in their own spaces (that is, outside the boundaries of home, school or other adult-controlled institutions) and without the presence of adults (except, of course, for the ethnographer herself); although slightly earlier Ervin-Tripp and Mitchell-Kernan (1977, p. 7) had observed, in a similar vein to Opie and Opie (1969), that 'many of the speech events in which children engage typically occur among children apart from adults, and they are explicitly taught, in many cases, by children'.

One of the upshots of research on talk in the peer group is to demonstrate the ways in which children's talk represents an oral culture specific to childhood. But the aim is not only to reveal such a childhood-specific oral culture, but more generally to show the ways in which children competently manipulate the resources of language and interaction in managing their participation in a wide range of social situations. Seen outside the adult ambit, children of even very young ages are shown to be highly competent social interactants, who use a wide array of language resources in complex negotiations over power, access, and participation in joint activities. In this view, being a competent language user is not so much a case of passing through developmental stages as of laminating skills and competencies gained through involvement in the manifold social situations of everyday life.

Related to this is a third important arena of action: what is described in Part III of this volume as 'institutional knowledge'. This refers both to the ways in which the adult-defined discourses of social institutions may function to constrain and construct children in institutional terms; and to the types of alternative and possibly oppositional knowledge deployed by children in articulating the cultural spaces of social institutions with their own, more or less autonomous spaces for action.

In her paper comparing children as actors in both home and school environments, Mayall (1994b) outlines two distinctive models of the child which emerge in these different settings. In the home, the child tends to be constituted relationally and is viewed as a 'subject' or 'person'. In school, by contrast, the child is constructed as a 'project' for adult work — the work of education — and children come to view themselves as the 'object' of this project. What this suggests is that in important respects, children within the physical and social bounds of the school are subject to, and defined by, specific bodies of institutional knowledge which play a key role in separating their school existence off from their home existence.

Many of Mayall's remarks on this are reminiscent of Erving Goffman's famous observations on 'total institutions' (Goffman, 1961). Goffman defined total institutions such as the prison, the monastery or the mental asylum in terms of their wholesale control over the organization of the inmate's existence, from the forms of clothing to be worn to the times at which lights are switched off at night and on in the morning. Total institutions aim to subject the inmates to regimes of power in which the routines of everyday life are radically separated from the world outside and even the smallest details of existence are incorporated into an overall institutional rationale. In a similar sense, Mayall (1994b) asserts that school 'is a closed, complete system, where goals and practices cohere, and where the activities of the teachers (during the school day) are limited to a focus on the teaching and training of the children' (p. 125). Viewing the school in this way as a form of total institution emphasizes the extent to which children can be constructed by its institutional discourses, and foregrounds what Mayall found to be children's conception that

> they are powerless to reconstruct the school as a social institution to meet their own ideas about what would constitute a child-friendly educational setting. For them, the school is indeed an impervious, congealed construction of social norms. (*ibid.*, p. 124)

However, as Mayall suggests, this is of course only one side of the coin. As Goffman showed in his research on asylums, viewed from the perspective of the institution, the inmates were either well-integrated into the norms of the institution or were 'nuisances'. But viewed from the perspective of the inmates, life in the institution was something for which competent, rational strategies were needed:

while the institution staff saw themselves as moulding the inmates to some socially approved purpose, the inmates utilized an array of strategies for retaining their sense of self and of self-respect.

In a similar sense, it is possible to see how children, while being subject to construction in the terms of institutional knowledge and practices, can deploy their own knowledge of institutional regimes to create spaces of autonomy and even resistance. For instance, Danby and Baker (this volume) show how children in a kindergarten respond to a teacher's intervention in their conflicts by engaging in two parallel strategies. In the teacher's presence, they comply with her programmatic attempt to alleviate the conflict and get the children to 'make up'. But once the teacher has departed, the children deploy their own procedures for dealing with the conflict.[6] Thus, teacher-defined knowledge in which conflict is a 'hurtful' thing and in which the one who is hurt must be comforted by the perpetrator, exists in parallel with alternative knowledges which are defined by children themselves and can be brought into play in the interstices of the school's institutional regime.

'Institutional knowledge' overlaps in numerous ways with the other arenas of action we have discussed. For instance, the family can itself be seen as an institution, knowledge about the workings of which can be mobilized in children's activities. Various aspects of institutional knowledge also come into play in the kinds of conversational interactions discussed by sociolinguists and conversation analysts, especially when these refer to, or are situated within, institutional settings themselves, such as television studios (Thornborrow, this volume) or paediatric clinics (Silverman, 1987). Similarly, the forms of institutional knowledge discussed in, for example, Christensen's study of family medicinal practices (this volume) cross between institutional knowledge (knowledge about different medicines and their appropriate use), discourse competence, and the family order in which the medicinal practices are situated.

A unifying issue which emerges from these considerations of varying arenas of action relates to the recurrent differences between the agendas which inform adults' actions and those which inform children's. Whether in the family arena, the arena of talk and interaction or the arena of institutional knowledge, a basic question in investigating the real-world situatedness of children's social competence is that of how far children construct and people cultures that are autonomous from or dependent upon those of adults. Indeed, this 'autonomy-dependency' axis is one around which the vast majority of work in the new social studies of childhood (including the present volume) can be said to revolve. One possible interpretation of this would be to suggest, in a rather simplistic way, that children's social competence can be equated with their autonomy from adult-controlled culture and that dependency equals non-competence. However, that is most certainly not the way we would see it. Rather, what we have tried to stress is that the issue of children's social competence is an empirical question. This is what lies behind our repeated emphasis on *situating* social competence in actual everyday praxis. The question of children's social competence cannot ultimately be settled a priori: it has to be investigated in situ.

Conclusion

In this chapter we have outlined a particular conception of the competence paradigm in social studies of childhood. We have argued for the primacy, within that paradigm, of empirical research which situates children's social competence as a practical accomplishment in the ordinary circumstances of everyday life. This implies a phenomenological (Waksler, 1986) or ethnomethodological (Garfinkel, 1984) perspective in which the aim of the researcher is to describe the organization of the social world from the participants' point of view and to see that organization itself as a participants' accomplishment. While we are not suggesting that research on children should adopt all the paraphernalia of ethnomethodological theorizing (see Boden, 1990), the basic empirical standpoint we are arguing for is 'ethnomethodological' (in quotes) in that it attempts to see children's social action for what it is, as a knowledgable, agentic, active accomplishment of children themselves in interaction with co-present others.

We outlined two methodological approaches which respond to the difficulties intrinsic to the attempt to view children's social action from the participants' perspective: ethnographic observation and conversation analysis. Ethnography can provide a great deal of insight into children's social competence as a situated phenomenon. Its principal contribution is that it allows us to see action as 'structurated' (Giddens, 1984; Alanen, this volume): the competencies involved in social action are both situated within and reproductive of the structural and institutional patterns of everyday life. Conversation analysis can be seen as adopting an essentially similar theoretical stance (see Hutchby, 1996); however, rather than taking as its data the observations and interviews carried out by the ethnographer, conversation analysis stresses the importance of *recording* behaviour in naturally occurring settings, and basing analytic accounts on the observable details of participants' jointly constructed activities.

We suggest that a combination of these approaches, aiming to describe participants' methods for making sense and organizing co-present activity in a way that is informed by a critical concern for the relationship between action and social structure, represents the best means for forwarding the competence paradigm in the social study of childhood. Some of the chapters in the present volume demonstrate the kinds of findings that can be generated using such an approach (Gardner, Sanders and Freeman, Thornborrow, Danby and Baker, Silverman et al.).[7] But there remains enormous scope for future explorations in this mode of situating children's social competence, both in the arenas of action we have identified and in others yet to be explored.

Notes

1 Similar to this is the conception of 'double-voice discourse' which has been worked out by Amy Sheldon in a number of papers (for example, Sheldon 1992a and 1992b).

2 This is not to imply that such an aim is anything other than laudable: in order for the child to make their way ultimately in the world, the ability to pronounce words in the conventional way is of course crucial.

3 Also relevant here is the work of Carolyn Baker (1982, 1984 and chapters 8 and 11 in this volume).

4 The joke involves three sisters who get married on the same day. Repairing to their parents' house for their wedding night, the mother patrols outside the bedrooms listening for the sounds of nuptials. Hearing satisfactory noises from two rooms but nothing from the third, in the morning she asks the third daughter to explain the silence: hence the punchline. The joke is told, in Sacks' data, by a group of teenage boys, who manifestly do not find it funny. Significantly, however, the joke has been introduced by its teller as a joke which his (12-year-old) sister told him. This poses Sacks his problem: it is evident why teenage boys (especially those who, like this group, characterize themselves as rebellious) would find such a joke 'obvious' and unamusing. But why would 12-year-old girls enjoy it? It is worth pointing out that Sacks' sophisticated answer to this question has been criticized by Thompson (1984) who claims that Sacks wilfully misses the point that this joke is merely an example of the ideological perpetuation of patriarchy: a joke 'in which women are presented as objects of pleasure whose capacity to satisfy male desire is enhanced by their incapacity to distinguish between a dinner table and a bed' (p. 117). Of course, as Montgomery (1986) points out in a rejoinder, Sacks was well aware of this aspect of the joke (see Sacks, 1992, vol. 2, p. 493). However, seeing it this way does not solve the question he poses, which has to do with its circulation among 12-year-old girls; unless, of course, one wants to argue that the girls in question are ideological dupes who unwittingly collude in the oppression of their gender, a view which those within the competence paradigm would doubtless find it hard to accept.

5 That the family is viewed as adult-centred by children themselves is nicely demonstrated in Hallden's (1994) analysis of children's fictional accounts of future family situations.

6 In Danby and Baker's account, there are significant differences between boys and girls in the ways in which both these things are done.

7 By no means all of these authors would describe themselves as using 'conversation analysis' in the strict sense, as outlined, for instance, by Hutchby and Wooffitt (1997). This, we think, is clear from the methodological discussions each contribution itself provides.

References

ALDERSON, P. (1993) *Children's Consent to Surgery*, Buckingham: Open University Press.

ALDERSON, P. (1994) 'Researching children's rights to integrity', in MAYALL, B. (ed.) *Children's Childhoods: Observed and Experienced*, London: Falmer Press.

BAKER, C. (1982) 'Adolescent-adult talk as a practical interpretive problem', in PAYNE, G. and CUFF, E. (eds) *Doing Teaching: The Practical Management of Classrooms*, London: Batsford.

BAKER, C. (1984) 'The search for adultness: Membership work in adolescent-adult talk', *Human Studies*, **7**, pp. 301–23.

BODEN, D. (1990) 'The world as it happens: Ethnomethodology and conversation analysis', in RITZER, G. (ed.) *Frontiers of Social Theory: The New Syntheses*, New York: Columbia University Press.

COOK-GUMPERZ, J., CORSARO, W. and STREECK, J. (1986) *Children's Worlds and Children's Language*, Berlin: Mouton de Gruyter.

ERVIN-TRIPP, S. and MITCHELL-KERNAN, C. (1977) 'Introduction', in ERVIN-TRIPP, S. and MITCHELL-KERNAN, C. (eds) *Child Discourse*, New York: Academic Press.

GARFINKEL, H. (1984) *Studies in Ethnomethodology*, Cambridge: Polity Press.

GARFINKEL, H. and SACKS, H. (1970) 'On formal structures of practical actions', in McKINNEY, J.C. and TIRYAKIAN, E.A. (eds) *Theoretical Sociology*, New York: Appleton-Century-Crofts.

GARVEY, C. (1984) *Children's Talk*, Cambridge, MA: Harvard University Press.

GIDDENS, A. (1976) *New Rules of Sociological Method*, London: Hutchinson.

GIDDENS, A. (1984) *The Constitution of Society*, Cambridge: Polity Press.

GILLIGAN, C. (1982) *In a Different Voice: Psychological Theory and Women's Development*, Cambridge, MA: Harvard University Press.

GOFFMAN, E. (1961) *Asylums*, New York: Doubleday.

GOODE, D. (1991) 'Kids, culture and innocents', in WAKSLER, F. (ed.) *Studying the Social Worlds of Children*, London: Falmer Press.

GOODWIN, M.H. (1990) *He-Said-She-Said: Talk as Social Organisation Among Black Children*, Bloomington, IN: Indiana University Press.

HALLDEN, G. (1994) 'The family — A refuge from demands or an arena for the exercise of power and control — Children's fictions on their future families', in MAYALL, B. (ed.) *Children's Childhoods: Observed and Experienced*, London: Falmer Press.

HAMMERSLEY, M. and ATKINSON, P. (1983) *Ethnography: Principles in Practice*, London: Routledge.

HOPPER, R. (1989) 'Conversation analysis and social psychology as descriptions of interpersonal interaction', in ROGER, D. and BULL, P. (eds) *Conversation*, Clevedon: Multilingual Matters.

HUTCHBY, I. (1996) *Confrontation Talk: Arguments, Asymmetries and Power on Talk Radio*, Mahwah, NJ: Erlbaum.

HUTCHBY, I. and WOOFFITT, R. (1998) *Conversation Analysis: Principles, Practices and Applications*, Cambridge: Polity Press.

JAMES, A. (1993) *Childhood Identities: Social Relationships and the Self in Children's Experiences*, Edinburgh: Edinburgh University Press.

JAMES, A. and PROUT, A. (eds) (1990a) *Constructing and Reconstructing Childhood: Contemporary Issues in the Sociological Study of Childhood*, London: Falmer Press.

JAMES, A. and PROUT, A. (1990b) 'Introduction', in JAMES, A. and PROUT, A. (eds) *Constructing and Reconstructing Childhood*, London: Falmer Press.

KITZINGER, J. (1990) 'Who are you kidding: Children, power and the struggle against sexual abuse', in JAMES, A. and PROUT, A. (eds) *Constructing and Reconstructing Childhood*, London: Falmer Press.

LAKOFF, R. (1975) *Language and Women's Place*, New York: Harper.

MACKAY, R. (1973) 'Conceptions of children and models of socialisation', in DREITZEL, H.P. (ed.) *Childhood and Socialisation*, London: Collier-Macmillan.

MANDELL, N. (1991) 'The least-adult role in studying children', in WAKSLER, F. (ed.) *Studying the Social Worlds of Children*, London: Falmer Press.

MAYALL, B. (ed.) (1994a) *Children's Childhoods: Observed and Experienced*, London: Falmer Press.

MAYALL, B. (1994b) 'Children in action at home and school', in MAYALL, B. (ed.) *Children's Childhoods: Observed and Experienced*, London: Falmer Press.

MEHAN, H. (1991) 'The school's work of sorting students', in BODEN, D. and ZIMMERMAN, D. (eds) *Talk and Social Structure*, Cambridge: Polity Press.

MOERMAN, M. (1988) *Talking Culture: Ethnography and Conversation Analysis*, Philadelphia, PA: University of Pennsylvania Press.

MONTGOMERY, M. (1986) 'Language and power: A critical review of "Studies in the Theory of Ideology" by John B. Thompson', *Media, Culture and Society*, **8**.

OAKLEY, A. (1994) 'Parallels and differences between children's and women's studies', in MAYALL, B. (ed.) *Children's Childhoods: Observed and Experienced*, London: Falmer Press.

OCHS, E. (1988) *Culture and Language Development*, Cambridge: Cambridge University Press.

OCHS, E. and SCHIEFFELIN, B. (1979) *Developmental Pragmatics*, London: Academic Press.

OCHS, E. and SCHIEFFELIN, B. (1983) *Acquiring Conversational Competence*, London: Routledge and Kegan Paul.

OPIE, I. and OPIE, P. (1969) *The Lore and Language of Schoolchildren*, Oxford: Clarendon Press.

PARSONS, T. (1951) *The Social System*, New York: Free Press.

PIAGET, J. (1926) *The Language and Thought of the Child*, London: Kegan, Paul, Trench, Trubner and Co.

PROUT, A. and JAMES, A. (1990) 'A new paradigm for the sociology of childhood? Provenance, promise and problems', in JAMES, A. and PROUT, A. (eds) *Constructing and Reconstructing Childhood*, London: Falmer Press.

QVORTRUP, J. (1990) 'A voice for children in statistical and social accounting: A plea for children's rights to be heard', in JAMES, A. and PROUT, A. (eds) *Constructing and Reconstructing Childhood*, London: Falmer Press.

QVORTRUP, J., BARDY, M., SGRITTA, G. and WINTERSBERGER, H. (1994) *Childhood Matters: Social Theory, Practice and Politics*, Aldershot: Avebury.

SACKS, H. (1978) 'Some technical considerations of a dirty joke', in SCHENKEIN, J. (ed.) *Studies in the Organisation of Conversational Interaction*, New York: Academic Press.

SACKS, H. (1992) *Lectures on Conversation* (2 volumes, edited by G. Jefferson), Oxford: Blackwell.

SCHEGLOFF, E.A. (1982) 'Discourse as an interactional achievement: Some uses of "uh huh" and other things that come between sentences', in TANNEN, D. (ed.) *Analysing Discourse: Text and Talk*, Washington DC: Georgetown University Press.

SCHEGLOFF, E.A. (1990) 'On the organisation of sequences as a source of "coherence" in talk-in-interaction', in DORVAL, B. (ed.) *Conversational Organisation and its Development*, Norwood NJ: Ablex.

SCHEGLOFF, E.A. (1992) 'Repair after next turn: The last structurally-provided defence of intersubjectivity in conversation', *American Journal of Sociology*, **97**, pp. 1295–345.

SCHIEFFELIN, B. (1990) *The Give and Take of Everyday Life*, Cambridge: Cambridge University Press.

SHELDON, A. (1992a) 'Conflict talk: Sociolinguistic challenges to self-assertion and how young girls meet them', *Merrill-Palmer Quarterly*, **38**, pp. 95–117.

SHELDON, A. (1992b) 'Preschool girls' discourse competence: Managing conflict', in HALL, K., BUCHOLTZ, M. and MOONWOMON, B. (eds) *Locating Power*, Berkeley, CA: University of California, Berkeley Linguistic Society.

SHELDON, A. (1996a) 'Special Issue: Constituting Gender Through Talk in Childhood', *Research on Language and Social Interaction*, **29**.

SHELDON, A. (1996b) 'You can be the baby brother but you aren't born yet: Preschool girls' negotiation for power and access in pretend play', in SHELDON, A. (ed.) 'Special Issue:

Constituting Gender Through Talk in Childhood', *Research on Language and Social Interaction*, **29**, pp. 57–80.

SILVERMAN, D. (1987) *Communication and Medical Practice*, London: Sage.

SILVERMAN, D. (1993) *Interpreting Qualitative Data*, London: Sage.

THOMPSON, J.B. (1984) *Studies in the Theory of Ideology*, Cambridge: Polity Press.

THORNE, B. (1993) *Gender Play*, Buckingham: Open University Press.

WAKSLER, F.C. (1986) 'Studying children: Phenomenological insights', *Human Studies*, **9**, pp. 71–82.

WAKSLER, F.C. (1991) *Studying the Social Worlds of Children: Sociological Readings*, London: Falmer Press.

WALKERDINE, V. (1984) 'Developmental psychology and child-centred pedagogy: The insertion of Piaget into early education', in HENRIQUES, J., HOLLOWAY, W., URWIN, C., VENN, C. and WALKERDINE, V. (eds) *Changing the Subject: Psychology, Social Regulation and Subjectivity*, London: Methuen.

Part I

Competence and Family Structures

Chapter 2

Children and the Family Order: Constraints and Competencies

Leena Alanen

Introduction

A denaturalization of children and childhood takes place when children begin to be seen as real and active members of the societies in which they live. A sociology of childhood is interested in accounting for this fact and in writing it into its discourse. In recent years, sociologists and social anthropologists have begun to deal with the issue and have suggested different starting points and ways of proceeding in this. The present chapter seeks to contribute to that debate.

I take for granted that children are competent social actors. That is, I do not question children's competencies — social, or cultural — nor do I explore them empirically in order to challenge and expand existing views on the range of activities and environments in which children are involved in modern societies. Such work is being done particularly well in ethnographies of childhood and I want to start from the vision opened by such work that there are hardly any limits to the extent and the kinds of children's participation in ongoing social life, including the shaping of childhood itself. The kinds of competent participation that we may empirically find in researching children's social worlds are, however, constrained by the social practices surrounding this participation. Therefore, rather than focusing directly on children's competencies, my aim is to explore the structuring of childhood in modern societies, in order to see how possibilities for and limitations on such competencies are contained in observed and experienced childhoods.

My agenda has grown out of reflecting on and reworking two research projects. The first is the Childhood as a Social Phenomenon (CSP) project based at the European Centre, in Vienna, and the second a collaborative Nordic project on the organization of everyday life in one-parent families (OPF), in which my special focus was on the kinds of childhoods that such households make available for children to live and shape — or in other words, what children make of family. At first it seems that the methodologies employed in these two sociological projects were different and even in opposition to each other. The CSP standpoint was one of 'looking down' at children from the level of social structures in order to see how children's lives are implicated in those structures and what the consequences of this are both for children's lives and other lives. In contrast, the OPF study started from the everyday level of lived childhoods and proceeded by 'looking up' from there, in order to detect the ways in which children are involved in the construction of the social order that determines modern childhoods.

I will end up by arguing that neither of these methodological standpoints alone will help to advance a plausible sociology of childhood. Their usefulness is that they serve as critiques to each other and may therefore keep in check and contribute to the understandings emerging with each methodology.

The sociology of childhood is a project in an early stage. Much of the most innovative work in this new field has focused directly on children as social actors in their everyday worlds. Much less has been done to link children's childhoods to other structures of social life in modern societies in ways that preserve children's agency. This is the central theme of this chapter: it aims to contribute to a sociology of childhood that is both structural and agentic.

The Standpoint of 'Looking Down'

In the Childhood as a Social Phenomenon project, the theoretical perspective was structural from the very beginning: childhood was seen as a structural form that is integrated in society (for example, Qvortrup, 1990, pp. 7–8 and 1994, p. 23). Such a standpoint holds the viewer firmly on a societal macrolevel, as if looking 'downwards' in order to see and analytically describe the kinds of childhood(s) as they become visible from there. The presumption is that children are included in social life as its 'ordinary' members.

Such an analysis begins by presenting one or another social system that is interpreted as including children as its members; that is, children are seen as competent social (inter)actors within that system, and the functioning of that system as dependent on children's work. Jens Qvortrup has argued, in several texts (for example, Qvortrup, 1985 and 1995), that children are, and have always been, socially useful in that they participate in the social divisions of labour characteristic of their societies; these systemic divisions have changed over time, but children's participation has remained their permanent feature. In David Oldman's analyses (Oldman, 1994a and 1994b) childhood is presented as a mode of production (essentially of human capital). This production takes place in and through a particular system of stratification in which children take a central place as its active members. Through an extension of the Marxist conception of class, Oldman then presents this membership as a class position of 'children', linked to that of 'adults' and so the mode of production defines a generational system in which children are organized to work for their own 'self-capitalization'.

Conceptualized in this way, 'generation' is made to refer to a social system comparable with 'gender' (also 'gender system', or 'gender order' in feminist theory), and with the more conventional sociological 'class'. In Göran Therborn's (1995) analytical terms, both Qvortrup and Oldman focus on a particular structuration (structural formation/structure in formation) of social relations. Here the term 'structure' refers to 'a patterning of resources and constraints available to people as social actors' (Therborn, 1995, p. 8; cf. Giddens, 1984), and these patterings, in turn, define the system's immanent positionalities. In Qvortrup's case, the actors in question are all doing one or another type of useful labour; for children of modernity that labour consists of large amounts of scholarly work (this is also the core of children's self-capitalization, in Oldman's terms). Because school labour is so obviously children's, and not adults' work, children and adults also make up the two generational categories that become embedded in a systemic interdependency wherever schooling has differentiated into a specific kind of work. Oldman (1994b), elaborating the notion of the mode of production, specifies his case as one in which (some) adults are doing 'childwork' (working 'on children') while children also work although this work is mostly misrepresented as their activities of growing up. The systemic interdependency maintained through these generational relations can now be specified as existing between the 'childworkers' and (simply) 'children' — because all children are constrained to participate in those relations.

Generational relations (like gender or class relations) are not meant to name a specific sphere of social relations that would exist over, or beyond, the relationships of children's (and adults') everyday lives and determine them; rather, they are best understood as historically constructed social logics that become observable through their structuring effects in many (or any) sites of everyday life. Through this capacity they also become real, and even material (Hennessy, 1993). Oldman (1994b) picks up for closer examination the sites of school and child-care, but he also emphasizes that family itself is best understood as one site in among these three social systems of stratification which, in their interplay, produce the structuring of social relations known as 'family'.

The constituents of structure can be specified in more detail as: (i) a bounded social system; (ii) a regulated membership; and (iii) a 'situs pattern', or a set of interrelated positions within the system (Therborn, 1995, p. 8). All of these constituents are also present in the systems proposed by both Qvortrup and Oldman for a structural interpretation of childhood: they effect a generational ordering of children into the systemic positions which then define modern childhood. Therborn, however, wants to go beyond a description of structured positioning and goes on to specify how such structures are transformed over time, by people active in those structures. Individual and collective actors act not only in and upon such structures, he argues, but also in and upon the cultures of their social systems. Therborn therefore makes an analytic distinction between structurations and enculturations, and regards them as two sets of interlinked systemic processes through which human social relations are formed and transformed. The systemic frames presented so far (Qvortrup and Oldman) take up structurations, or the hard material dimensions of generational ordering. A more comprehensive structural analysis of childhood would need to consider and link to such structurations: in particular, (i) the identities of the system immanent actors, as well as (ii) the particular knowledges and perspectives, and (iii) the valuations (values and norms) which accrue to the actors in the system as the constructive effects of their ongoing structuration (see Therborn, 1995, p. 228).

By placing enculturations on the same analytic level as structurations, Therborn underlines the systemic character of enculturations: they, too, give direction and shape to social action, and thereby make those involved (for present purposes, children) into participants in systems of cultural relations. As participants children also contribute to the maintenance, expansion, contraction, and even disappearance of those relations. They participate in knowledges and in the construction of identities, for themselves as well as for other participants, and they share sets of values and norms and registers of emotions. They do all this in interaction with other participants, although normally not as their equals. Power is inherent in cultural systems — a central lesson from Foucault and many others, but amazingly easy to forget as soon as we begin to think about children in their peer relations.

The enculturation aspect of the reproduction and transformation of the generational orders is significant in emphasizing children's practical, experiential knowledge of the generational system in which they are constrained to participate: children are 'knowers'. For the sociologist, the insight should be that such knowledge is valuable data for investigating those generational orders, from a child's standpoint. What exactly is included in this knowledge, and how it gets articulated, remains a problem for both sociological theory and the methods of child research. Notwithstanding this, the insight gives substance to the claim that a sociology from a children's standpoint is conceivable.

The analytical division of social systems into structurations and enculturations is meaningful in as much as it summarizes the complex of ways through which children may exert their active membership in their own societies. Social and cultural systems hardly ever reach total compatibility with each other, and their constant movement allows numerous opportunities for actors to think and act differently, to confront, resist, oppose and change existing conditions. The upshot for childhood research is that a structural-cultural frame invites researchers to investigate empirically the ways in which children deploy the material, social and cultural resources that are available to them in different combinations, and what they make of them in terms of particular childhoods.

This invitation to (multidimensional) empirical research on childhood is the strong point in the 'looking down' approach that begins on a social and cultural system level, assumes and preserves children's agency, and then proceeds to investigate how these systems are lived and reenacted in children's every day lives, in the various settings which children traverse. The weak point in employing this method is linked to the inherent perspectivity of all knowledge (including the sociological). The second methodological approach is based on a critical awareness of this.

The Standpoint of 'Looking Up'

This approach turns the analytical gaze around. The grounds for doing so have been developed and intensively discussed within academic feminism under the heading of 'standpoint' — the perspectives from which women's lives can be known. Among sociologists in particular, Dorothy Smith has worked on standpoint as a method for constructing sociological knowledge which would preserve women's agency (Smith, 1988, 1990a and 1990b).

Feminists' interest in standpoint grew out of the need to theorize women's participation in ongoing social life. In the early stages, concepts and categories were simply borrowed from the mainstream discourses that had generally failed to include women and were therefore criticized as being 'malestream'. The central claims of these discourses were reinterpreted and their intended domains extended to include women and gender relations — essentially a method of choosing to look 'down' at women's lives from the conceptual heights of the discipline. This strategy soon proved inadequate. The complexities of women's lives could not be covered and in the process the original discourses were often felt to become distorted. Questions were now in place about the hidden (gendered) meanings of the concepts and categories of social science and its structural agendas: what lies behind and at the origin of the (hegemonic) concepts, what do the terms refer to, how were they originally generated, in response to what problems and issues, and in whose interests? Answering such questions would both explain the distorting effects and mark the limitations of existing sociology for understanding women's lives.

Such work has exposed sociological (or any) knowledge as ideological, culturally constructed, contextual and in this sense political: a perspective from one or another structured location is contained within it. Perspectivism is inherent in all knowing, therefore it should also be the starting point of all knowledge production and systematically built into its strategies. For feminist sociologists this has meant to begin from the social locations of women and to address society and social relations from the perspective of women's lives and experiences.

In the same way, a new sociology of childhood would begin from the actual everyday locations and activities of its subjects, and from there turn 'upwards' to account for social relations that overdetermine childhoods as they come into view. The parallel aims would be to:

> express women's (children's) experience and yet embed our [their] experience as women (children) in the generalizing relations of society. The general aim is to explicate the social processes and practices organizing people's everyday experience. It means a sociology in which we do not transform people into objects but preserve their presence as subjects. It means taking seriously the notion of a sociology concerned with how phenomena are brought into being through the actual activities of individuals and of exploring how those activities are organized in social relations. . . . It means an inquiry that will disclose how activities are organized and articulated to the social relations of the larger social and economic processes. (Griffith and Smith, 1987, p. 89)

Because women have largely been outsiders in the creation of the concepts and categories that constitute sociology (Smith, 1988, p. 257), a feminist sociology will need to resist them and generate its knowledge by using as its resource the knowledge of the social world that women have through their participation (or work) in the daily construction of that world. And because the processes and relations outside their immediate daily lives (in our kind of societies) help to create the conditions of those lives and the experiences of living in those places, a feminist sociology will link these two in order to make society known from the point where women stand, and explain to them how their 'everyday/everynight' lives are implicated in the actual organization of the totality of social relations — or the 'relations of ruling' (Smith, 1988). A sociology from a women's standpoint will then go beyond merely listening to and describing what women are able to tell about their lives. In analysing the sections of the social world that women know as its insiders the sociologist also comes to problematize the concepts and theories of her sociology that represent the 'extra-local and abstracted organization of ruling'.

Thus the idea of standpoint defines a method for research: it begins from outsiders' experience and proceeds from there towards the social processes and practices that structure that experience, preserving all the way the presence of outsiders as knowers and actors. It aims to provide different information which will be summarized in a set of new, alternative categories for use in further research (Longino, 1993). Finally, as it also questions the discursive practices by which the conventional adult-centred sociology orders children's everyday lives, it can show how knowledge is constructed and how power is exercised and reinforced through that construction of knowledge.

Children and the Family Order

Possibly even more than women, children are cultural outsiders in the above sense. The critique of adult-centred conventional knowledge about children and childhood is a clear parallel to the male-centred tendencies in social science: it claims, first, that social scientists have looked at children from the perspectives of various adult groups, such as parents, teachers, authorities of nation-states, or other actors that are institutionally positioned to organize and coordinate children's lives. Secondly, these perspectives or standpoints have actually been built into their concepts and theories of children and childhood (Thorne, 1987; Alanen, 1992, pp. 53–5).

'Family' is one of the most powerful social science concepts through which the discursive ordering of children has been effected; in Therborn's terms, 'family' has been a central medium in the structuration and enculturation of modern (Western) childhoods. It has defined, through the historically specific construction of the modern nuclear family, a bounded private sphere to which the child 'naturally' belongs, a membership in a family of his/her own, and a position in the family system which both gives the child responsibilities and entitles him/her to access to a range of resources. The cultural and material familialization of childhood in the Western world is an excellent example of structuration and enculturation.

The normative and normalizing construction of familialized childhood provides the cultural common-sense through which childhoods, children's lives and the actual conditions of their living are described and assessed in the Western world. The standpoint methodology aims to question this ruling of childhood through family and suggests that we begin from the everyday locations of real active children and 'look upwards' from there, to detect how children's social relations are actually structured along a generational axis. Through living their daily lives in their generationally defined locations children have particular situated knowledge of the particular social relations within which such lives are lived. This the standpoint-conscious researcher will explore as serious knowledge, and attempt to proceed from there upwards towards the institutional relations that 'rule' those childhoods. In all of this, the researcher will preserve children as active members of their societies and their activities as the work through which they participate in the construction of a modern generational order.

The Study

The Childhood in One-Parent Households study was part of a larger empirical project, designed to be a qualitative analysis of the organization of everyday life in families of divorced or separated women and their children, and to contribute to a critical reflection of sociological analyses of the family phenomenon and of social-ization theory. The motivating idea for the study was, from the very beginning, to resist the conventional picture of mother-headed families as it appears in social science literature: as a deficient or deviant family form. Its construction as such takes place by way of comparison to the normal, 'intact' family made of the two generations of 'parents' — the heterosexual adult couple — and their dependent children. This normalizing family concept in which children appear as their parents' dependents, with all its implications, dominates in research focusing on children who live in one-parent households. The 'deficient' family structure has been said to risk a child's development as it is thought best to take place, that is: in and through the family, nested in turn within a larger organization of social relations. Consequently, the agendas of research focusing on children in one-parent house-holds have aimed to register manifestations of dysfunctional, maladjusted and even pathological behaviours. Far from trusting children to be active subjects and know-ing actors in their own lives they have been studied as objects and victims of their social environments.

The data in the OPF study was collected through interviewing 100 children, aged 9–13 years, and their mothers in four Nordic countries (Denmark, Finland, Norway and Sweden). Care was taken in the interviews to regard the children them-selves as the main informants on their own particular experience and their position-ing as a child in relation to the larger world. This was done by asking the children to talk with the interviewer about their daily activities and relationships within the household, the availability for their use of various material and social resources in their daily lives, and the kind and quality of their relations to other people and to the institutions of the adult world in general as they came into view. Talking about such matters would take place in children's everyday language, carefully avoiding the kind of institutional talk that already permeates children's life-worlds in general, and perhaps even more strongly the life-worlds of children living in one-parent households. The wording of questions and comments also aimed to avoid inviting children to talk specifically in the terms of a family discourse — which the culturally competent children certainly could have done. Instead, the aim was to bring into discussion all the social relationships that children maintain and are maintained with them by others in practical everyday activities, in all possible sites of their everyday life, formal and informal.

Next, the interview data were organized into written accounts describing in detail the children's everyday lives. Each account included information on the child in terms of (i) life history; (ii) everyday life: activities during weekdays, weekends, vacations; (iii) personal economy, property and access to other material resources; (iv) relations to school and generally to the adult world; (v) access to and use of space, both inside and out-of-doors; and (vi) personal relationships with parents and relatives, as well as friendships with other children and adults. Also, in writing these accounts, children were to be preserved as acting, feeling, knowing subjects. Based on these accounts, as well as background material from both mothers' and children's interviews, two structural dimensions of children's everyday lives were constructed.

Social Dimensions of Child Life

The significance of this mode of organizing the interview data is that it allows us to see children's lives apart from (in this case) their mothers' everyday life and, consequently, to identify the extent to which the two are in fact integrated. Integration and autonomy of child life in relation to mother's life were defined in this study by the degree to which mothers and children share (i) their free-time and (ii) their friends and acquaintances (including kin), (iii) with whom the child prefers to discuss and share his/her personal matters like problems and sorrows and (iv) the extent to which the mother is informed about events, people and things, in the general flow of the child's daily activities. On this information two types of relational child life were identified: integrated and autonomous.

Out of twenty-five Finnish children, it appeared that sixteen led a daily life that is closely related to that of their mothers, while nine seemed to be more autonomous in the running of their daily life. There is no clear difference between 'integrated' and 'autonomous' children in their average age and, therefore, it cannot be concluded that autonomy would follow from the child's increasing 'maturity'. Therefore, it is also possible to say that a child's life that is integrated with the mother's is not necessarily 'childish', and autonomy at a younger age need not make children into (premature) adults; both autonomy and integration are social constructions (cf. Solberg 1990 and 1994). There is, however, a slight gender difference as the 'autonomous' children turned out more often to be boys than girls. Yet, again, this does not mean that an integrated life is a 'girl-life', for half of all the children whose everyday life is integrated with that of their mothers' are in fact boys.

A second dimension that differentiates the children concerns the organization, or the agentic management of a child's daily life. The significance of this dimension follows from acknowledging children as social actors. This includes the possibility of children largely managing their affairs on their own. Modern childhood tends to be — or is expected to be — familialized in the sense that children are seen to depend on their parents for the basic conditions of their lives. Parents are normally in command of more material, social and other resources than children, and thus in a more powerful position to shape the everyday conditions of child-life. Therefore the expectation is that parents are in fact the main organizers of children's everyday lives (outside school and other formal institutions). Also the predominant ideological normalization of a familial childhood and its parental counterpart — culturally normative motherhood — includes the expectation that mothers are responsible for the general management of their children's life outside school.

But how is it in fact? It has been argued that the social status of 'being a child' has radically changed and that the practices of modern childhood have repositioned children apart from their families — childhood has been modernized by being individualized (Büchner, 1990; du Bois-Reymond et al., 1994). This means, for children, increased opportunities but also constraints to move daily between many social sites, and to manage the social demands of each by themselves. The one-parent household structure may well add to this general individualization of the child's life. The decomposition of families, through parental divorce or separation, may in fact leave children with more opportunities, and more resources, to pursue activities and build up social relations more autonomously than is the case with children in two-parent households.

An American study by Weiss (1979) revealed such an instance of dissolving the generational superordinate-subordinate structure when there is only one parent left in the household. In the new situation, novel intergenerational partnerships may emerge and even assert themselves between parent and child. Weiss describes the redistribution of rights and responsibilities in one-parent households, and shows that this can provide children with the useful and appreciated experience of 'growing up a little faster', whereas it may be that a two-parent household prevents children from having the same experience. The recent discussion on children's rights and increased arguments for greater respect for children in directly deciding matters that concern them also provides some mothers with the cultural justification for adopting this kind of family reorganization, whether it takes place by force of circumstance or out of mothers' conscious wish to provide their children with more influence in their (shared) daily life.

The availability and use of various familial and non-familial resources such as (i) time, (ii) space, (iii) money, (iv) people (parents, neighbours, relatives, school teachers, other adults, peers) and (v) social and commercial services were examined in order to detect the variation among children on this dimension of their daily life.

The two candidates for principal organizers of children's free time, money use, and contacts with other people were, of course, the mother and the child. The mother carried the task of managing these things for the child in ten out of the twenty-five mother-child households, while the child appeared to be the main organizer in five cases. Finally, there were ten mother-child households in which the organization was managed jointly. Age appeared to be only weakly related to organization: children's daily lives are organized by mother somewhat more often when the child is younger, and children themselves are more active with the management of their daily course of activities and social contacts when they are older. A gender difference can be more clearly seen: there are more boys than

Table 2.1   Patterns of children's daily life

| | | Child's everyday life in relation to mother's | |
		Autonomous	Integrated
	By mother	2	8
Organization of child's everyday life	Jointly	4	6
	By child	3	2

girls among both the co-organized and self-organized children than among the mother-organized.

Constructions of Child Life

These two dimensions of autonomy vs. integration and mother- vs. self-organization vary independently of each other. Mothers may actively organize both integrated and autonomous everyday life for their children, and children themselves may in turn pursue autonomy in their daily activities but may also choose to stay closely connected to their mothers' everyday life. By cross-tabulating these two dimensions six categories of possible patterns of children's daily life are created and can now be used to account for the diversity of child life in one-parent households.

The placing of children into the six categories shows that even in a small sample of twenty-five children all of the possible patterns exist (Table 2.1 gives the number of cases in each type). The most frequent combination is the mother-organized child life which is integrated to that of the mother. Out of the twenty-five cases, 32 per cent display this pattern. The autonomous lifestyle proves to be least frequent overall (36 per cent of cases as against 64 per cent), but it is nevertheless present in nine cases. Suvi (9 years) is one of the children belonging to the largest group whose everyday life is both closely integrated with that of her mother's, and mother-organized. Here is the (shortened) account of her everyday life.

When Suvi's parents separated several years ago she and her mother moved to their present home town. Her father wanted to live near her, so he, too, found a new job for himself in the same town and moved there. Suvi now lives with her mother in a suburb, and her father in an apartment in another suburb of the town. Since last year her father lives with a new partner.

Suvi's school is quite far from home and she needs to be taken there in the mornings and fetched from there in the afternoon. She does not particularly like school, but all her friends are from school, and friends make school OK. As her friends live around the town, she doesn't see them outside school unless special arrangements are made and adults help the children to meet. When mother needs to be away for the weekend Suvi stays with a school friend's family or her father. She has never been left alone in the house.

Mother and Suvi spend a lot of their free time together, either at home or visiting other families. Once a week mother takes her to a music lesson and every second week to a riding lesson. Together they may also go to the big city library or just downtown for shopping. Suvi gets very little pocket money; her mother thinks she has no need yet for her own money. They try to be back home by 8 o'clock so as to have Suvi in bed early. Once a week they have an evening together at home, taking first a sauna and then eating and chatting.

There are not many things for Suvi to do at home: her mother looks after their tiny household. There are no children living near them with whom Suvi could play. Summers are spent visiting Suvi's aunt's family in the country. They may also make short visits to friends elsewhere but they rarely travel abroad.

Suvi sees her father once a week. Before her father had a new partner she spent more time with him. Parents call each other weekly and agree on visiting days and on travelling arrangements. Usually Suvi stays at her father's home overnight and if it is a weekday, goes straight from there to school. There are children living in the same block house, but Suvi rarely plays with them. She prefers to stay inside and read comic books, watch TV or play games with father and his partner. She has no things of her own at father's home and sleeps in the living room when staying overnight. She is quite satisfied with these arrangements.

The structure of daily activities of children belonging to the group integrated/mother-organized is determined essentially by school and by home: children's friends are mostly from school and after-school life takes place at home and its surroundings. Relatives live mostly elsewhere, so face-to-face contacts are more seldom whereas weekly contacts by phone are maintained. Contacts with mother's friends — most of whom live close by — are frequent. These friends are mainly women and there are also other single mothers among them. Children have also learned to know the homes and families of their mothers' friends, just as the mothers know most of their children's friends from school and many of their families as well.

The children in this group, however, make differential use of the resources available to them in these settings. For some of the children everyday life has previously resembled the home-based, family-centred life of Suvi but has since expanded beyond the boundaries of their own household. Sanna's daily life is also centrally organized around school and home and she, too, belongs to the group of mother-organized and integrated children. But she also moves daily within social relations that go beyond the frame of a protected (bi-)nuclear family childhood. Sanna's mother has made her own network of friends available to her daughter, by letting her get involved in the activities and interests of adults around her and leaving space for Sanna to use her own social resources. Suvi, in contrast, continues to live in a nuclear (more recently binuclear) family, with the result that her everyday world is both spatially and socially more bounded than Sanna's: Suvi is a family child. Sanna and some other children in the mother-organized and integrated group do not experience the boundaries of 'the family' as clear and particularly significant. Sanna's mother sees this, in fact, as a result of her enforced poverty during the time she was a student and a mother of two young children. Now she says she has grown accustomed to her 'lifestyle of poverty' and never thinks of settling down as 'only a family' — she thinks of it as a cage which she has now escaped forever. Her newly developed feminist orientation also supports her — and her two daughters' — present way of life in a sort of extended family, or 'familiality'. Both of her daughters have 'used' her personal networks of people for constructing the social frames of their own everyday worlds: they, too, live in her familiality.

The responsibility that many mothers feel for organizing their children's daily life, whether self-claimed or brought into their consciousness through public opinion, includes for most mothers the arranging and maintaining of a satisfactory contact for the children with their fathers. In cases where the father has totally disappeared from their child's lives, or is present only insignificantly, other strategies are employed to take the place of a missing relationship. Some mothers have included their children in their own personal networks and helped them to use it for launching their own familiality (Sanna's mother). Alternatively mothers may, from the beginning, channel various other resources to the child and support his/her own initiatives in organizing her daily activities and relationships: children are then more their mothers' partners than their dependents. Such strategies may be preferred by the mothers from the very beginning, and the interviews indicate that such mothers, more often than others, are satisfied with their present family arrangements and think generally that the one-parent family is a good, or at least a perfectly viable, form of living.

Those who think that the one-parent family form is a bad one tend to feel that it is mainly, or exclusively, their responsibility to organize the child's daily life. Their view of 'good mothering' is that this can take place only in a 'good family', and this is the conventional nuclear one. They nevertheless strive to follow this ideal of 'good mothering' in their own post-divorce conditions, and often work hard to assure their children a proper family childhood and still carry feelings of dissatisfaction.

The child-organized, autonomous pattern of everyday life may be seen as the other extreme to Suvi's kind of home-based and family-centred life pattern that is organized by the mother (sometimes with the cooperation of the father) within a social space bounded by the modern childhood institutions of family and school. Pete (11 years, self-organized and autonomous) is one of these children.

> When Pete wakes up in the morning his mother is already away at her work. His mother is self-employed and works mostly in people's homes. She starts early and stops late because she wants to minimize the inconvenience that her presence means to the dwellers. She travels by car and now and then during the day takes short breaks to come home, take a nap or see that everything is fine. Before leaving in the morning she leaves the alarm clock to wake Pete up for school. Pete then makes his own breakfast — but sometimes doesn't — and looks through the morning paper before leaving for school.
>
> School is fine for Pete: he likes the teachers and the children there. Other children, however, are the best thing in school and Pete has many friends. They play together during the breaks, walk back home together after school and see each other in their free time.

Mother may be at home when Pete comes back from school. If she isn't there, he makes himself a snack. Mother leaves on the table some money for him to go and buy something to eat. Mostly he buys ready-made food.

In the afternoons and evenings Pete meets his friends — he mentions at least ten of them by name — and he plays with them out-of-doors, goes with them to their homes and meets their families. He may well stay there also for the evening meal. People in the neighbourhood know Pete and his mother well, because she has done things for many of them in their homes and has also helped many of them when dealing with the municipal offices and authorities. Pete thinks of some parents of his friends as also his friends and he visits these families particularly often. Neighbours may take Pete along with their own children to see games or movies or to the swimming hall and never ask if he's got money to buy his ticket. Once in a while Pete baby-sits for a neighbouring family and recently went for a weekend trip with the little girl and her family to their summer cottage. When Pete's mother made a few days' trip abroad Pete stayed with another local family. According to his mother he is very good with people and has a lot of friends: 'He seems to look particularly for families with two adults and in a way makes the fathers his own as well. They then take him to places along with their own kids.'

Pete's parents were divorced when he was a baby and his father lives alone. Pete sees him very infrequently, but sometimes his father rings him up and they talk over the phone. Sometimes he comes around and drops tickets through the letter slit in the door for him and his friends to go to see a game.

Pete seems to have had more extensive opportunities to use his time and explore his social environments than most of the children. His mother leaves for him many resources to use: money to use according to his daily needs, but particularly her familiarity with the neighbourhood and its people. He now 'practically knows everyone living here'. As a result, an elaborate system of material and social exchange has emerged between Pete and many people living in the area. There is mutual giving and taking without much asking who pays, and Pete seems to cross freely the boundaries that usually mark the privacy of other children, adults and whole families. Pete's father, living in another suburb, has remained a complete outsider to this elaborate exchange system.

Pete may be exceptionally good in relating to people and places, having had an exceptional resource for developing this in his mother. But he is not the only one with this pattern. Because he spends most of his free time in the locality where there is limited access to activities other than free play and to people that are not first and foremost mothers, fathers and children, his daily life seems to take a pronounced familial character, not unlike that of Sanna's. This, however, may derive more from his young age at the moment. Other children in this group, while one or two years older than Pete, display more clearly the fact that their life pattern is organized through essentially non-familial relationships and they have, more than Sanna and other children, moved into institutional arenas that are beyond the family, school and local child cultures. One of the older boys, for instance, was originally led by his mother to take on his present interests in art and oriental sports. Since then they are his favoured activities which now also provide him with new and autonomously maintained relationships, among them (adult) friendships that he does not share with his mother.

Children's Childhoods

The written accounts of the everyday lives of twenty-five children clearly support the claim that children actively construct their everyday lives. They do this under various circumstances and with a variety of material, social and cultural resources at hand. Parents' separation in itself implies a rearrangement of such resources and children's subsequent access to and actual use of them is anything but predictable from the mere fact of their parents being divorced. Thus living in a one-parent family does not entail a certain kind of childhood; there are many childhoods and children, too, participate significantly in their making.

The structures of everyday lives do not simply follow from the distribution of resources, however. Choices are made and opportunities to choose are socially structured. A range of social factors have an effect on the variety of childhoods that become possible. In addition to age — itself a subsystem of generation — and gender, these factors include, for children in the studied age range, the origins and nature of children's personal network, the area where they live and the locations for free-time activities (indoors–outdoors, homes–public facilities), the opportunities to move between locations, the amount of money that is available for their own use, as well as the presence of a father or other adults (besides mothers) in the child's daily life.

Two particular categories of child life — the mother-organized autonomous type (the upper left corner in Table 2.1, p. 38) and the self-organized integrated type (the lower right corner) — display a pattern of daily life that corresponds more closely than the other groups to the 'classical' idea of a family childhood in which the nuclear family (including the binuclear family structure and the contracted minimal mother-and-child unit) provides the main frame of daily life. Other adult contacts are provided mainly by relatives and the main part of daily activities (besides school) takes place with peers that live in the neighbourhood and are often also school-mates. This is the *classical childhood* in the sense of Ariès: the parent-child relationship is the central generational axis of their everyday lives and this has also continued in the post-nuclear situation. Living in a one-parent household does not make any great difference to them personally, and children do not mention their family situation as anything particular. Their mothers have, moreover, made great efforts in order to secure that their children may live the kind of 'normal', playful and carefree life that they think every child is entitled to because they are children. The troubles and consequences of divorce are for adults to bear.

The co-organizing children, whether they live a fairly autonomous life or more integrated with that of their mothers, in turn belong to the group of *modern (sub) urban children*. Their most active sphere of life is with peers. Some of them — especially the more autonomous ones — actively explore public spaces and facilities, often in couples or larger groups of other children, and also make active use of clubs and other facilities that are municipally organized and located in their suburb. In a country like Finland, such resources are made available for children to use predominantly by the welfare state. Many of these 'modern children' live in suburbs and prefer to stay there, meeting lots of friends of their own age and moving about in groups, into homes and out again, perhaps listening to music in the local library or just strolling around the area, 'doing nothing'. They draw a clear line between themselves as young people with their own activities and opinions, and adults. Living in a one-parent family is nothing particularly special. However, a problem related to this and mentioned by some of them is the shortage of money: being dependent on a typically low-income mother gives fewer opportunities to acquire the necessities of proper social life: music, instruments, travelling, rock festivals etc.

The third group of children might be named (familial) *innovators*. This group includes both mother-organized, integrated children (Sanna) as well as self-organized, autonomous children (Pete). The resources made available to children in this group to develop and use are slightly different and so are the results in terms of everyday life patterns. By exploiting the resources originally made available to him through his mother, Pete has expanded the boundaries of his daily life beyond the merely familial relationships around which Sanna's everyday world is organized. He is also one of the children who ignore the rigid boundaries that are conventionally drawn around the world of the paradigmatic child, optimally developing within a safe and protected family sphere. In this sense everyday social worlds clearly reach beyond the culturally constructed 'family' and, in some cases, even familiality. The pronounced individualization that their lifestyles seem to display may help to depict these children as the most modern of them all (cf. du Bois-Reymond et al., 1994). In the light of the present study, however, this would be based on a simplification of the structural and cultural processes through which modern childhoods are constructed.

Conclusion

The sociological study of childhood is predicated on its being a historical and social phenomenon: childhood has a beginning and a history, both of them intertwined with the general dynamics of social life — it is not a world apart. Histories of childhood indicate that since the beginning its locus has been within the modern construction of the (nuclear) family. Since then, childhood has been discursively (re)constructed essentially as a position of relative incompetence and dependency within the family.

This chapter has attempted to bring children back to full membership in social life. For this, a double strategy has been proposed, both sides of which take children seriously as social actors and as constructors of their social worlds. The first strategy begins from the macro-level of social relations and brings children into them positioned within such social and cultural systems. This opens a vision for constructing a second research strategy, which begins from the level of children's everyday lives and knowledges and from there moves upwards to link those everyday lives and experiences to the social processes and practices that structure those lives. Both these structural approaches take children seriously as active members and competent participants in their social worlds. Both of them accomplish different things, and each may therefore complement, and correct, the achievements of the other, as the analytical 'downwards' gaze from within the structurations and enculturations of social life meets unthought-of realities of children's everyday lives and then turns 'upwards', to challenge and reconstruct the conceptual apparatus of the sociology of childhood.

References

ALANEN, L. (1988) 'Rethinking childhood', *Acta Sociologica*, **31**, pp. 53–67.

ALANEN, L. (1992) *Modern Childhood? Exploring the 'Child Question' in Sociology*, Jyväskylä: University of Jyväskylä, Institute for Educational Research. Publication Series A, 50.

BJÖRNBERG, U. (1992) *One-Parent Families: Lifestyles and Values*, Amsterdam: SISWO: Netherlands Universities Institute for Coordination of Research in Social Sciences.

BUISSON, M. and MERMET, J.-C. (1986a) 'Le divorce: Une nouvelle forme de socialisation familiale?' in *Groupe de Recherches sur le Proçes de Socialisation, Cahiers de Recherche*, No. 6, Lyon: Université de Lumière Lyon 2, pp. 103–41.

BUISSON, M. and MERMET, J.-C. (1986b) 'Des circulations d'enfants: De la famille à la familialité', *Le Groupe Familial*, **112**, pp. 38–43.

BUISSON, M. and MERMET, J.-C (1988) 'Mobilite et socialisation familiale: Le divorce', in *Groupe de Recherches et d'Etudes Sociologiques et Ethnologiques, Cahiers de recherche*, Numéro speciale, Mai, Lyon: Université de Lumière Lyon 2, pp. 35–48.

BÜCHNER, P. (1990) 'Growing up in the eighties: Changes in the social biography of childhood in the FRG', in CHISHOLM, L. et al. (eds) *Childhood, Youth and Social Change. A Comparative Perspective*, London: Falmer Press.

DU BOIS-REYMOND, M. et al. (1994) *Kinderleben. Modernisierung von Kindheit im interkulturellen Vergleich*, Opladen: Leske and Budrich.

GIDDENS, A. (1984) *The Constitution of Society*, Cambridge: Polity Press.

GRIFFITH, A.I. and SMITH, D.E. (1987) 'Constructing cultural knowledge: Mothering as discourse', in GASKELL, J.S. and McLAREN, A.T. (eds) *Women and Education. A Canadian Perspective*, Calgary: Detselig.

HENNESSY, R. (1993) *Materialist Feminism and the Politics of Discourse*, London: Routledge.

LONGINO, H.E. (1993) 'Feminist standpoint theory and the problems of knowledge', *Signs: Journal of Women in Culture and Society*, **19**, pp. 201–13.

OLDMAN, D. (1994a) 'Adult-child relations as class relations', in QVORTRUP, J. et al. (eds) *Childhood Matters. Social Theory, Practice and Politics*, Aldershot: Avebury Press.

OLDMAN, D. (1994b) 'Childhood as a mode of production', in MAYALL, B. (ed.) *Children's Childhoods: Observed and Experienced*, London: Falmer Press.

QVORTRUP, J. (1985) 'Placing children in the division of labour', in CLOSE, P. and COLLINS, R. (eds) *Family and Economy in Modern Society*, London: Macmillan.

QVORTRUP, J. (1990) *Childhood as a Social Phenomenon. An Introduction to a Series of National Reports*, Eurosocial Report, Vol. 36. Vienna: The European Centre for Social Welfare Policy and Research.

QVORTRUP, J. (1994) 'Childhood matters: An introduction', in QVORTRUP, J. et al. (eds) *Childhood Matters. Social Theory, Practice and Politics*, Aldershot: Avebury Press.

QVORTRUP, J. (1995) 'From useful to useful: The historical continuity in children's constructive participation', in AMBERT, A.-M. (ed.) *Sociological Studies of Children, Vol. 7*, Greenwich, CT: JAI Press.

SMITH, D. (1988) *The Everyday World as Problematic: A Feminist Sociology*, Milton Keynes: Open University Press.

SMITH, D. (1990a) *Texts, Facts and Femininity*, London: Routledge.

SMITH, D. (1990b) *The Conceptual Practices of Power*, Boston, MA: Northeastern University Press.

SOLBERG, A. (1990) 'Negotiating childhood: Changing constructions of age for Norwegian children', in JAMES, A. and PROUT, A. (eds) *Constructing and Reconstructing Childhood*, London: Falmer Press.

SOLBERG, A. (1994) *Negotiating Childhood. Empirical Investigations and Textual Representations of Children's Work and Everyday Life*, Stockholm: Nordic Institute for Studies in Urban and Regional Planning NORDPLAN.

THERBORN, G. (1995) *European Modernity and Beyond: The Trajectory of European Societies, 1945–2000*, London: Sage.

THORNE, B. (1987) 'Re-visioning women and social change: Where are the children?', *Gender and Society*, **1**, pp. 85–109.

WEISS, R.S. (1979) 'Growing up a little faster: The experience of growing up in a single-parent household', *The Journal of Social Issues*, **35**, pp. 97–111.

Chapter 3

Runaway Street Children in Nepal: Social Competence Away from Home

Rachel Baker

Anthropological Perspectives on Children and Social Competence

Much of the anthropology written about children focuses on how they are 'socialized' into adult society and on the sociopolitical nature of childhood.[1] These lines of inquiry provide an informative context for a debate on social competence and are summarized below.

The first line of inquiry taken by anthropologists addresses the learning process that enables individuals to select appropriate behaviour and use certain skills to participate in society. Ethnographic studies highlight the cultural specificity of the changes in young peoples' status and relationships with adult members of society while they are growing up. The value of ethnographic investigation is demonstrated by Schieffelin (1990) in her study of socialization and language acquisition among Kaluli children. Her analysis is based on observation of interaction between adults and children and the explicit instructions of parents. For example, children are taught not to use 'child-like' appeal, but to be assertive in their demands so that they can participate in everyday 'adult' exchange. She proposes that language acquisition is at once deeply influenced by the process of becoming a competent member of society and also the means by which children attain such competence (Schieffelin, 1990, p. 15).

Contributors in a recent anthropological conference on child-focused research agreed 'to jettison the old concept of "socialization", which assumes that the end-point of learning is known, and what remains to be found out is how the child comes to acquire it' (Benthall, 1992, p. 23). The alternative is to view learning not as a progression regulated solely by time — such that greatest sophistication is achieved in adulthood, but as a process of participation within various social contexts. Many children, and particularly street children, operate in a broad range of social settings. We can therefore learn something about their social competence by investigating the type and degree of their participation in these contexts.

This approach rejects the notion that the individual learner is 'a discrete body of abstract knowledge which (s)he will then transport and reapply in later contexts. Instead, (s)he acquires the skill to perform by actually engaging in the process', which is akin to an apprenticeship (Hanks in Lave and Wenger, 1991, p. 15). Emphasis is given to children's participation as novices and as experts within their peer groups and as subordinates in adult-regulated social arenas. Within this frame-work learning is not restricted to the acquisition of propositional knowledge but includes the ability to 'play various roles in various fields of participation', to anticipate, improvise and to manipulate actions relative to changing circumstances.

The second strand in anthropological inquiry centres on childhood not as a biological lifestage but as a construction of the dominant sociopolitical environ-ment. Past and present ideologies interact to form the current ideas and practices that comprise various childhoods found in different societies. Thus, we may expect variation in ideas about the nature of children's capabilities.

The definition of 'the family' as the appropriate context in which children should live and learn is widespread among Western and non-Western societies. In stating that 'ideologically the child is somebody whose individuality must develop in family surroundings to be availed of when they become adults', Qvortrup high-lights the structure imposed on children's life course by their role as family mem-bers (Qvortrup, 1994, p. 10). Drawing on ethnographic data from Western societies, Hockey and James suggest that the power differences between parents and children that rest on perceptions of children's dependency, result in a denial of children's personhood. Here personhood refers to 'an individual's socially constituted iden-tity, not with respect to his uniqueness but with respect to a particular set of cultural ideas about what it means to be fully human' (Hockey and James, 1993, p. 48). Therefore children are held to be incompetent in an adult sphere and requiring protection from external risk factors. Children's 'need' for care serves as a means of control by adults in families or institutions. Moreover general assumptions of children's vulnerability prompt these adults to take protective measures out of con-cern for their welfare. However in the bid to protect, children are thereby defined at worst as adults' possessions and at best as 'a separate, non-adult population' (Musgrove in Hockey and James, 1993, p. 70).

An evolutionary perspective points out that humans are unique among higher primates in having a long period of childhood dependency. Bogin (forthcoming) defines childhood as the period up to the age of 7 years when children need adults to process their food in order to survive. Physical survival aside, notions about the emotional and social attributes necessary to function in society vary cross-culturally. A general cut-off age for childhood dependency is therefore inapplic-able; in some societies, children take on 'adult' tasks at an earlier age than in others. In contrast to the Western practice of controlled and restrictive dependency of children, the Asian context is one of extended families 'where the social unit reigned supreme over its individual members and of which children are simply a part' (Hockey and James, 1993, p. 70). Hence while the presence of other depend-ants (for example grandparents) may give greater autonomy to the individual child, there is a pervasive transition from dependent to provider and again to dependent within the traditional life course. Children may therefore be forced into certain roles by adults who need their assistance as productive workers. They are expected to uphold the unity and honour of the extended family.

The rhetoric of child advocacy often contains the notion of 'agency'. Defined as 'the initiation of action by choice', the term carries woolly political overtones and is of doubtful analytical value (Wartofsky, 1981, p. 199 quoted in Qvortrup, 1994, p. 3). Yet it provokes the question of whether children's competence is restricted to their own social milieu or is effective within the wider society. In a comparative study of British children's interactions in the home and the school, Mayall demonstrates children's ability to influence and modify their social environments. She qualifies this conclusion by stressing the significance of the particular context which governs adult constructions of childhood and 'the precise nature of the power relationship between the child and adults in any given setting' (Mayall, 1994, p. 117). Thus her findings confirm that a notion of children's social competence is only meaningful when set in the context of social interaction among children and adults.

Aims and Structure

An anthropological contribution to this volume seeks an understanding of social competence from children's perspectives and within particular social and cultural contexts. There are thus two aims in this chapter.[2] Firstly, to find out what a notion of social competence means for Nepali street children. I will elucidate their own ideas about coping on the streets and of a successful lifestyle. Secondly, to examine the similarities and differences in street children's and others' perspectives on maturity, responsibility and social competence.

Street children do not form their opinions in isolation from their home or host communities. They are formed in interaction with adults and children who see some aspects of a street child's lifestyle as unacceptable and needing change. Adults are held to be more socially competent by virtue of their greater experience. This chapter focuses on children who have considerable breadth of experience in varied social and physical environments and hence may have an alternative perspective to that of the adults who intervene in their life course. I inquire further into the differences in children's and adults' notions of competent behaviour by exploring the views of street children's peers. Research to date does not yield a very clear picture; children sometimes evaluate competence on the basis of adult norms and other times they do not.

I begin by defining my use of the term 'social competence' and how it can be investigated. Next a brief description of the Nepali street children and popular views of their lifestyle provides the necessary context to the discussion. In the four sections that follow, I will trace the career of one Nepali child named Dilip and address these questions:

(i)   What are the features of Nepali childhoods?

(ii) Is leaving home and becoming a street child a demonstration of social competence?

(iii) Are homeless street children competent in the social settings in which they interact?

(iv) Are children competent if they cannot sustain a change in lifestyle that they desire?

Investigating Social Competence

The following journal entries illustrate contrasting ideas about children's competence. Dilip, aged 13, appears to be incompetent in the first but competent in the second. He spent one year living on the streets in Kathmandu before he joined a local boarding school with a group of street friends.[3] A year later, shortly after Dilip ran away from school for the second time, I wrote:

> It was getting light when I saw Dilip and his friend Tulke, sacks in hand, warming themselves by a fire near a rubbish skip. Unlike one previous meeting, Dilip did not run away. However he did not want to talk and avoided looking at me. Knowing that Dilip had told me of his wish to return to school, Tulke turned to Dilip and said 'Off you go then . . . I'm going now'. I asked gently what he wanted to do. He seemed bewildered and unable to voice what he felt, and walked slowly away from me. This time, there were no crowds of onlookers to cause embarrassment and all three of us knew about his movement between school and the street. Yet Dilip still seemed unable to resolve a decision between the immediate advantages of remaining on the streets with Tulke and the desire to return to what he, and those who he respects, view as 'the good life' at school.

> (Two weeks later) I spotted Dilip walking alone down a busy street dotted with tourists. He looked cheerful and was wearing a new, but already dirty, set of clothes. I called him and, seeming a little disconcerted, he waited to chat. I told him that his place at school was still available and that he should contact me if he wants to go back. We discussed how we might meet. He knows the telephone numbers of the school and the NGO centre[4] in his head and at his request I wrote mine on a piece of paper. He said that when either of us had found his classmate who recently ran away, he would return with him. As he walked away with a happy and confident stride, I suspected that this plan was made in order to keep me happy. I still knew little about his own intentions.

How do we respond to children who are at the same time vulnerable and capable? What do we make of children who reject a lifestyle that offers benefits now and for the future? These are not easy questions. But firstly, what is social competence?

Social competence is understood not as the mastery of a specific task by a pre-defined formula, but as the demonstration of a general aptitude to cope with one's social surroundings. It comprises firstly the ability to select appropriate behaviours from acquired knowledge and secondly the ability to use them towards personal goals in a changing social environment. Thus, individuals are not universally competent. Rather they are competent to do certain tasks or to perform within certain spheres and may show incompetence in other areas.

Who then judges an individual to be competent? Competence is generally ascribed according to adult criteria. Yet we cannot assume that adults are competent all of the time. We can expect that a Nepali street child's opinion of his own behaviour might differ from those of his family and neighbours, and among adults and children. I suggest that a debate on children's competence must be tied to their goals and the products of their actions within particular social settings.

Social competence is demonstrated in relations between the self and others (interpersonally) but is affected by a person's self-awareness (intrapersonal competence). Interpersonal and intrapersonal competence are mutually interactive and formative. Popular belief holds that an individual without some degree of self-awareness and self-esteem is unable to maintain positive social relations. Equally it could be said that such intrapersonal qualities are generated during interaction with others. Naturally, competence at both levels is affected by experience and evolves over time.

Intrapersonal competence is defined as 'an individual's sensitivity to, and understanding of, his own needs, desires, anxieties, and the like' (Gardner, 1984, p. 264). I add a sense of self-worth and control over one's life to this definition, the reasons being that I found these notions to be pertinent to Nepali street children and that they are generated by the positive views of others concerning an individual's actions. Western concepts of self-esteem cannot be directly transferred across cultures. Moreover, the subjective nature of these criteria forces us to ask if the observations of an adult can infer the meanings of intrapersonal competence among children.

Interpersonal competence is 'a sensitivity to the needs, desires and fears of other individuals and capacity to collaborate with them and thus achieve one's goals in a communal situation' (*ibid.*). The immediate social network for Nepali children may be their family, peer group, staff at school or an NGO centre. Members of this group have a primary role in supporting the individual physically, socially and emotionally. Lasting bonds are likely to be formed between the individual and each member of this group. Homeless children are very mobile and may interact only sporadically with individuals in their wider social network. Nonetheless, contact in this sphere was important for street children who aspired to achieve the lifestyles of adults they respected.

Who are the Nepali Street Children?

The term 'street children' is one adopted globally to describe children who are 'out of place' but it incorrectly implies that children have no other social environment but the urban streets. In Nepal homeless street boys[5] include orphans and 'abandoned' children. The majority of the latter group have natal homes but for a variety of reasons live independently. The local term khate describes children who rag-pick or beg, live in groups, sleep rough and are apparently detached from their families.

In Nepal, 'competence' for a street child comes down to simply coping with hardships; like hunger, sickness, the cold and being beaten by local people or the police. In addition, street children may experience worry about their family and the future and periods of loneliness or ostracism from their peers. Thus, although we may see examples of remarkable adaptability among street children, in debating their competence there is a danger of overlooking the latter costs to well-being defined by children themselves.

Certain behaviours and characteristics are commonly attributed to khate by local adults and children. They are perceived to be vulnerable to society's ills and responsible for their deviant lifestyle. Moreover khate themselves, as well as confronting such stigmatism, often reiterate some of these definitions to explain why they cannot improve their lifestyle. Thus, in popular discourse notions of moral acceptability colour ideas about children's competence:

> There are two types of street kids. One type is rude and unruly. They usually quarrel with each other, go for pick-pocketing, annoy by-passers (sic.) and passengers in buses. But the other type is humble and polite. They mind their own business and, at times, even mediate the quarrelling kids. (*The Kathmandu Post*, 18 December 1993)

Children who show that they can live on the streets provoke unease among the general public. They threaten the status quo because they fail to fulfil their roles and acquire competence. Following Gardner (1984, p. 257), not only do these children restrict their own potential but that of the group or the overall culture.

Perspectives on Street Children and Their Social Competence

Popular perspectives on children form two alternative paradigms that present contrasting notions of their competence. The first prioritizes children's dependence on adults and connects potential competence to stages in development towards adulthood. Children are viewed as lacking in the knowledge that, in due course, will become available to them through a process of socialization. Hence they are deemed vulnerable to adult vices for example crime, prostitution and substance abuse. This rationale has guided aid programmes for street children. In striving to provide for their 'needs'; adequate shelter, food, protection and adult care, it is difficult for these initiatives to avoid fostering dependency. A healthy diet and education are means to improving quality of life. Yet focusing on their provision conceals children's competence within their own spheres of interaction.

The opposing paradigm is one of children's liberation from adult dominance. Children are recognized as capable in situations of adversity.[6] Their means of coping are seen as different to those of adults but nonetheless competent. Hence, effective programme work is achieved if adults learn about and bolster street children's own competence. Moreover, dependence does not preclude competence; everyone relies on other people to some extent. Individual children and adults can therefore be both dependent and competent through participation in social relationships. Hence 'children are neither small adults nor property. Rather they are resourceful humans. Like adults, they are capable and caring and need relationships and support' (Ennew, 1994a, p. 201).

Yet, there are important limitations of an approach that promotes children's liberation from adult control. First and foremost, children are implicitly viewed as 'special' and distinct from adults. Thinking about 'street children' as a discrete category masks the social and political aspects of homelessness. Street children share the constraints imposed by poverty with the majority of Nepali families. For many, the need to earn for their families is a first step to becoming a street child. Furthermore, the second paradigm is explicit in granting power, agency, choice and efficacy to children. Yet relatively little attention is paid to the moral responsibilities that arise from these capabilities. If children are viewed as competent social actors then they must also be accountable for their actions and words.

Nepali Childhoods

Local views about children who leave home are contingent on general ideas associated with childhood in Nepal. Portrayals of children in the media contrast what can be broadly described as the traditional childhood in Nepal and a Western childhood. The former is influenced by particular cultural beliefs and an agricultural economy. The latter has become the experience of wealthy urban Nepalis, but remains an ideal for the majority of Nepal's population. The newspaper extract and advertisement below indicate what are perhaps the polar extremes of children's experiences and cultural models of appropriate childhoods.

> Navraj Neupane, aged 13, was engaged with Ambika Bhattarai soon after his birth. Despite his disapproval for early marriage, he was forced to marry her a year ago when they were both 12. The marriage was fixed because they were both born on the day of the new moon. 'Villagers think that if the marriage between these two does not take place then they will both die' Navraj says. (*The Kathmandu Post*, 13 September 1994)

> Has your child been missing?
> Missing........the Montessori methods of teaching?
> Missing........the audio visuals?
> Missing........the trained and qualified staff?
> Missing........the good, clean and hygienic environment?
> Missing........the fun and play?
> If YES the....Montessori Child Care Centre . . . is here for your child. (*Ghorkapatra*, 2 April 1995)

Nepali adults and children emphasize the immaturity of young children who require discipline and care from adults within the home. Further parallels to the Western model lie in Nepali perceptions of young children's limited abilities, even in the context of their contribution to household production. For example Dilip's stepmother has three children at home under the age of 5. She says that because they are incapable of cooking rice or washing pots, she gives them wool to spin, a task which they can do successfully.

Adolescents living on the streets said that NGO centres providing facilities and a disciplined environment were appropriate for 'small' (sano) or orphan street children. The adolescents distinguished themselves from these children by their ability to work independently. Being 'small' implies vulnerability due to physical size, age and inferior social status. The street children talked about becoming 'big' (thulo) in the future by achieving a greater age and a job with social status.

Western notions about children's dependence on the home extend into early adolescence. The scope of parental responsibility, the constraints imposed on parenting by poverty and children's roles within a Nepali family were illustrated during an interview with Dilip's stepmother:

— What happens if your children don't obey you?
I can't do anything but in a few years they will grow up and find other work.
(....)
— When do you think that a child becomes an adult and can look after himself?
Maybe 7 or 8 years. ... once they are 10 or 11 years they can work with their hands but before that they can't really do anything can they?
— What kinds of qualities do you want your children to have?
They should listen to what their mother and father tell them and work hard shouldn't they? If they did this then I would be so happy.
— Who teaches them?
Their mother and father must show them what is good but they sometimes don't stay here. If we go and look for him it costs 150 rupees, that is one month's worth of my husband's wages so what can we do? If we bring him home then his friend says 'let's go' so off he goes!

For girls and boys, responsibilities in the household begin early. For boys above about 10 years, these are accompanied by a freedom to participate in labour migration or opportunities to travel outside the natal family and village. Girls, in contrast, are usually kept at home because they are needed for domestic tasks and in order to protect their purity and assure a good marriage.

The common patterns in children's experiences and adults' views regarding what Nepali children ought to be doing should not be viewed as prescriptive norms. Rather they partly explain the background to apparently unusual behaviour — such as children leaving home. The parents with whom I spoke did not wish for their children to leave. But they acknowledged that they could not provide for their children materially (or sometimes emotionally) according to their own standards.

Homeless children too reported desperate circumstances in which they had no choice but to leave their villages to seek a livelihood in the city. Often the whole family moved to find a source of income. Evidently, it is neither unusual nor disapproved of for a poor, 13-year-old boy such as Dilip, to leave home in order to look for work. Yet children expressed the pain, loneliness and injustice of leaving home in interviews and poems about being a street child. When they look back, such experiences are significant elements of their childhoods.

From Home to the Street: A Demonstration of Social Competence?

Dilip's family came to Kathmandu when he was 7-years-old after their land in East Nepal was flooded. They now live in one of the squatter settlements on the city's periphery. His stepmother described her difficulties in feeding the family. Their lack of money was exacerbated by the heavy cost of hospital treatment for Dilip's mother, who subsequently died. Like all squatters, they lack security because they do not own the land on which their house is built and face possible eviction by the government. Although there are other families living in worse conditions nearby, Dilip's family depend on his father's irregular employment as a builder, supplemented by the stepmother and her children's wool spinning.

A reliance on retrospective accounts makes it difficult to determine whether Dilip's departure was primarily prompted by choice or by force of circumstance. When asked what he remembered liking about home life, Dilip spoke of his friends with whom he played and of meals shared with his family. He disliked feeling lonely when there were no friends in the neighbourhood and the occasional beatings from his stepmother for failing to take adequate care of his younger siblings. The views of Dilip and his stepmother concerning his role in the family are detailed below and shed light on whether Dilip was a competent household member.

Dilip's perspective on his present and future role in the family home is somewhat ambiguous. He said that he wants to save money to bring home and intends to live at home in the future. What he actually does is to spend the majority of time away from home, visiting occasionally, reportedly to see his siblings. Children often do not verbalize a conscious decision that conflicts with normal practice. Their actions are therefore more effective indicators of their purpose than their words. Dilip's actions vis-à-vis his home suggest that while he values his independence, he appears to maintain some sort of ongoing relationship with his family and a positive view of home life.

There are similar ambiguities in Dilip's stepmother's comments about his behaviour. By seeking his own livelihood, he has done what she says is expected of children over 10 years old. However the manner in which she describes his lack of obedience and her attempts to keep him at home portray his independence as problematic. Such statements are of course likely to be influenced by the presence of an educated NGO worker whose questions imply that something is amiss with her stepson and that she is partly to blame. Although she does not describe him as competent in his relationships to the home and his behaviour is taken to be unacceptable, both Dilip's parents appear to recognize his autonomy. Not knowing how to keep Dilip at home, they planned to send Dilip to live in East Nepal with his uncle. His father decided against the plan because he thought that Dilip would come back to Kathmandu at the first opportunity.

Some of the tensions inherent in perceptions of parental responsibilities and children's independence are apparent in Dilip's stepmother's response to the following question:

> —Have you ever been to get Dilip from the streets?
> Once his elder sister tried to bring him home and when he was struggling to get away from her fell and hit his nose so it started bleeding. People said to her 'let him go, why are you taking him home where his stepmother will scold him and his father will beat him? He can go his own way'.

Here adults outside the family acknowledge Dilip's competence to live in the city, supporting his independence in preference to the abuse he may suffer at home.

The widespread belief that parents have responsibility in guiding their children raises important issues relating to the interdependence of children's and adults' competence. In the West and in Nepal, there is a pervasive notion that children rely on adults to provide for them and to define limits of appropriate behaviour. From a child's perspective, failure to fulfil these expectations is an indication of adult incompetence. A study of children's long-term responses to parental divorce indicates that children benefit from being with adults who demonstrate that they are in control. The study (Hetherington, 1991, p. 126) found that authoritative parenting, defined as 'involving warmth and firm but responsive control' played a protective role against the adverse effects of marital transitions on children. Such parenting 'was associated with high social competence and low rates of behavioural problems, especially with low externalising problems, and especially among boys . . . Thus, in coping with stressful life events, a supportive, structured, predictable parent-child relationship plays a critical protective role' (*ibid.*).

It could be argued that due to a severe lack of resources and changing family relationships caused by death, elopement and remarriage, the parents of Nepali street children were unable to offer the regularities and certainties described above. If so, can an individual be competent in a social environment of uncertainty? When household income and family relationships are unpredictable, children are likely to seek stability outside the home. Alternatively, children may know that the home situation is unlikely to improve and take the opportunity to experience a world of greater possibilities outside an otherwise limited and predictable life course. Approximately one third of the Nepali street children surveyed in 1993 reported a desire for independence or to see the city, as the reason for leaving home (Baker et al., 1997).

Living on the Streets: Evidence of Social Competence?

Arriving in a busy city is a lonely experience for children without a travelling companion. Boys describe feeling confused and frightened while wandering through the streets trying to find work or a contact from the village. Some found a job in a small restaurant while others were quickly approached by other homeless children and taught how to earn by rag-picking or begging. Such apprenticeships benefit both the novice who learns through participation and the more experienced child who gains economically.[7]

With time, newcomers become familiar with the city's geography and identify people who they meet regularly in certain places. Unlike other poor urban children, they grow to depend on resources found in a number of diverse social domains (Lucchini, 1996). These include networks of peers and adults in city centre streets, peripheral slum areas and various NGO programmes, and for most, their home. Like adults, children who move to a different physical and social environment are unlikely to sever their ties with the people they leave behind.

Over a two-year period, Dilip moved between his home, the streets, the NGO centre and two schools. While on the streets he visited his home and the NGO centre periodically. Then, encouraged by the staff to think about his future, he lived in the centre before moving to a local boarding school. After a year at school he ran back to the streets twice. On the second occasion he refused the option of returning, saying that he wanted to attend a different school. After much persuasion by NGO staff, he settled in the centre then was transferred to another school where he has been for the past six months.

I have argued earlier that a socially competent individual is someone who is not only able to survive, but to generate a positive sense of his own well-being out of others' approval of his actions. To what extent does Dilip achieve such competence? In an interview before he began attending school, he described rag-picking as easy. After he ran away, he was often seen walking the streets with his sack, making fires at the roadside and selling scrap in various junkyards; apparently comfortably engaged in a well-practised lifestyle. His words and actions recorded in the following journal entry suggest that Dilip considered himself not just to be coping but to be doing well in what he set out to do:

> Dilip had just weighed his scrap when I arrived in the junkyard and I heard him announce as if to himself and those around him: 'Fifty rupees this morning and what did you say that sack-load was worth? sixty? so I've earnt a total of one hundred and ten rupees today'. He folded his sack, tucked it under his arm, took the money from the owner and bought a donut which he ate immediately. (Baker, fieldnotes)

From the point of view of learning to read and write, running away from school is incompetent and frowned upon by society. But in Dilip's immediate economic and social context, he demonstrates competence in his knowledge of the opportunities on the street and the sources of support that are still available to him. He regularly rag-picked, sometimes begged from tourists and local shoppers and was reported to have found several thousand Indian rupees on the pavement that he quickly spent with three friends. In addition to the series of strong friendships formed with peers in which work, eating and sleeping arrangements were shared, Dilip had other safety nets. He visited home occasionally, joined other homeless boys who ate on credit in cheap restaurants and knew that in times of need he could rely on the NGO centre for a place to sleep or medical care. He rarely used the latter services, instead he slept with friends on temple steps or pavements and bought his own medicines. He told me that he avoids older boys who walk about in gangs and start fights. These many factors enable Dilip to both cope with and, as far as I could tell, often enjoy living outside his home or an institution.

Not all street children have equal access to the range of social environments used by Dilip. Moreover, the extent to which individual children can gain in a given setting partly depends on learning to present themselves according to the opinions about 'street children' prevalent in each setting. Children who beg are often skilled in using their appearance and Western adult perceptions of vulnerability in order to elicit donations. Dilip's peers were anxious to tell me of Dilip's whereabouts or that Dilip was 'stupid' (badmas) to run away. Having experienced the negative attitudes of the NGO staff towards running away, they expressed a 'responsible' outlook on his behaviour thereby making themselves deserving of anything that I could offer them. The consistency of current street children's reactions to runaways indicates that they too were of the opinion that Dilip and others like him were not acting in their own best interests.

I sought the views of older street youth in a discussion about the work of the NGO centre. While they acknowledged the problems of making rules in the centre, one commented that 'children who smoke should be taught good habits, to brighten their future'. His friend added 'it is our moral duty (dharma) to do this'. They agreed that children who run away from school or work opportunities given to them are responsible for their actions. In addition they cautioned that giving children too much (for example a financial guarantee to employers should any mishap arise), was unwise because they would take advantage of the situation. These young people did not question the capabilities of younger children per se. Rather they suggest that competence can be either positive or negative; depending on its effect on the individual concerned and those who are trying to improve his quality of life.

I now turn to the relationships between street children's social competence and their ideas about adult behaviour. Younger children voiced respect for NGO staff who maintained good humoured and sensitive but firm control. Such adults were not immune to accusations by children of unjust treatment. Yet my observations of daily interaction matched street children's positive comments about these individuals. Without exception those who have worked with street children would stress the importance of consistency and integrity. Street children in Manila stated that they did not like staff who were gullible or who had double standards. For example, they complained that staff pretended to care when there were visitors, but were not truly caring and that they demanded that the children should follow strict schedules that they themselves did not follow (Street Children in Asia, 18–19 cited in Ennew, 1994b, p. 139). The insecurities experienced by children in the home environment (described earlier) may have been replaced by greater autonomy on the streets. In their mobility between social environments children witness disparate value judgments about their lifestyles and behaviour which influence intrapersonal competence. Someone in authority who reacts consistently to children's actions, aspirations and fears may therefore provide the sense of stability necessary to engender social competence. Junkyard owners also offer facilities and a consistent opinion on rag-picking, although their emphasis on its income earning potential contrasts with the NGO perspective. Rag-pickers tend to base themselves in one junkyard where they store any possessions, keep an account with the owner, (usually of debts to him), and may even build a shelter in which to sleep.

The discussions between Dilip and I about his possible return to school were witnessed by a number of his street friends. Their reactions showed an appreciation of different perspectives on Dilip's situation. Although they were not personally involved in the immediate problem, the comments of several boys indicated to me that they understood both Dilip's position and the 'adult perspective'; represented in the dilemma that I was faced with. (The latter can be summarized as not knowing whether to encourage Dilip to return to school or to leave him to pursue the street lifestyle that he apparently chose.) The words and actions of Dilip's friend Tulke reported at the beginning of the chapter are a case in point. On a previous occasion, when I met both boys late at night, Tulke asked if he could ride my bike while I talked with Dilip. By making himself scarce he spared Dilip the embarrassment of my presence and his indecision being made public.

Dilip ran away from school with a younger boy, Laxman, and they worked, ate and slept together. In an interview designed to detail children's social networks, Laxman named Dilip as a playmate, someone who comforted him when he felt worried and the person he would like to be accompanied by on a long journey. It could be argued that Dilip became competent by being treated as if he was competent by Laxman. For example, his competence as a carer was evident in Laxman's dependence on him. Shortly after Dilip had returned to the NGO centre I spotted Laxman holding onto railings in a busy street. His loneliness was evident in his readiness to accompany me to the centre to see Dilip, despite genuine fear of the scolding he would receive. A focus on Dilip's role in their partnership indicates that children's competence, when demonstrated independently from adults, can easily be overlooked. However with regard to Laxman's behaviour, it is clear that competence is contingent on the support of friends. In the absence of friends who can be relied on, children display and feel a sense of vulnerability.

What then are the social and emotional costs of street living as perceived by Dilip, his friends and adults with whom he interacts? They include an overriding sense that running from the school to the streets has negative consequences for the individual and is a deviant form of behaviour. Rejoining the khate way of life is taken as proof that children cannot break the negative habits associated with this social category. The vocabulary used to describe khate includes the notion of being spoilt or broken (bigreko), being dirty and involved in thieving.

Staff in the NGO centre identify a 'live for the moment' mentality amongst street children that is based around short-term desires, immediate spending and a lack of routine, planning or anticipation of the future. Much of the literature on street children in South America frequently refers to such a mentality, known as imediatismo (Ennew, 1994a). Such behaviours have clearly developed in response to the short term nature of resources. But they entail possible costs in terms of children's inability to make long-lasting and effective relationships. Hence these behaviour traits are, in many ways, the antithesis of social competence and we must ask how such labelling by society affects individual children's self-image and esteem.

There is some doubt on the extent to which Dilip is able to manage successful relationships with his family members while living independently. For, although he expresses positive feelings towards his home, he says that on the occasions that his father has met him in the streets, he has been beaten by him, his stepmother scolds him at home and he is sometimes reluctant to visit home. In response to questions about their sources of support, a number of children said 'if I feel sad or alone, I go and watch a film'. Not having someone to talk to in times of distress suggests a cost of independence, although children at home may not discuss these matters with family members. Distancing from family relationships and greater investment in peer relations is common among pre-adolescents across cultures. These trends have been shown to be heightened under circumstances of family stress, for example parental divorce. Hetherington's study (1991, p. 122) confirmed previous research findings, namely that disengagement from the family is one way in which children cope with divorce.

Competence to Make Changes?

The Nepali street children recognize a conflict between what they prioritize in the short term, whether through need or desire, and their aspirations for the future. They therefore describe a range of competent behaviour in their peers that has positive or negative connotations. There are no cultural models of post-street life hence individual children cannot position themselves in the life-course in terms of career, marriage and settling in a community. None of the street children I met envisaged rag-picking, begging or sleeping rough in the future. Some street children said that they wanted jobs with high status, (for example film star, police officer and bank manager), which they were unlikely to obtain. Yet many spoke of attending school, setting up a small business, seeking waged government employment or returning to their home village and could envisage opportunities to do these.

By living independently in the city, street children experience elements of an urban, middle-class childhood that are inaccessible to their parents and peers in the rural village or urban slum. They see wealthy children going to school or shopping, they watch television and Hindi films, they talk with tourists and they experience the philosophy and provision of the NGO centre. While only a small minority are able to participate directly in this alternative childhood, (through school sponsorship or skill training programmes), street children's exposure to different lifestyles may influence their views on their own future career. In terms of intergenerational differences in experience and children's changing expectations, there are parallels in the outcomes of running away to the city and attending school in the village.

Skinner and Holland (1996) found that village children in Central Nepal drew sharp contrasts between those people who were uneducated and those who had some formal education. Many described the former as living in a 'traditional, superstitious and conservative world', linking it to their parents way of life that 'was oriented more to farming and local affairs' (p. 280). In contrast, the 'educated' person was able to look outward and forward beyond the village because their 'eyes had been opened' to personal opportunities and the prospect of 'development' in the community (*ibid.*, p. 282). Schooling therefore offered opportunities for emancipation from the traditional oppression of gender, caste and state control. Yet the school produced new forms of privilege and disdain: 'We saw an ever-increasing validation of formal education as a source of symbolic capital, giving those who possessed it claims to superior position and statuses' (*ibid.*, p. 274).

Some street children described their move to the city as similarly progressive and liberating. We may therefore expect that these children view farming, tailoring or other traditional livelihoods in their home communities, as inferior to occupations in the urban sector. Most children expressed a preference for work in the city because they saw opportunities for a greater cash income. However many said that, should they fail to find a job, they will go home where their parents will find work for them. Parental alcoholism and family discord prompted one 14-year-old Damai (tailor caste) boy to run to the streets. He later reported that he preferred to learn to sew than attend school 'because tailoring is my family trade'. Problems in family relationships and the likelihood that returning children will be unskilled in traditional livelihoods, may prevent children from realizing some career plans. To date, we know relatively little about the career outcomes of street children in Nepal. A significant number have settled in the urban poor community or gone back to their home villages. The majority are still on the streets.

Dilip's behaviour raises important questions about the assumed costs incurred to children's future by spending time on the streets. Economically it is currently viable and sometimes lucrative. There are potential longer term income sources in the squatter and junkyard communities, for example butchery, municipal sweeping and small-scale craft and retail businesses. In terms of social relations and status, the outcomes are mixed. Children show that they are able to participate successfully within several immediate social spheres, including family, peers and staff at the NGO centre. Nevertheless the negative associations prevalent within the wider social sphere are influential in children's immediate social relations. For example many children expressed difficulty in going home because it may have become known in the community that they were khate.

It is therefore quite plausible that children's unsuccessful attempts to integrate into wider society have had negative effects on their sense of control in their own lives. Because they failed to meet the responsibilities that come with a job or school placement, children said that they were incapable of moving out of the street lifestyle. Thus, they expressed disappointment in what they viewed as their own incompetence in wider society.

Enrolling at school is a step termed as 'progress' by the rest of society. But the children who joined boarding school after living on the streets, were quick to point out the sacrifices they had to make. In school they must live by rules that govern their routine, types of food and even manner of speech and behaviour. Also they must forego their mobility between places and social networks. To be a competent school child from the point of view of staff and other children, one must act in such a way to demonstrate both subordinance to and dependence on adults in authority. Unsurprisingly on expeditions out of school some of these 'ex-street children' made persistent demands in the expectation that I, an adult and sponsor to one of them, should now provide them with clothes and food. Staff described these children as potentially problematic because their expressive behaviour could disrupt other children and running away was not infrequent.

Yet the staff also acknowledged the expertise that children developed in the streets; cleverness and cunning had ambiguous qualities but leadership skills were valued and fostered. Within a peer group there is not room for everyone to be a leader. One 15-year-old 'ex-street boy' who was respected and called 'older brother' (dai) by his friends, displayed competence in school and outside. He was often sent by staff to look for runaway children. His uncontested position as elder and group leader suggests that his self-image and social skills grew together and were valued equally by his peers and adults. In contrast, Dilip's behaviour seems to have been influenced by the restrictions in the school setting. When asked to give a reason for his departure from school he said that a teacher had beaten him. As we might expect, 13-year-old street children who are learning basic literacy in a class of much younger children, are easily discouraged. The daunting prospect of five years of study before they are deemed educated is confounded by their awareness that even then, there is no guarantee of a salaried job.

Conclusion

After several months of observing Dilip on the streets after he ran away, I viewed his social competence in this arena as no less sophisticated than that of adults. Realizing the limits of what was accessible to me, I compared his quality of life — his demeanour, degree of control in shaping events and how he was valued by others — on the streets and as a school pupil. In terms of immediate prospects the street environment had clear advantages so I challenged Dilip to think about the future and returning to school. Was I unfair to expect him to be able to choose one or the other?

NGO staff commented that children often ran away 'for no real reason, but say that the teachers have beaten them just to give us an answer'. Adults often perceive children as unable to debate either the reasons behind their actions or the relative advantages of career options. If adults then unconsciously add these perceptions to their opinion that running away is inappropriate, the conclusion is one of children's incompetence.

I have argued that a salient characteristic of homeless street children is that they do not currently invest in, nor are they forced into, one particular lifestyle. Rather they move between diverse physical and social environments in which their competence is judged according to different criteria. If children are to profit from these various social interactions they must present themselves differently in each environment. As has been demonstrated, children find immediate advantages in maintaining personal involvement in a number of social groups such as the junk-yard, NGO centre and various peer networks. Those who do so successfully may be described as socially competent.

My discussion has addressed the notion of social competence among children in a Nepali social and cultural context. It has demonstrated that 'social competence' is a nebulous term that derives its meaning from the particular context in which it is used. Like the term 'deviance', social competence is 'not a quality that lies in behaviour itself, but in the interaction between the person who commits an act and those who respond to it' (Becker, 1963, p. 14). In this chapter, the term 'social competence' has been applied to individuals whose behaviour is viewed as abnormal and challenging to the status quo. I have shown that ideas about a person's capabilities are affected by value judgments of appropriate forms of behaviour. These ideas are instrumental in forming children's own perceptions of their competence within wider society and a sense of self-worth.

Thus the Nepali street children acknowledge their competence in daily life but perceive the street lifestyle and its advantages as only temporarily appropriate. Dilip's inability to decide which lifestyle to pursue was distressing to observe and perhaps from my own perspective, the most poignant demonstration of his vulnerability. This analysis has shown that children are amply aware of the consequences of their actions even if they are, on occasion, unable or unwilling to voice them. Nevertheless, if children consider themselves to have failed in their ambition to be educated at school or secure a job, life-courses that are socially acceptable, these may have negative effects on their self-esteem which should not be overlooked.

Notes

1   I thank the children and adults interviewed in Nepal, the staff of CWIN (Child Workers in Nepal) and especially my co-researcher Catherine Panter-Brick for her comments on this chapter. The research was conducted in affiliation with Tribhuvan University, Kathmandu and funded by a Durham University studentship.

2   This chapter draws on fieldwork conducted in Nepal over twenty months between 1992 and 1995. I used participant observation, semi-structured interviews and group discussions with pre-adolescent children, older street youth and adults including parents and NGO staff. I did not set out to research social competence *per se* and thus my discussion is based on my own observations of street children's behaviour and the judgements of their friends, parents and adult care-givers in the context of prevalent ideas about childhood in Nepal.

3   The arrangement was made within an established sponsorship programme run by a Nepali Non-Governmental Organisation (NGO). My position as Dilman's sponsor is nonetheless important in our relationship. It is likely that he viewed me as either more supportive or more threatening than other adults, and his behaviour should be considered in this light.

4   The NGO (refered to in footnote 3) runs a drop-in centre where street children play, wash, eat and receive medical treatment. Non-formal education classes, a banking scheme and several skill training programmes also operate from the centre.

5   Due to the fact that a very small minority of the street children were girls (3 per cent), this study focuses solely on boys.

6   Research from South America shows a healthy resistence to adversity among homeless children in the form of a high degree of intelligence, a concern for each other, lack of drug use and a good self-esteem (Aptekar, 1994).

7   Although hierarchical relations exist within groups of children, exploitative pair bonds were apparently rare.

References

APTEKAR, L. (1994) 'Street children in the developing world: A review of their condition', *Cross Cultural Reserach*, **28**, pp. 195–224.

BAKER, R., PANTER-BRICK, C. and TODD, A. (1997) 'Homeless street boys in Nepal: Their demography and lifestyle', *Journal of Comparative Family Studies*, **28**.

BECKER, H.S. (1963) *Outsiders: Studies in the Sociology of Deviance*, London: The Free Press.

BENTHALL, J. (1992) 'Child focused research', *Anthropology Today*, **8**.

BOGIN, B. (forthcoming) 'Evolutionary and biological aspects of childhood', in PANTER-BRICK, C. (ed.) *Biosocial Perspectives on Childhood*, Cambridge: Cambridge University Press.

ENNEW, J. (1994a) 'Parentless friends: A cross-cultural examination of networks among street children and street youth', in NESTMAN, F. and HURRELMAN, K. (eds) *Social Networks and Social Support in Childhood and Adolescence*, Berlin: De Gruyter.

ENNEW, J. (1994b) *Street and Working Children: A Guide to Planning*, Save the Children.

GARDNER, H. (1984) 'The development of competence in culturally defined domains: A preliminary framework', in SHWEDER, R.A. and LeVINE, R.A. (eds) *Culture Theory: Essays on Mind Self and Emotion*, New York: Cambridge University Press.

HETHERINGTON, E.M. (1991) 'Coping with family transitions: Winners, losers and survivors', in WOODHEAD, M., LIGHT, P. and CARR, R. (eds) *Growing Up in a Changing Society*, London: Routledge.

HOCKEY, J. and JAMES, A. (1993) *Growing Up and Growing Old: Ageing and Dependency in the Life Course*, London: Sage

LAVE, J. and WENGER, E. (1991) *Situated Learning: Legitimate Peripheral Participation*, New York: Cambridge University Press.

LUCCHINI, R. (1996) 'The street and its image', in CONNOLLY, M. and ENNEW, J. (eds) 'Children out of place: Special issue on working and street children', *Childhood*, **3**.

MAYALL, B. (1994) 'Children in action at home and school', in MAYALL, B. (ed.) *Children's Childhoods: Observed and Experienced*, London: Falmer Press.

QVORTRUP, J. (1994) 'Childhood matters: An introduction', in QVORTRUP, J. et al. (eds) *Childhood Matters: Social Theory, Practice and Politics*, Aldershot: Avebury Press.

SCHIEFFELIN, B. (1990) *The Give and Take of Everyday Life: Language Socialisation of Kaluli children*, New York: Cambridge University Press.

SKINNER, D. and HOLLAND, D. (1996) 'Schools and the cultural production of the educated person in a Nepalese hill community', in LEVINSON, B.A., FOLEY, D.E. and HOLLAND, D. (eds) *The Cultural Production of the Educated Person: Critical Ethnographies of Schooling and Local Practice*, Buffalo, NY: SUNY Press.

Chapter 4

Protest–despair–detachment: Questioning the Myth

Helen Barrett

The claim that protest–despair–detachment is the typical pattern of young children's responses to major separations appears to have attained the status of a truism, being still firmly believed by many clinicians and featuring in many psychology textbooks. Yet, premised on a conceptualization of children as considerably more socially inept than they actually are, it does not appear to fit well with the facts as a general description of children's separation responses. In this chapter I argue that, even during its inception in the period from the 1940s to the 1980s, empirical evidence did not support this interpretation and that there is a need to reconceptualize separation responses. Taking into account the possibility that the initial stages of separation are characterized by a far greater range of individual differences than was previously recognized, I propose that the protest–despair–detachment framework be replaced by an account more capable of accommodating the evidence.

Doubts expressed concerning many aspects of Bowlby's early theories of attachment and separation have given rise to modifications (for example, O'Connor, 1956; Schaffer and Emerson, 1964; Yarrow, 1961 and 1964; Morgan, 1975; Clarke and Clarke, 1976). Many of these modifications have been documented (for example, Rutter, 1972, 1979a and 1991) and incorporated into Bowlby's later theorizing. Yet one aspect appears to have received little consideration. This is the notion that, on being separated from an attachment figure, 'There is good evidence that many (but not all) young children show an immediate reaction of acute distress and crying (what has been called the period of "protest"), followed by misery and apathy (the phase of "despair"), and finally there may be a stage when the child becomes apparently contented and seems to lose interest in his parents ("detachment" in Robertson's and Bowlby's terms) . . . That these reactions occur is well established' (Rutter, 1972, p. 29 and 1981, p. 31).

Despite, or perhaps because of, the difficulty of creating the conditions under which all three stages of separation response can be reliably observed, this account of separation responses appears to have acquired the status of a doctrine which has never been seriously debated. It features in teaching programmes and texts within the fields of developmental psychology, psychiatry and related disciplines and is often also present even in current literature related to separation targeted at lay audiences (for example, Tolfree, 1995; Lansdowne, 1996). In addition, the causal implications embedded within the protest–despair–detachment account continue to influence thinking about separation within both academic and non-academic traditions. Two causal links are implied: first, that separation leads to despair or depression and, second, that prolonged separation leads to detachment which is viewed as a serious threat to social and emotional development.

Within mainstream psychology, these simple links have been challenged. For example, it has been suggested that the link between early separations and depression may be largely spurious and likely to be mediated by extraneous influences such as pre- and post-separation relationships (Bifulco, Harris and Brown, 1992; Bemporad and Romano, 1993). More generally, however, separation continues to be viewed as inextricably associated with unacceptable risk. Many childcare policies, including arrangements for the care of children in hospital, health care advisor training, day care and educational provision, and decisions with regard to the care and custody of young children, have been and continue to be informed by concerns about the effects in early life of separation on children's mental well-being and subsequent emotional development. And within this social context, particularly in respect of the care of young children, encouragement to invest in wider social support networks has been relatively lacking while public fears about the damaging effects of separation have tended to be reinforced. Perhaps typical of advice reinforcing a negative view of separation are the following passages written by an author whose child care manuals (Leach, 1989, 1991a and 1991b) have proved to be extremely popular: 'It is clearly and certainly best for babies to have something close to full-time mother care for six months at least — conveniently linked with breast-feeding — and family care for a further year or better two. Using financial or career penalties to blackmail women into leaving infants who are scarcely settled into life outside wombs that are still bleeding is no less than barbarous' (Leach, 1994, pp. 78–9); 'Whoever it is who cares for infants, they need to have permanence, continuity, passion and a parent-like commitment that is difficult to find or meet outside the vested interests and social expectations of family roles and cannot be adequately replaced by professionalism' (*ibid.*, p. 83).

Views such as these seem clearly to be rooted in a discourse in which separation in early childhood is viewed as a negative experience. It is this issue which this chapter sets out to address. I argue that accounts such as the protest–despair–detachment (PDD) account, which can be viewed as a prototypically negative account of separation, have now passed into folklore and continue to exert a potent influence which needs to be reexamined, disputed and replaced. Three arguments are advanced in respect of the PDD account: first, that the evidence for the PDD pattern was never substantial; second, that there is now and has for some time been ample evidence for alternative accounts of separation responses; third, that the PDD account, being premised on a model of the very young child as far less socially competent than recent research has indicated, stands in need of refinement.

The PDD Pattern and Attachment

Initially, Bowlby and Robertson identified separation-protest in a specific group of children: 'When a child of 18–24 months of age, who has previously had a normal relationship with his mother and has not been separated from her for more than a few hours, is parted from her and cared for in an impersonal environment (that is, an environment which does not provide substitute mothering) he commonly progresses through three phases of emotional response which we describe as the phases of *protest, despair,* and *denial'* (Robertson, 1953, p. 383). In a series of papers in which Bowlby developed his theory of separation anxiety (for example, Bowlby, 1953, 1958, 1961, 1962, 1968, 1969 and 1973; Robertson and Bowlby, 1952), Bowlby reiterated this description but renamed the final phase *detachment* in keeping with his theory that the whole sequence of responses constitutes a reaction to disruption of attachment bonds or loss of the primary attachment figure (Bowlby, 1960a). Bowlby considered that the PDD description applied to all types of separation in infants and young children, even children cared for at home: 'When they (*infants and young children of over six months*) for any reason lose their loved object the three phases of mourning described are experienced. At all ages, we now see, the first phase of mourning is one of Protest, the second one of Despair, and the third one of Detachment' (Bowlby, 1961, p. 338). Though he acknowledged that 'The initial phase, that of protest, may begin immediately or may be delayed' (Bowlby, 1969, p. 49), Bowlby did not seek further explanation concerning what may underlie this variability.

Bowlby located the source of his conclusions deep within a range of theoretical arguments and empirical evidence. For example, he argued (Bowlby, 1960a) that PDD was pre-figured in Freud's work and fitted well with Freud's final theory of anxiety as 'missing someone who is loved and longed for' (Freud, 1926, p. 293). Bowlby mapped the continuum of responses in relation to loss of an object in Freud's scheme onto the three phases of separation responses: anxiety, the reaction to the danger of losing the object, gives rise to protest; the pain of mourning which is engendered by retreat from the lost object gives rise to despair; defence, which relates to dealing with anxiety and pain, leads to detachment. He saw this enforced detachment as the potential source of later difficulties in establishing close relationships.

Whilst the long-term detachment outcome has been challenged in relation to a range of separation experiences (for example, Quinton and Rutter 1976), it is still considered a possible consequence of more severe separation situations. In addition, work instigated by Bowlby on attachment has tended to reinforce the belief that poor social and emotional development is associated with ambivalent or avoidant attachment relations. It is notable that the three major attachment patterns identified by Ainsworth and colleagues in association with Bowlby (Ainsworth et al., 1978) map very closely onto the three phases of PDD. Broadly speaking, secure attachments can be associated with determined attempts to regain access to the caregiver (protest), the ambivalent resistant pattern with despairingly mixed feelings (a mixture of protest and despair) in relation to the caregiver and avoidant attachment with detachment. PDD, though relatively unfashionable as a research issue, has therefore retained a strong covert influence within current thinking about attachment.

These concerns about potential damage to attachment relationships also feature highly both in the research literature on day care and in the thoughts of day care users and providers (Barrett, 1991). The averred link between extensive day care in infancy and avoidant attachment (Belsky, 1988; Belsky and Rovine, 1988; Belsky and Braungart, 1991) reflects similar concerns and tends to support a negative view of substitute care. Interestingly, Bowlby and Robertson sometimes differed in their opinions on this issue. While Robertson agreed that protest was the initial response to hospitalization for most children, particularly those under 5 (Robertson, 1953; Robertson and Robertson, 1971b and 1989), he did not accept Bowlby's assertion (Bowlby, 1980) that the presence of a substitute attachment figure only attenuated and made less intense but did not alter the basic PDD response (Robertson and Robertson, 1971). Failure to resolve such a fundamental difference can be seen perhaps to reflect the predominantly theory-driven process through which the PDD pattern was identified.

The Origins of the PDD Model of Separation Responses

Studies of Young Children

For obvious ethical and practical reasons, research on the effect of long-term separation on young children has not involved carefully controlled experiments. Rather, as Bowlby acknowledged (Bowlby, 1969 and 1973), the empirical basis for his account of separation responses was derived from accounts, often patchy and anecdotal, of children admitted to residential nurseries or homes (Burlingham and Freud, 1942 and 1944; Freud and Dann, 1951; Spitz, 1945, 1946a and 1946b; Spitz and Wolf, 1946; David et al., 1952; Aubry, 1955; Heinicke, 1956; Heinicke and Westheimer, 1965; Robertson and Robertson, 1971b) and hospitals (Robertson and Bowlby, 1952; Robertson, 1952 and 1953; Bowlby, 1953; Prugh et al., 1953; Illingworth and Holt, 1955; Douglas and Blomfield, 1958; Schaffer, 1958; Schaffer and Callender, 1959; Mićić, 1962; Vernon et al., 1967; Davenport and Werry, 1970; Stacey et al., 1970).

As has been stressed elsewhere (for example, Pinneau, 1955; Vernon et al., 1967), the data presented in these studies was rarely either systematically collected or fully reported. With regard to non-hospital studies (since hospital studies were always confounded by additional trauma such as illness, unfamiliar environments and routines, frightening institutional practices, etc.), few of these included observations made at the crucial point of separation, an omission which must weaken any inferences concerning initial responses to separation. Reports also omitted crucial details such as how many children were involved, their ages at the time of study or at the point of separation, pre-separation experience, previous separation experience, length of separation, reasons for separation, the nature of the separation experience. Few studies took into account whether siblings were kept together or parted. Some were also unclear about the extent to which the mother was available (Burlingham and Freud, 1942 and 1944; Spitz and Wolf, 1946). Further, few reports contained details of adequate control group comparisons and this lack was compounded by the failure to control observer bias. An additional, fundamental problem which lent a distinctly subjective quality to many studies was the failure to develop reliable or valid measures of infant distress or to describe clearly how measures (for example, frequency of crying) were applied. Finally, due to the brevity of most studies, the stage of despair or depression was rarely documented and, where it was identified, either was not manifested by the majority of children within samples (Spitz and Wolf, 1946; Bowlby, 1953) or seemed not to be have been preceded by protest (Spitz and Wolf, 1946; David et al., 1952).

Studies of Animals

Bowlby's theoretical position was considerably strengthened by his demonstration of its compatibility with control systems theory and evidence from ethological studies. Arguing that it is possible to understand the behaviour of human infants within an ethological framework, Bowlby postulated the existence of an attachment behavioural system (as distinct from reproductive, nutritive or affiliative systems) which functions to preserve the species, irrespective of individual members' inherent sociability. Within this system, he saw separation anxiety as the primary instinctive response to rupture of attachment to the mother which is present in all species. By designating separation anxiety as a primary instinctive response in this way, Bowlby freed himself to generalize across species and to use the more accessible experimental data on animal responses to social isolation to support his theories. Comparing primate and human responses to separation, he argued that 'These naturalistic accounts show plainly not only that the attachment behaviour of young non-human primates is very similar to the attachment behaviour of young children but that their responses to separations are very similar also' (Bowlby, 1973, p. 83). This position leads to problems in relation to theory-generation and data-analysis for over-reliance upon animal models can lead to a tendency to place so much emphasis on similarities that differences can be overlooked. Also, even if overt behaviours appear alike, and this is still much disputed particularly with regard to the detachment phase (Berman, Rasmussen and Suomi, 1994; Hoff, Nadler, Hoff and Maple, 1994), the assumption that the cognitive processes mediating them and the emotional states accompanying them are very similar cannot be justified. In the following section, it is argued that closer attention to relevant data may have led to rather different conclusions.

Alternative Interpretations of Early Data

Where studies did include observations of initial responses, even in settings where separation was compounded by trauma, many children's first responses seemed to be characterized by something other than protest. Due to the paucity of data contained within most of the early studies, this section draws mainly upon the films made by the Robertsons of children experiencing separation.

Several studies fleetingly drew attention to the variety of coping strategies adopted by children on admission to institutions. For example, David et al. (1952,

p. 69), in their study of children admitted to a residential institution, commented upon 'the surprisingly valiant manner' in which the children in their study endured 'what seemed to us an intense shock'. In a follow-up report, Aubry (1955) noted that the first signs of distress usually only appeared at the exact moment of separation if the separation itself was accompanied by an additional traumatic feature, such as the sudden illness of the mother or the sudden disappearance of one of the parents from home. She, like several other authors, identified the onset of distress as contiguous with routines such as undressing, bathing or putting to bed which were usually carried out by mother. This pattern seems well illustrated in the film 'A 2-year-old goes to hospital' (Robertson, 1952; Bowlby et al., 1952) which consists of time-sampled episodes during a child's eight-day stay in hospital for treatment of an umbilical hernia. Scenes from Laura's stay are accompanied by a narrative which is closely related in the account which follows.

A 2-year-old Goes to Hospital

Talks with her parents prior to hospital admission had aimed at preparing Laura for separation. On the bus which brought her and her mother to the hospital, she is 'very lively'. On arrival, when the nurse invites her to come and see the rocking horse, Laura says, 'you come too mummy' but 'goes quite cheerfully' without her. Immediately after this, at 10 a.m., the nurse takes Laura into the bathroom and proceeds to undress and bath her (this is not her usual bath-time). At this point, Laura cries and calls 'I want my mummy' several times but, after ten minutes, 'has regained her composure'. She talks to the nurse as she is dressed. But she looks rather serious and, on being put to bed, first asks why other children are in bed, then objects to having her temperature taken, saying, 'Don't like it. I want my mummy.' However, at this point, she cuddles the nurse and does not cry again until her mother comes to say goodbye. She quietens before her mother leaves and, once on her own, looks around the ward as though worried and perhaps a bit sad but also intrigued.

The following morning, Laura is filmed singing to herself, 'Boatie, boatie, boatie' (a boat is one of her favourite toys which accompanied her to hospital). She greets the nurse with 'Where's my mummy gone?', then is described as going on playing 'as if unconcerned'. During her stay, she 'often asks for her mother like this with little feeling in her voice, asking this question on almost every occasion when she is given attention by a sympathetic person'.

During the remainder of her stay, although she is described as having cried very little, Laura protests in response to distressing hospital procedures such as the surgeon's manual exploration of her abdomen and the rectal anaesthetic given on the day of her operation. On this day, Laura is distinctly wary of what the nurses are going to do to her, very aware of distress in other children and is showing signs of crossness with her teddy. On the day after the operation, she is described as very subdued and quiet and, from this point on, her emotional state appears to be one of lightly suppressed distress. Her continued attempts to control her feelings lead to bed-wetting, more attacks on her teddy and the hospital doll, and the appearance of some nervous mannerisms (clutching objects, picking and scratching at herself). By day seven, she is gloomy and withdrawn and on day eight needs some persuasion before she is prepared to believe that she is really going home.

The film clearly documents the stressfulness of this kind of stay in hospital. At the same time it illustrates the resourcefulness of a very young child in highly threatening circumstances. Laura's way of coping with separation, particularly on day one, seems to be characterized more by stoicism and a determination not to evoke concern than by protest. It is not until several intrusive events have taken place and she has been subjected to unpleasant surgical procedures that Laura's initial attempts to calm herself really seem to give way. The emergence of singing on day one could be viewed as a creative attempt to control the strange environment by filling it with pleasant and familiar sounds. That the subject of the song was a favourite transitional object also suggests that Laura continued at this stage to believe or want to believe that a familiar transitional space was still available to her, irrespective of her physical circumstances. At this point, too, she still seemed prepared to accept the nurse as a playmate. She seemed able to retain an imaginary inner world which outer reality had not yet impinged upon so that protest and rejection of alternative caregivers was not yet necessary. Even after the untimely bath, the speed with which Laura recovered her stoical attitude and accepted the nurse's attentions seems to suggest that at this stage her behaviour was characterized more by resilience, stoicism or coping than by protest.

Another case, described by Robertson and Bowlby (1952), appears to fit far more closely the separation–protest pattern. In this case, Barbara, whose age is not given, is described as being undressed and put into a cot in sight of her parents who are not allowed to respond to her, to say goodbye or to visit for five days. Barbara protests vigorously and immediately. Whether her protests were in response to a severe violation of expectations in relation to her parents' behaviour or to being separated and subjected again to hospital (she had had a previous experience of hospitalization), or both, it is not possible to determine. It is also conceivable that, if hospital procedures routinely required parents to act in such an upsetting manner, Robertson may have observed a far higher incidence of protest behaviour than would be expected under more favourable circumstances.

Other Films by the Robertsons

Robertson made five other films during the period 1967 to 1973 of children in residential or foster care while their mothers were in hospital having a baby. Four of these children were fostered, one at a time, in the Robertsons' home; the fifth child was placed in a residential nursery. The four children fostered by the Robertsons were introduced to Joyce Robertson, the principal substitute carer, before the fostering arrangement began. None of these four children manifested acute distress on being separated but, rather, each adopted a range of coping strategies which the Robertsons refer to as 'defensive activity' (Robertson and Robertson, 1976, p. 21). The children persisted with these coping attempts for variable lengths of time.

Kate (29 months) (Robertson and Robertson, 1967), the first child to be filmed in the Robertsons' care, was in foster care for twenty-seven days. For the first six days, she is described as 'unusually cheerful, cooperative and active'. She engages in activities which she may have helped with at home, such as cleaning the windows.

Jane (17 months) (Robertson and Robertson, 1968) was fostered for ten days and appeared to become 'very attached to her foster mother' (Robertson and Robertson, 1976, p. 9). Throughout the first three days Jane is described as 'active and cheerful. But she makes intense efforts to get smiles from her caretakers. Her smiling is so exaggerated and artificial, alternating with a confused and tense expression, that it cannot be mistaken for humour or happiness' (*ibid*.). The narrative accompanying the film at this point describes her as 'gay and lively', directing 'intense, purposeful smiles to foster family' and engaging in 'gay overactivity' with 'intense smiling'.

Thomas (28 months) (Robertson and Robertson, 1971a) was also fostered for ten days and, though showing clear signs of strain by day nine, seemed more able than the other children to use his intellectual understanding to maintain positive images of his parents and his situation. Throughout the separation, 'for most of the time he is good humoured, in friendly contact with his caretakers, and able to enjoy play and the activities offered' (Robertson and Robertson, 1976, p. 17). Nevertheless, for the first two days he is 'overactive' and 'pseudocheerful'.

Lucy (21 months) (Robertson and Robertson, 1973), who was fostered for nineteen days, is described as, prior to separation, having a sombre expression. She leaves her mother 'without a protest and without a change of facial expression'. But throughout the first few days she is 'increasingly active and the glumness gives way to a lively range of feelings — petulance, gaiety, and affection' (Robertson and Robertson, 1976, p. 13). By the fifth day, she is 'bright and cheerful' and 'appears to be in a better state than immediately before the separation'. On reunion, Lucy shows mixed strong feelings and signs of a conflict of loyalties between her mother and the foster mother though this appears to resolve itself as her positive feelings towards both predominate.

In all four of these children, then, the initial stage of separation appears to be characterized not so much by protest but by determined attempts to cope and to continue to keep alive a sense of self-efficacy in meaningful social interactions. All four appeared to go through a phase where, although aware that something was not as usual, they distracted themselves from it rather than feeling it and protesting. Eventually each child began to show signs of strain and the two older children, Kate and Thomas, were able to voice their sense of missing their parents. But even at this point, protest did not appear to become their predominant mode of expression. This does not appear to fit well with Bowlby's assertion that, 'Throughout the latter half of his first year and during the whole of his second and third he is closely attached to his mother-figure, which means that he is content in her company and distressed in her absence. Even momentary separations often lead him to protest; and longer ones always do' (Bowlby, 1962, p. 263). While, as Bowlby emphasized, these children all eventually showed distinct signs of strain, it does not seem accurate to describe their response as protest. This seems even more clear in the case of the next child to be discussed.

John (17 months) (Robertson and Robertson, 1969) spent nine days in a busy residential nursery. Disturbed in his sleep by being admitted in the night, he cried, then slept. During his first two days, he is described as behaving much of the time as he did at home, 'confident that people in the environment will respond to his needs as his parents had done. When this does not happen he is increasingly bewildered and confused, but he does not immediately break down. He makes more determined efforts to get attention from the nurses, but he cannot compete with the more assertive institutionalized children and his quiet advances are usually overlooked' (Robertson and Robertson, 1976, p. 25). During these first two days, therefore, he makes many attempts to continue as though everything was normal. Realization that it is not is only gradual.

By the third day, John's distress is very much more evident, he plays less and he shows anger when his father visits. Subsequently, his anguish intensifies, he stops eating, is constantly miserable and spends much time buried under a huge teddy, in quiet and deep despair. By the last days of his stay, he is described as dull, blank and unresponsive, inconsolable and distrustful of his parents on reunion.

Even though John has a placid, rather passive temperament, his active attempts to continue to engage in positive social interactions are evident during the first days of his separation. He tries to utilize familiar coping strategies but quickly finds them ineffective. His predominant expressive state at this point is bewilderment and confusion and it is notable that it is only when he has given up trying to interact with the nurses that he refuses food and drink, stops playing and cries a great deal. In other words, in John's case, the protest phase began after an earlier phase during which he struggled to cope.

Further Challenges to the PDD Account of Separation Responses

The discussion above has raised several possibilities in relation to the PDD pattern of separation responses. First, it has been suggested that the initial phase of response is not best described as a phase of 'protest' but rather as a phase in which children use all the strategies at their disposal to retain a sense of self-efficacy. Second, it has been recognized that protest may not only be delayed but may be absent completely or superseded by other types of coping strategy. Third, it has been suggested that despair or depression, when it does occur, is often not preceded by protest. Evidence from two other sources, namely research on adult experiences of separation and loss and more recent research on separation in early childhood, lends further support to the notion that the PDD account of separation may be incomplete.

Adult Mourning

Bowlby's original model of adult mourning comprised three main phases (Bowlby, 1961): pining or yearning and searching for lost object; disorganization and despair;

reorganization or recovery. The parallel between this pattern and the pattern proposed for separation responses in young children is clear: the searching phase links with protest, disorganization with despair, reorganization/recovery with detachment. But, in relation to adult mourning, further research and reflection indicated that an 'important first phase, which is usually fairly brief' (Bowlby and Parkes 1970, p. 198) had been omitted. This first phase was described as disbelief or numbness (Bowlby and Parkes, 1970; Parkes, 1972; Bowlby, 1980).

Interestingly, although workers in the field of adult grief responses have not always agreed on an overall pattern of responses, most have postulated an initial period during which the bereaved person is unable to accept the reality of the loss (for example, Averill, 1968; Kübler-Ross, 1975; Kalish, 1988). It has also been recognized that this initial period may recur at later stages, such as in instances of false recognition or the sensation that a dead person is still present.

Separation from an attachment figure in early childhood has been considered to be very similar to mourning in adulthood. Yet the PDD account overlooks the possibility of an intervening phase between separation onset and commencement of protest. This may be understood as due to differences between the nature of experiences or experiencers (or both) though there are arguments against both these positions which will be addressed later. Perhaps more relevant is Bowlby's insight that: 'always in the history of medicine it is the end result of a pathological sequence which is first to be noted. Only gradually are the earlier phases identified, and it may be many years before the exact sequence is understood' (Bowlby, 1960a, p. 91).

Job-related Marital Separations

In an extensive review of studies of chronic separation experiences during marriage, Vormbrock (1993) drew attention to findings from three sets of workers who suggested that women experiencing job-related separation tend to go through four stages of adaptation: initial shock/numbness, protest, despair, detachment/reorganization (Hill, 1949; Bey and Lange, 1974; Bermudes, 1977). These four stages are clearly more similar to adult mourning processes than to the pattern proposed for childhood separation. Yet, interestingly, Pearlman (1970), in a separate study, asserted that, without exception, each of the 485 naval wives who consulted him in his practice as a military psychiatrist exhibited the PDD pattern of responses in relation to marital separation. Pearlman was the only worker who attempted to link observations directly with attachment theory: failure to find evidence of initial numbness or shock as well as the unusually high proportion of subjects manifesting PDD suggest that the discrepancy between findings was more closely associated with theory- than data-derived differences.

Vormbrock (1993) also drew attention to the fact that, although partners may, for the same reason, share a separation experience, the responses of the home-based spouse are often quite different to those of their non-home-based partner. While home-based wives often experienced very ambivalent feelings during separation and reunion and tended over time to distance themselves from relationships, husbands were generally eager to reestablish intimacy and, though often anxious, were considerably less likely to feel angry on reunion. This finding again indicates the importance of taking into account the social context in which separation occurs. It also suggests that the potential of any specific type of separation to disrupt an attachment relationship may be related more to the individual's perception of control over accessibility to an attachment figure than to the type of separation (though this may still have an influence), that is, negative effects may be related more to perceived than to actual availability of attachment figures.

Separation in Early Childhood

Since the original formulation of the PDD account, research on separation responses in infancy has been extensive. In the main, the focus has been on attachment relationships between infants and their principal caregivers and the effect of these on social development. There has also been a number of studies of different kinds of separation. My intention in this section is not to present an extensive review or critique of this literature but rather to illustrate by way of examples how, since the PDD account was formulated, information from a variety of sources has led to altered perspectives on child development within which the validity of the PDD account appears tenuous.

Separation and Attachment

A large body of data has been gathered using instruments designed to measure attachment, most notably the Strange Situation Procedure (Ainsworth and Wittig, 1969). During this procedure, infants (usually aged between 12 and 18 months) are exposed to a novel play environment and separated twice from their carer, first in the company of a stranger, then alone. Infants' behaviour throughout the procedure and particularly towards carers on reunion is analysed and, using a forced classification method, the attachment relationship between baby and carer is assessed. Originally, eight attachment patterns were identified (Ainsworth et al., 1978) plus a proportion of interaction patterns which were considered unclassifiable (approximately 3 per cent of each sample). Of the eight original patterns, four were described as secure (B1–B4) and four as insecure: anxious-avoidant (A1–A2) and anxious-ambivalent/resistant (C1–C2). Analysis of 'unclassifiable' cases has since led to identification of a disorganized/disoriented pattern (Main and Solomon, 1990) or patterns (Lyons-Ruth et al., 1991). Zeanah, Mammen and Lieberman (1993) have further proposed that disorders of attachment can be classified as non-attached, inhibited, role-reversed and indiscriminate.

In view of these large individual differences in attachment pattern and in response to separation even within the restricted setting of the Strange Situation Procedure, few workers familiar with attachment research would now consider one pattern sufficient to describe separation responses in young children. In the Strange Situation setting, the majority of 1-year-olds, on the first separation, and a signific- ant proportion on the second separation, do not show overt distress, although the presence of stress may be indicated by physiological measures (Belsky and Braungart, 1991; Spangler and Grossman, 1993). Nevertheless, cross-cultural studies have shown that separation anxiety appears to peak during the second year of life and that, although there is very considerable inter- and intra-cultural variation, the majority of infants (40–65 per cent) in most samples tend to fall into the secure (B) category within which more expressive (B3–B4) infants often predominate. This raises the possibility that the PDD account, being based on less systematically gathered data, may simply reflect a normative bias and that only children who have not developed secure attachments would fail to demonstrate the PDD pattern of response to separa- tion. This hypothesis is difficult to test but, even if it were supportable, a viable model of separation responses in young children seems to require the capacity to account for both normative and non-normative data.

Separation, Attachment, Temperament and Emotion Regulation

Relationships between attachment and temperament (Kagan, 1982), between attach- ment and emotional self-regulation (Bridges and Grolnick, 1995) and between attach- ment classification and separation anxiety (Frodi and Thompson, 1985) have long been the subject of controversy. Noting that separation protest was neither confined to nor shown by all securely attached (B-classified) infants, Frodi and Thompson (*ibid.*) suggested that temperamental differences such as reactivity (higher in B3– C2 than in A1–B2 infants) may predict separation anxiety better than attachment classification. While some researchers have supported this position (Belsky and Rovine, 1987; Fish and Belsky, 1991), others have not done so (Vaughn et al., 1989). Small sample sizes in many studies of attachment and the fact that few studies report findings relating to attachment subgroups mitigate against speedy resolution of these differences. Some evidence also suggests that qualitatively different pat- terns of reactivity may be associated with infants classified as resistant compared with infants classified as avoidant and that ability to self-regulate emotionally may mitigate negative effects of reactivity in some infants (Fox and Calkins, 1993).

Whilst, therefore, at this stage, it is difficult to draw firm conclusions about the relationship between temperament, emotional self-regulation and responses to separa- tion, it does seem clear that there are far greater individual differences in response than the PDD account proposes.

Separation and Coping Skills

Distinctive individual styles of coping begin to be evident early in infancy (Kagan 1982; Kagan et al., 1993). Although younger children may employ fewer and less elaborate coping strategies (Maccoby, 1983; Werner, 1990) and are more likely to be adversely affected by traumatic events (Pynoos and Eth, 1985), recent research has drawn attention to the active constructive nature of coping responses in early infancy.

Perturbation studies employing the 'blank face' technique (for example, Tronick et al., 1978; Murray and Trevarthen, 1985) have shown how, even in the first few months of life, in these situations, infants invariably try to reanimate the mother by, at first, employing coping mechanisms which are not a defence: 'He turns to face her and establish mutual contact. He raises his eyebrows and opens his eyes and mouth wide in invitation to interaction. He vocalizes, smiles, gestures, and is often very creative with humor and invention. When all this doesn't work, he turns his head away for a moment and then turns back to try again' (Stern, 1994, p. 14). These and other studies (for example, Baillargeon et al., 1985) indicate that infants have considerable ability to generate event expectancies and that, in coping with disruption of expected interactive sequences, infants typically deploy a far wider range of strategies than had previously been thought to be within their social repertoire (Trevarthen, 1993).

It has also been increasingly recognized that mother-infant separations become part of many young infants' experience very early in life: they occur for a wide range of reasons and with much greater frequency than was formerly acknowledged (Suwalsky and Klein, 1980; Smith and Turner, 1981; Presser, 1982; Hill, 1987 and 1989; Suwalsky et al., 1987). This raises the possibility that mechanisms for coping with the experience of separation in early childhood may be more sophisticated than the PDD account assumed. One set of studies in this area (Field and Reite, 1984; Field, 1991) seems to lend support to this view.

Field and Reite (1984) observed the behaviour of children whose mothers were in hospital during the birth of another child. They noted increases in negative affect, activity level, night wakings, and crying during the hospital period and depressed behaviour and activity after mothers' return, i.e. their initial observations confirmed the view that separation was a negative event in the life of young children. However, noting that separation was confounded in this earlier study with the effect of altered family and extrafamilial environment, Field later observed children separated for the purpose of mothers' conference attendance (Field, 1991). In this study, children remained at home and day care arrangements were unchanged. Increased activity (referred to as 'agitation' rather than 'protest') was observed both during and after separation but, in these circumstances, the negative behaviours observed in the earlier study were not found to be associated with repeated separations. Field concluded that 'At the very least, these data highlight the complexity of early separation stress. The stressors and the children's responses to them are apparently very dependent upon the separation context and the children's coping skills' (*ibid.*, p. 546).

It is well established that there are enormous individual differences in coping skills and these have been conceptualized as stemming from three very variable sources: the extrafamilial environment within which events occur, the family context and the child's disposition and abilities (Garmezy, 1983). There is not space here to discuss these extensively and the reader must be referred elsewhere for a fuller discussion (for example, Compas, 1987; Garbarino, 1993; Miller et al., 1994). What does seem clear is that, with regard to separation experiences, the influence of each of these dimensions will be both considerable and highly variable. For example, the experience of separation in an extrafamilial environment or culture where separation experiences are encouraged is likely to be very different from that in an environment where non-familial care is discouraged; similarly, different family contexts will influence the nature of children's separation experiences and impact on the meaning of the separation experience to the child as well as the child's ability to cope with the separation; finally, many aspects relating to disposition and ability will influence the child's ability to respond to the stress of separation.

The purpose of this brief discussion is to give some indication of the extent to which individual differences in ability to cope with separation may be expected to vary. Again, this variability of responses is likely to be far greater than the PDD account proposes.

Separation Responses and Models of Child Development

Recent research has tended to reflect a move away from models of child development in which children are viewed as more or less passive recipients of experience and a move towards social interactionist or constructivist models (Lerner, 1986) in which the child is viewed as having an active role in constructing experience within his/her unique social context. In accounts of development based on models of this kind, which were less prominent at the time when the PDD account was first developed, responses to environmental change are not viewed as well described without reference to the individual's unique history of social interaction. In comparison with contextualist models, simple effects models, particularly those which assume the existence of universal age-related stages of development, while perhaps moderately predictive in terms of autogenically determined normative data, are much less capable of accuracy in respect of a fuller data set. In other words, more complex contextualist models acknowledge and predict a much wider variety of developmental trajectories within the range of normal behaviour. For this reason, an account of separation responses in young children such as the PDD account would be very unlikely to emerge from this kind of model.

Towards a Revised Model of Separation Responses in Young Children

These challenges to the PDD account of separation responses in young children appear to suggest two possibilities: either the PDD account should be allowed to fade into oblivion as more research findings amass to contradict it (an option which some current attachment researchers may find attractive) or an attempt could be made to construct an alternative account in the light of more recent research findings. Given the difficulty of ensuring the first, the second option is taken here, more with a view to opening up than to settling discussion since research is still needed

Figure 4.1   Young children's responses to separation from a primary caregiver

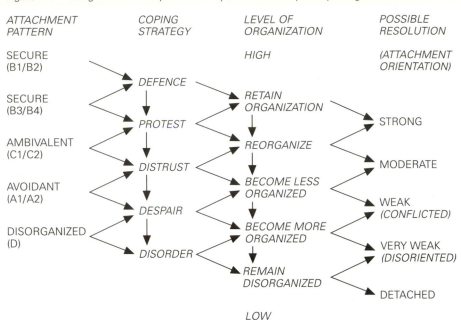

in some areas. Essentially, it is proposed that the PDD account be replaced by a more complex account such as that illustrated in Figure 4.1. In this more complex account it is recognized, first, that there will be considerable variability in responses and that this variability will stem both from factors inherent within the individual (for example, disposition, ability, interactive experience) and from factors inherent within the social context of the separation experience (for example, availability and accessibility of alternative carers, nature of separation); these two sets of factors will also interact.

Second, this account is based on a model of the child as a constructive agent, considerably more able and active even in infancy than the PDD model allowed so that, even if detachment from the primary caregiver occurs, this detachment will rarely generalize across all social relationships. Instead, in most separation situations, the number of opportunities to employ coping strategies will be sufficient for the PDD pattern not to emerge, even where separations occur during the first two or three years of life. Many children will therefore go through an initial phase characterized by markedly prosocial behaviours during which they may appear not to acknowledge a threat to their status quo, may employ a wide range of strategies designed to protect them from the necessity to acknowledge any threat and may, through this defensive behaviour, facilitate the making of meaningful new relationships or attachments which may resemble earlier patterns of relating to caregivers but which may also be permeable to change.

This account of separation responses therefore differs quite radically from the PDD account in that it views young children not as dominated by separation anxiety and the need to cling to one principal carer but rather as capable of forming multiple attachments and of having skills which may facilitate, given favourable conditions, the formation of new attachments. To this extent, it is not a negative account of separation effects but neither is it a wholly positive one for it recognizes that there will be considerable variation in the nature of attachments formed and that these will reflect, as infant-mother attachments reflect, the extent to which the child's coping strategies permit 'felt security'. In some emotionally vulnerable or socially shy children, this sense of security may be threatened even by relatively mild separation experiences.

Bowlby, perhaps more than any other single individual, has contributed enormously to our appreciation of the significance of attachment and separation in early childhood. Much of his achievement depended upon his openness to new ideas and his ability to incorporate new evidence into theoretical frameworks which he constantly revised and developed. This chapter represents an attempt to continue in this spirit. It acknowledges that evidence has accumulated which cannot easily be accommodated by the protest-despair-detachment account and proposes that it is time to begin to develop an alternative framework.

References

AINSWORTH, M.D.S., BLEHAR, M.C., WATERS, E. and WALL, S. (1978) *Patterns of Attachment: A Psychoanalytical Study of the Strange Situation*, Hillsdale, NJ: Erlbaum.

AINSWORTH, M.D.S. and WITTIG, B.A. (1969) 'Attachment and exploratory behavior of one-year-olds in a strange situation', in Foss, B.M. (ed.) *Determinants of Infant Behaviour, IV*, London: Methuen.

AUBRY, J. (1955) *La carence des soins maternels*, Paris: Presses Universitaires de France.

AVERILL, J.R. (1968) 'Grief: Its nature and significance', *Psychological Bulletin*, **70**, pp. 721–48.

BAILLARGEON, R., SPELKE, E.S. and WASSERMAN, S. (1985) 'Object permanence in five month old infants', *Cognition*, **21**, pp. 191–208.

BARRETT, H. (1991) 'The social experience of childminded children', unpublished PhD thesis, Birkbeck College, University of London.

BELSKY, J. (1988) 'The "effects" of infant day care reconsidered', *Early Child Development Quarterly*, **3**, pp. 235–72.

BELSKY, J. and BRAUNGART, J.M. (1991) 'Are insecure-avoidant infants with extensive day-care experience less stressed by and more independent in the Strange Situation?', *Child Development*, **62**, pp. 567–71.

BELSKY, J. and ROVINE, M. (1987) 'Temperament and attachment security in the Strange Situation: An empirical rapprochement', *Child Development*, **58**, pp. 787–95.

BELSKY, J. and ROVINE, M. (1988) 'Non-maternal care in the first year of life and security of infant-parent attachment', *Child Development*, **59**, pp. 157–67.

BEMPORAD, J.R. and ROMANO, S. (1993) 'Childhood experience and adult depression: A review of studies', *American Journal of Psychoanalysis*, **53**, pp. 301–15.

BERMAN, C.M., RASMUSSEN, K.L.R. and SUOMI, S.J. (1994) 'Responses of free-ranging rhesus monkeys to a natural form of social separation: I. Parallels with mother-infant separation in captivity', *Child Development*, **65**, pp. 1028–41.

BERMUDES, R.W. (1977) 'Separation: Its effects and adaptations', *The Chaplain*, **34**, pp. 18–34.

BEY, D.R. and LANGE, J. (1974) 'Waiting wives: Women under stress', *American Journal of Psychiatry*, **131**, pp. 283–6.

BIFULCO, A., HARRIS, T. and BROWN, G.W. (1992) 'Mourning or early inadequate care? Reexamining the relationship of maternal loss in childhood with adult depression and anxiety', *Development and Psychopathology*, **4**, pp. 433–49.

BOWLBY, J. (1953) 'Some psychopathological processes set in train by early mother-child separation', *J. Ment. Sci.*, **99**, pp. 265–72.

BOWLBY, J. (1958) 'The nature of the child's tie to his mother', *International Journal of Psychoanalysis*, **39**, pp. 350–73.

BOWLBY, J. (1960a) 'Separation anxiety', *International Journal of Psychoanalysis*, **41**, pp. 89–113.

BOWLBY, J. (1960b) 'Grief and mourning in infancy and early childhood', *Psychoanal: Study Child*, **15**, pp. 9–52.

BOWLBY, J. (1961) 'Processes of mourning', *International Journal of Psychoanalysis*, **42**, pp. 317–40.

BOWLBY, J. (1962) 'Childhood bereavement and psychiatric illness', in RICHTER, D., TANNER, J.M., LORD TAYLOR and ZANGWILL, O.L. (eds) *Aspects of Psychiatric Research*, London: Oxford University Press.

BOWLBY, J. (1968) 'Effects on behaviour of disruptions of an affectual bond', in THODAY, J.D. and PARKES, A.S. (eds) *Genetic and Environmental Influences on Behaviour*, Edinburgh: Oliver and Boyd.

BOWLBY, J. (1969) *Attachment and Loss, Volume 1: Attachment*, (reprinted 1981) Harmondsworth: Penguin.

BOWLBY, J. (1973) *Attachment and Loss, Volume 2: Separation: Anxiety and Anger*, (reprinted, 1975) Harmondsworth: Penguin.

BOWLBY, J. (1980) *Attachment and Loss, Volume 3: Loss: Sadness and Depression*, (reprinted 1985) Harmondsworth: Penguin.

BOWLBY, J. and PARKES, C.M. (1970) 'Separation and loss within the family', in ANTHONY, E.J. and KOUPERNIK, C. (eds) *The Child in His Family, Vol. 1*, New York: Wiley.

BOWLBY, J., ROBERTSON, J. and ROSENBLUTH, D. (1952) 'A two-year-old goes to hospital', *Psychoanal: Study Child*, **7**, pp. 82–94.

BRIDGES, L.J. and GROLNICK, W.S. (1995) 'The development of emotional self-regulation in infancy and early childhood', in EISENBERG, N. (ed.) *Social Development, Review of Personality and Social Psychology, 15*, Thousand Oaks, London and New Delhi: Sage.

BURLINGHAM, D. and FREUD, A. (1942) *Young Children in Wartime*, London: Allen and Unwin.

BURLINGHAM, D. and FREUD, A. (1944) *Infants Without Families*, London: Allen and Unwin.

CLARKE, A.M. and CLARKE, A.D.B. (1976) *Early Experience: Myth and Evidence*, London: Open Books.

COMPAS, B.E. (1987) 'Coping with stress during childhood and adolescence', *Psychological Bulletin*, **101**, pp. 393–403.

DAVENPORT, H.T. and WERRY, J.S. (1970) 'The effect of general anaesthesia, surgery and hospitalization upon the behavior of children', *American Journal of Orthopsychiatry*, **40**, pp. 806–24.

DAVID, M., NICOLAS, J. and ROUDINESCO, J. (1952) 'Responses of young children to separation from their mothers: I. Observations of children aged 12 to 17 months recently separated from their families and living in an institution', *Courrier Centre Internationale de l'Enfance*, **2**, pp. 66–78.

DOUGLAS, J.W.B. and BLOMFIELD, J.M. (1958) *Children Under Five*, London: George Allen and Unwin.

FIELD, T.M. (1991) 'Young children's adaptations to repeated separations from their mothers', *Child Development*, **62**, pp. 539–47.

FIELD, T. and REITE, M. (1984) 'Children's responses to separation from mother during the birth of another child', *Child Development*, **55**, pp. 1308–16.

FISH, M. and BELSKY, J. (1991) 'Temperament and attachment revisited: Origin and meaning of separation intolerance at age three', *American Journal of Orthopsychiatry*, **61**, pp. 418–27.

FOX, N.A. and CALKINS, S.D. (1993) 'Pathways to aggression and social withdrawal: Interactions among temperament, attachment, and regulation', in RUBIN, K.J. and ASENDORPF, J.B. (eds) *Social Withdrawal, Inhibition, and Shyness*, Hillsdale, NJ: Erlbaum.

FREUD, A. and DANN, S. (1951) 'An experiment in group upbringing', *The Psychoanalytic Study of the Child*, **6**, pp. 127–68.

FREUD, S. (1926) *Inhibitions, Symptoms and Anxiety*, Harmondsworth: Penguin.

FRODI, A. and THOMPSON, R. (1985) 'Infants' affective responses in the Strange Situation: Effects of prematurity and quality of attachment', *Child Development*, **56**, pp. 1280–90.

GARBARINO, J. (1993) 'Children's response to community violence: What do we know?', *Infant Mental Health Journal*, **14**, pp. 103–13.

GARMEZY, N. (1983) 'Stressors of childhood', in GARMEZY, N. and RUTTER, M. (eds) *Stress, Coping and Development in Children*, New York: McGraw-Hill.

HEINICKE, C.M. (1956) 'Some effects of separating two-year-olds from their parents: A comparative study', *Human Relations*, **9**, pp. 105–76.

HEINICKE, C.M. and WESTHEIMER, I.J. (1965) *Brief Separations*, London: Longmans.

HILL, M. (1987) *Sharing Child Care in Early Parenthood*, London: Routledge and Kegan Paul.

HILL, M. (1989) 'The role of social networks in the care of young children', *Children and Society*, **3**, pp. 195–211.

HILL, R. (1949) *Families Under Stress*, New York: Harper.

HOFF, M.P., NADLER, R.D., HOFF, K.T. and MAPLE, T.L. (1994) 'Separation and depression in infant gorillas', *Developmental Psychobiology*, **27**, pp. 439–52.

ILLINGWORTH, R.S. and HOLT, K.S. (1955) 'Children in hospital: Some observations on their reactions with special reference to daily visiting', *The Lancet*, 17 December, pp. 1257–62.

KAGAN, J. (1982) *Psychological Research on the Human Infant: An Evaluative Summary*, New York: W.T. Grant Foundation.

KAGAN, J., SNIDMAN, N. and ARCUS, K. (1993) 'On the temperamental categories of inhibited and uninhibited children', in RUBIN, K.J. and ASENDORPF, J.B. (eds) *Social Withdrawal, Inhibition, and Shyness*, Hillsdale, NJ: Erlbaum.

KALISH, R.A. (1988) 'The study of death: A psychosocial perspective', in WASS, H., BERARDO, F.M. and NEIMEYER, R.A. (eds) *Dying: Facing the Facts*, Washington, DC: Harper and Row.

KÜBLER-ROSS, E. (1975) *Death: The Final Stage of Growth*, New Jersey: Prentice Hall.

LANSDOWNE, R. (1996) *Children in Hospital: A Guide for Family and Carers*, Oxford: Oxford University Press.

LEACH, P. (1989) *Baby and Child: From Birth to Age Five*, Harmondsworth: Penguin.

LEACH, P. (1991a) *Babyhood: Infant Development from Birth to Two Years*, Harmondsworth: Penguin.

LEACH, P. (1991b) *The Parents' A to Z: A Guide to Children's Health, Growth and Happiness*, Harmondsworth: Penguin.

LEACH, P. (1994) *Children First: What Our Society Must Do — And Is Not Doing — For Our Children Today*, Harmondsworth: Penguin.

LERNER, R.M. (1986) *Concepts and Theories of Human Development*, New York: Random House.

LYONS-RUTH, K., REPACHOLI, B., MCLEOD, S. and SILVA, E. (1991) 'Disorganized attachment behavior in infancy: Short-term stability, maternal and infant correlates, and risk-related subtypes', *Development and Psychopathology*, **3**, pp. 377–96.

MACCOBY, E.E. (1983) 'Social-emotional development and response to stressors', in GARMEZY, N. and RUTTER, M. (eds) *Stress, Coping and Development in Children*, New York: McGraw-Hill.

MAIN, M. and SOLOMON, J. (1990) 'Procedures for identifying infants as disorganized-disoriented during the Ainsworth Strange Situation', in GREENBERG, M., CICCHETTI, D. and CUMMINGS, E.M. (eds) *Attachment in the Preschool Years: Theory, Research and Intervention*, Chicago, IL: University of Chicago Press.

MIĆIĆ, Z. (1962) 'Psychological stress in children in hospital', *International Nursing Review*, **9**, pp. 23–31.

MILLER, P.A., KLIEWER, W., HEPWORTH, J.T. and SANDLER, I.N. (1994) 'Maternal socialization of children's postdivorce coping: Development of a measurement model', *Journal of Applied Developmental Psychology*, **15**, pp. 457–87.

MORGAN, P. (1975) *Child Care: Sense and Fable*, London: Temple Smith.

MURRAY, L. and TREVARTHEN, C. (1985) 'Emotional regulation of interactions between two-month-olds and their mothers', in FIELD, T.M. and FOX, N.A. (eds) *Social Perception in Infants*, Norwood, NJ: Ablex.

O'CONNOR, N. (1956) 'The evidence for the permanently disturbing effects of mother-child separation', *Acta Psychologica*, **12**, pp. 174–91.

PARKES, C.M. (1972) *Bereavement: Studies of Grief in Adult Life*, London: Tavistock.

PEARLMAN, C.A. (1970) 'Separation reactions of married women', *American Journal of Psychiatry*, **126**, pp. 946–50.

PINNEAU, S.R. (1955) 'The infantile disorders of hospitalism and anaclitic depression', *Psychological Bulletin*, **52**, pp. 429–52.

PRESSER, H.B. (1982) 'Working women and child care', in BERMAN, P. and RAMEY, E. (eds) *Women: A Developmental Perspective*, Washington, DC: Department of Health and Human Sciences.

PRUGH, D.G., STAUB, E.M., SANDS, H.H., KIRSCHBAUM, R.M. and LENIHAN, E.A. (1953) 'A study of the emotional reactions of children and families to hospitalization and illness', *American Journal of Orthopsychiatry*, **23**, pp. 70–106.

PYNOOS, R.S. and ETH, S. (1985) 'Developmental perspective on psychic trauma in childhood', in FIGLEY, C.R. (ed.) *Trauma and its Wake*, New York: Brunner/Mazel.

QUINTON, D. and RUTTER, M. (1976) 'Early hospital admissions and later disturbances of behaviour: An attempted replication of the findings', *Developmental Medicine and Child Neurology*, **18**, pp. 447–59.

ROBERTSON, J. (1952) Film: *A two-year-old goes to hospital*, London: Tavistock Child Development Unit.

ROBERTSON, J. (1953) 'Some responses of young children to loss of maternal care', *Nursing Times*, **49**, pp. 382–6.

ROBERTSON, J. and BOWLBY, J. (1952) 'Responses of young children to separation from their mothers: II. Observations of the sequence of response of children aged 18 to 24 months during the course of separation from their mothers', *Courrier Centre International de l'Enfance*, **2**, pp. 131–42.

ROBERTSON, J. and ROBERTSON, J. (1967) *Young Children in Brief Separation, Film No. 1: Kate, 2 years 5 months: In foster care for 27 days*, London: Tavistock Child Development Research Unit.

ROBERTSON, J. and ROBERTSON, J. (1968) *Young Children in Brief Separation, Film No. 2: Jane, 17 months: In foster care for 10 days*, London: Tavistock Child Development Research Unit.

ROBERTSON, J. and ROBERTSON, J. (1969) *Young Children in Brief Separation, Film No. 3: John, 17 months: For 9 days in a residential nursery*, London: Tavistock Child Development Research Unit.

ROBERTSON, J. and ROBERTSON, J. (1971a) *Young Children in Brief Separation, Film No. 4: Thomas, 2 years 4 months: In foster care for 10 days*, London: Tavistock Child Development Research Unit.

ROBERTSON, J. and ROBERTSON, J. (1971b) 'Young children in brief separation: A fresh look', *Psychoanalytic Study of the Child*, **26**, pp. 264–315.

ROBERTSON, J. and ROBERTSON, J. (1973) *Young Children in Brief Separation, Film No. 5: Lucy, 21 months: In foster care for 19 days*, London: Tavistock Child Development Research Unit.

ROBERTSON, J. and ROBERTSON, J. (1976) *Guide to the Film Series: Young Children in Brief Separation*, London: Robertson Centre.

ROBERTSON, J. and ROBERTSON, J. (1989) *Separation and the Very Young*, London: Free Association Books.

RUTTER, M. (1972) *Maternal Deprivation Reassessed*, Harmondsworth: Penguin.

RUTTER, M. (1979a) 'Maternal deprivation, 1972–1978: New findings, new concepts, new approaches', *Child Development*, **50**, pp. 283–305.

RUTTER, M. (1979b) 'Separation experiences: A new look at an old topic', *Journal of Pediatrics*, **95**, pp. 147–54.

RUTTER, M. (1991) 'A fresh look at "maternal deprivation" ', in BATESON, P. (ed.) *The Development and Integration of Behaviour: Essays in Honour of Robert Hinde*, Cambridge: Cambridge University Press.

SCHAFFER, H.R. (1958) 'Objective observations of personality development in early infancy', *British Journal of Medical Psychology*, **33**, pp. 174–83.

SCHAFFER, H.R. and CALLENDER, W.M. (1959) 'Psychologic effects of hospitalization in infancy', *Pediatrics*, **24**, pp. 528–39.

SCHAFFER, H.R. and EMERSON, P.E. (1964) 'The development of social attachments in infancy', *Monographs in Social Research on Child Development*, **29**, p. 94.

SMITH, P.K. and TURNER, J. (1981) 'The measurement of shared care and its effects in a sample of working mothers and young children', *Current Psychological Research*, **1**, pp. 263–70.

SPANGLER, G. and GROSSMANN, K.E. (1993) 'Biobehavioural organization in securely and insecurely attached infants', *Child Development*, **64**, pp. 1439–50.

SPITZ, R.A. (1945) 'Hospitalism. An enquiry into the genesis of psychiatric conditions in early childhood', *Psychoanalytic Study of the Child*, **1**, pp. 53–74.

SPITZ, R.A. (1946a) 'Hospitalism: A follow-up report', *Psychoanalytic Study of the Child*, **2**, pp. 113–7.

SPITZ, R.A. (1946b) 'Anaclitic depression', *Psychoanalytic Study of the Child*, **2**, pp. 313–42.

SPITZ, R.A. and WOLF, K.M. (1946) 'Anaclitic depression: An enquiry into the genesis of psychiatric conditions in early childhood, II', *Psychoanalytic Study of the Child*, **2**, pp. 313–42.

STACEY, M., DEARDEN, R., PILL, R. and ROBINSON, D. (1970) *Hospitals, Children and their Families: The Report of a Pilot Study*, London: Routledge and Kegan Paul.

STERN, D.N. (1994) 'One way to build a clinically relevant baby', *Infant Mental Health Journal*, **15**, pp. 9–25.

SUWALSKY, J.T.D. and KLEIN, R.P. (1980) 'Effects of naturally-occurring non-traumatic separations from mother', *Infant Mental Health Journal*, **1**, pp. 196–201.

SUWALSKY, J.T.D., KLEIN, R.P., ZASLOW, M.J., RABINOVICH, B.A. and GIST, N.F. (1987) 'Dimensions of naturally occurring mother-infant separations during the first year of life', *Infant Mental Health Journal*, **8**, pp. 3–18.

TOLFREE, D. (1995) *Roofs and Roots: The Care of Separated Children in the Developing World*, Aldershot: Ashgate Publishing Company/Save the Children Fund.

TREVARTHEN, C. (1993) 'The function of emotions in early infant communication and development', in NADEL, J. and CAMAIONI, L. (eds) *New Perspectives in Early Communicative Development*, London and New York: Routledge.

TRONICK, E., ALS, H., ADAMSON, L., WISE, S. and BRAZELTON, T.B. (1978) 'The infant's response to entrapment between contradictory messages in face-to-face interaction', *Journal of the American Academy of Child Psychiatry*, **17**, pp. 1–13.

VAUGHN, B.E., LEFEVER, G.B., SEIFER, R. and BARGLOW, P. (1989) 'Attachment behavior, attachment security, and temperament during infancy', *Child Development*, **60**, pp. 728–37.

VERNON, D.T.A., FOLEY, J.M. and SCHULMAN, J.L. (1967) 'Effect of mother-child separation and birth order on young children's responses to two potentially stressful experiences', *Journal of Personality and Social Psychology*, **5**, pp. 162–74.

VORMBROCK, J.K. (1993) 'Attachment theory as applied to wartime and job-related marital separation', *Psychological Bulletin*, **114**, pp. 122–44.

WERNER, E.E. (1990) 'Protective factors and individual resilience', in MEISELS, S.J. and SHONKOFF, J.P. (eds) *Handbook of Early Childhood Intervention*, Cambridge: Cambridge University Press.

YARROW, L.J. (1961) 'Maternal deprivation: Toward an empirical and conceptual reevaluation', *Psychological Bulletin*, **55**, pp. 459–90.

YARROW, L.J. (1964) 'Separation from parents during early childhood', in HOFFMAN, M.L. and HOFFMAN, L.W. (eds) *Review of Child Development, Volume 1*, New York: Russell Sage Foundation.

ZEANAH, C.H., MAMMEN, O.K. and LIEBERMAN, A.F. (1993) 'Disorders of attachment', in ZEANAH, C.H. (ed.) *Handbook of Infant Mental Health*, New York/London: Guilford Press.

Part II

Contexts for Discourse Competence

Chapter 5

Children's Neo-rhetorical Participation in Peer Interactions

Robert E. Sanders and Kurt E. Freeman

It seems that as participants in social interaction, children under 7 can be far more adept comunicatively and socially than they get credit for.[1] We base this claim on having attended to a key aspect of social interaction: persons' achievement of social goals depends (in certain circumstances[2]) on their fashioning interactional turns proactively, not just reactively, i.e., in anticipation of and for the sake of their consequences for the course of the interaction. We do not refer here to children's adaptations of talk and behavior based on social cognitions about the other's competence, needs, dispositions, or the like. Our interest is whether, and in what ways, children adapt talk and behavior so as to constrain what can relevantly, coherently, be included in the interaction regardless of who the other is, on the basis of 'knowledge' about the formal interconnections among components of social interactions. The proactive aspects of children's participation in peer interactions in this sense has not been taken into account, or at least seriously examined, in most work on children's communicative and social development.

Using videotaped interactions between dyads of same-sex children playing with a Lego System building set[3], our analysis centers on whether, and how, the details of children's interactional turns were fashioned proactively (or as Sanders (1995a) has termed it, *neo-rhetorically*[4]). Against the backdrop of our instruction to the children that we wanted them 'to work together to build one thing', we focused on interactional turns that were fashioned in such a way that they constrained what would be relevant and coherent in the future interaction in favor of the assigned goal of achieving joint effort. Of particular interest were turns fashioned in a way that countered a potential produced by self or other in the local moment for the reverse, for example, for conflict, competition, or independent effort. Overall, at least one child in each dyad we analyzed fashioned interactional turns in that way repeatedly, and all the children cooperated, in such a way as to avoid overt conflict in the local moment and achieve coordinated effort for sustained periods of time, despite generally, recurrently, facing each other with conflicting wants, and issues of parity and control.

Of course, we may have artificially induced 'good behavior' by taking the children from their normal activities and putting them in front of a camera, in a play situation we initiated and, to an extent, structured. But even though children on their own do not always interact in the markedly civil ways we observed, one thing our data make plain is that it is not for want of the competence to do so.

Theory and research generally have missed this neo-rhetorical aspect of children's participation in interactions. In part this is an artifact of methodology (underlying substantive reasons are noted in the section below on the research context). The majority of studies have not attended to the sequential progression of what children say and do across turns, where the proactive aspects of children's participation lie. The focus instead has been on what are considered a priori to be noteworthy qualities of children's talk or behavior as those qualities are exhibited either in single interactional turns, or recurrently or additively across turns. As a result, much of interest here would not be visible to analysts: specifically, adjustments of what a child says and does progressively across a series of turns in anticipation of (to promote or interfere with) a particular consequence; also, phrasing, inflections, gestures and other microbehaviors, etc., or stock devices deployed in innovative ways, that might not be noteworthy in their own right but could be highly consequential in the local moment for where the interaction goes from there.[5]

In the relatively little work that *has* focused on the particulars and sequencing of what children say and do in interactions, the focus has generally been on what they respond to and not what they anticipate. This may be on the grounds that responsiveness and sustained engagement with the other are themselves noteworthy achievements, and perhaps also disbelief that children are capable of more (especially without theory or models that would predict it). Studies of children's achievement of topic continuity (Dorval and Eckerman, 1984; Hobbs, 1990), or the developing cohesiveness of children's turns in conversation (for example, McTear, 1985) are by definition concerned with the children's responsiveness to what has gone before, not their orientations to, and adjustments in anticipation of, what might happen next.

Of course, there are also some studies that are concerned as ours is with the efforts of children across a series of interactional turns to influence others and bring about preferred outcomes, sometimes when there is resistance from the other(s). But these studies too have tended to emphasize the personal wants, interactional antecedents, and social circumstances that dispose the children to react as they do, not potential interactional (as opposed to interpersonal) consequences they may be anticipating (for example, Eisenberg and Garvey, 1981; Goodwin, 1990; Sheldon, 1992 and 1996; Barnes and Vangelisti, 1995). Further, these studies tend to focus on what stock devices of expression and response the children utilize, creating the potential to miss it if turns are fashioned in adaptive or even innovative ways, or perhaps are fashioned to promote certain consequences or forestall them in combination with a progression of turns, sequentially, rather than in their own right. The unintended result of the methods and questions of most research, then, is that they conceal whether, and in what ways, the children produce and respond to talk and behavior as components of a larger, emerging whole — the interaction — by progressively adjusting what they say and do in anticipation of the larger whole that might result, i.e., what course the interaction might be taking in terms of what it includes and how it concludes.

Neo-rhetorical Participation in Interactions

In adult interactions, turns at speaking generally are not self-standing but are constructed, interpreted, and responded to as steps in the progress of the interaction towards some resolution. This is a central theme and datum in conversation analysis (for example, Atkinson and Heritage, 1984; Jacoby and Ochs, 1995). But beyond this, there is the neo-rhetorical aspect of participation in interactions, when persons fashion their turns to constrain the interaction to take a favored course, often progressively. Sanders (1983, 1984, 1987, 1991 and 1995a) has focused on the intricacy with which people do this, and also the systemic knowledge that people must have in order to project consequences and adjust their turns at speaking accordingly — knowledge of the way components of interaction and discourse cohere (are relevant to each other) to form wholes.

The evidence we have indicates that in peer interactions, children take part neo-rhetorically at least by the time they are 5, and thus must already have acquired that systemic knowledge (see Sanders 1987 on the formal character of this neo-rhetorical competence, and its relation to pragmatic competence; also Sanders, 1995b and forthcoming b). In the peer interactions we analyze below, some of the children detected and responded to the potential at specific turns for the interaction to take an unwanted course, at a level of intricacy and subtlety that surprised us.

Our aim in this chapter is to present these data in order to open the door to this line of inquiry: to show that children do participate neo-rhetorically in social interaction, that this is a competence they have.

A Note on the Research Context

The possibility that children's pragmatic competence has been systematically underestimated (and their neo-rhetorical competence overlooked) should be taken seriously, considering that even adults' pragmatic (and neo-rhetorical) competence can be misjudged, at least when there is a presumption that they are impaired and deemed functionally unable to make a case for themselves. Schegloff (1991) makes a strong case that neurologists — by having relied on faulty criteria for assessing pragmatic competence, and ignoring (or missing the significance of) details of individuals' participation in interaction — have been mistaken about the pragmatic competence of patients whose corpus calosum was severed (the neural link between right and left brain hemispheres). Goodwin (1995) analyzed a particular case where doctors and attending staff made a similar error involving an elderly stroke victim, Rob, who was rendered speechless, and whose efforts to gesture and vocalize they dismissed as meaningless. Rob's family did not accept medical opinion on this point and provided him with speech therapy. Rob learned to articulate three words, *yes, no,* and *and.* He proved to be pragmatically competent to deploy them in interactional sequences meaningfully, often creatively, along with intonation and bodily movement, to achieve communication with those around him.

If experts can be mistaken about the pragmatic (and neo-rhetorical) competence of adults, then this is all the more possible when it comes to children, considering how different from (most) adults they are intellectually and emotionally, and at very young ages how relatively limited their expressive abilities are. In our view, analysis has been held back in two ways. One is that the importance of the sequential aspects of the way turns at speaking in adult interactions are produced and responded to is only gradually becoming apparent, mainly through the work of conversation analysts. Thus, the need to regard this as an aspect of children's communicative development, and analyze children's turns at speaking in those terms (not as self-contained units of expression and social action), is relatively new.

But we regard the main problem as being the information-centered premise about language and communication (cf. Schegloff, 1995) that has dominated the way children's communicative development has been conceptualized. The information-centered premise is that speaking is a means of providing information to others about matters of interest, where others' responses are presumably oriented to 'realities' that are made salient by the information they have been given. From this perspective, children could not be expected to take an active, effective part in social interaction until they develop cognitively, socially, and linguistically enough to (a) comprehend their own experience in terms of distinct conditions, relationships, etc.; (b) be able to express the information involved with due clarity and accuracy; and (c) recognize what information the other does not have that a turn at speaking should provide (cf. Roberts and Peterson, 1983). If it is assumed that these are prerequisites for mature participation in social interaction, then research would most reasonably focus, as it has, on indices of children's acquisition of these prerequisites. There would be no reason to think that there is anything to be learned from taking into account the sequential progression of children's interactions, and whether children fashion their talk and behavior to progressively contribute to that.[6]

Analytic Protocol

The problem we face analytically is to warrant claims that particular turns at speaking were fashioned in anticipation of their consequences, strategically, so that one can then examine specifically what the person did in that regard. Heritage (1990–91) took the position that in general this is something we cannot accomplish, except by accident, because we cannot know what persons' preferences are about the course of the interaction and thus which particular turns if any were actively fashioned to promote them. However, while he was right to call attention to the need for due caution about this, and right to anticipate that we will miss some occurrences, in our view he overstated that case.

First, there are observational/analytic grounds for identifying specific turns as evidently having been fashioned neo-rhetorically, rather than reactively or expressively, apart from any considerations about what the person's preferences for the course of the interaction are. In brief, turns may have been fashioned neo-rhetorically to the extent that in their details they were not the most direct or efficient or self-consistent way in the local moment to produce what prior interactional turns had made relevant, and that in addition they changed what might relevantly follow in the interaction from what had been relevant beforehand.

For example, Schegloff (1995) analyzes an interaction between Debbie and Nick, where Debbie knew Nick was intending to buy a waterbed, and she made a 'pre-offer' to tell him about an ad in the newspaper she had seen for a waterbed. Her pre-offer started with 'guess what' and then was self-interrupted to ask whether he had got the waterbed yet. Nick said he had indeed got one, but did not ask why Debbie wanted to know. This made it irrelevant for Debbie to tell about the ad. Debbie asked three more times whether he really had got one and received the same reply each time. Her questions were not direct, efficient responses to Nick's answer, but in asking them she changed what would otherwise have been relevant (each reply by Nick made it irrelevant for her to tell about the ad, and each reiteration of the question made it potentially relevant again, depending on Nick's reply). On those grounds, there is reason to consider Debbie's questions to have been fashioned neo-rhetorically, in anticipation of the interactional consequences of Nick's replies and her reiterated questions.

Of course, the warrant for considering such turns as having been fashioned neo-rhetorically would be strengthened if they constrained what was relevant in the future interaction (or cancelled constraints) in a way that favored what the person in question preferred the interaction would include or how it would conclude. Consider that there are often circumstantial indications of what a person's preference(s) in that regard are. First, it may be the 'official,' assigned responsibility of one or more participants to constrain the interaction's course in a particular way (a responsibility usually based on person's institutional role-identities, but sometimes based on a particular directive, as in a judge's instructions to a jury or in our instruction to the children whose interactions we recorded). Another indication of a person's preference about the course of the interaction is overt statements he/she might produce about his/her preferences during the interaction, and/or what acts or information he/she accepts or resists for inclusion in the interaction, or as warranting closure. A third indication is if a number of the person's turns that seem to have been fashioned neo-rhetorically constrain the interaction in a uniform way.

These various indicators that an interactional turn has been fashioned neo-rhetorically are obviously more reliable in combination than singly. Accordingly, we specified and used the following three-part analytical protocol. An interactional turn was deemed to be fashioned neo-rhetorically if:

(a) The substance or manner of what the person said or did was not the most direct response to local antecedents, nor the most direct or accurate expression of the person's evident feelings or thoughts on the matter at hand, that the speaker could have produced; *and*

(b) The substance and manner of the person's turn changed what was otherwise relevant in the future interaction, and thus what course the interaction could otherwise have taken; *and*

(c) What the person's interactional turn made relevant or irrelevant is consistent with: (i) what the person would normatively prefer based on his/her role-identity and/or an assigned goal or responsibility; (ii) a preference about the course of the interaction that the person directly expressed; and/or (iii) what the person made relevant or irrelevant in one or more other turns at speaking.

Data: Peer Interactions Among Children Between 5 and 7 years old

The data examined below involve the interactions of the three dyads referred to previously. The dyad of older girls (Lorraine, 6;11, and Rashia, 6;7)[7] was situated in a private school; the younger girls (Lucy, 6;1 and Ruthie, 5;10) and the boys (Luke, 5;1, and Rick, 5;2) were situated in a summer daycare program. Based on a sociogram, the older girls were not part of the same friendship network, though they would have previously known each other and possibly interacted in school activities. The children in the two dyads of younger children were respectively in the same friendship networks.

Below we analyze each child's participation in detail, and find that there are notable variations in the extensiveness and complexity of their neo-rhetorical participation. The *extensiveness* of neo-rhetorical participation involves the number of a child's contiguous interactional turns that he/she fashioned in combination to constrain the interaction to favor a particular consequence. The *complexity* of neo-rhetorical participation involves the number and variety of details of expression — and particularly whether there were non-verbal as well as verbal aspects — that were monitored and/or adjusted to make particular interactional consequences relevant (or not relevant).

As noted above, the neo-rhetorical participation we examined was most extensive and complex in the case of each of the two older girls. In comparing extracts involving the younger girls and the still younger boys, one of the boys (Luke) was more extensive and complex in his neo-rhetorical participation than one of the girls (Lucy), and also more complex but less extensive than the other of the younger girls (Ruthie). While the other boy (Rick) was arguably least extensive and complex of all these children in his neo-rhetorical participation, he was not much less so than Lucy, who was a full year older. Beyond that, there were contrasts in terms of the children's adjustment of their talk and behavior so as to mitigate potential threats to their partner's or their own 'face' wants (see Goffman, 1967; Brown and Levinson, 1987). Both the older girls' and the boys' interactions exhibited such attention to face wants, in sharp contrast to the interaction of the younger girls.

Method

Because our interest was in a particular aspect of children's peer interactions that might not occur in all circumstances — neo-rhetorical participation — we sought to maximize the chances that it would occur by controlling the play situations we recorded, both in terms of the composition of dyads and the activity in which the children engaged. While controlling the situation in that way still yields naturalistic data that support claims about what children are competent to do in peer interactions, it prevents us from making claims about how typical it is for children to interact as we observed.

We controlled the composition of the dyads in two ways. First, we formed only same-sex dyads, to avoid interactions confounded somehow by gender differences. Second, based on prior interviews with the children individually, and with their teachers, we assigned each child a sociometric ranking (high, moderate, and low). Children were then paired with partners of roughly the same age, who were no more than one step higher or lower in sociometric standing, to minimize the chances of any social asymmetries before the fact that might reduce the need for neo-rhetorical participation.

We also took two steps to control the children's play activity. First, we gave the children a Lego System building set to play with, so that the activity and task across dyads was uniform, while leaving what the children could actually concern themselves with relatively open. There was a potential for divergent preferences and coordination problems to arise that would maximize the need for neo-rhetorical participation (for example, in regard to what the two would make, how to go about it, whether they were proceeding correctly, how to achieve equity, etc.). Second, we told the children that we wanted them to make one thing, working on it together, as a means of artificially inducing a uniform preference about the course of the interaction across dyads (in favor of achieving and sustaining joint effort). This was important for analytic purposes. On the basis of our analytic protocol, one warrant for identifying certain interactional turns as having been fashioned neo-rhetorically is if they serve to constrain the interaction in accordance with an assigned goal. The goal we induced thus made us privy to at least one preference the children had about the course of the interaction, insofar as they adopted that goal. We have grounds for believing they did, indicated below.

Our procedure was to bring each dyad to an unoccupied room that we furnished with the Lego set. The children were outfitted with wireless microphones before they began playing, while at the same time they were being shown the Lego set and told that we wanted them to make something working together. Each dyad was taped interacting for about fifteen minutes.

Analysis

In each of the dyads, the children adopted some 'stock forms' of expression and interaction that expressed their orientation to and adoption of the goal we induced of working together to make one thing. Our interest here in the children's production of these stock forms is only as evidence that the goal we induced was adopted, though their systematic deployment deserves attention in its own right (for example, Freeman, 1996, on children's use of tag questions). One of these stock forms was the heavy use of collective pronouns ('we', 'us', 'our') in place of first-person singular pronouns ('I', 'me', 'my'). Another was questions and statements to each other to consult or coordinate about what to do or how to proceed. Examples of the presence of these features in each interaction are given below (where collective pronouns are highlighted in boldface, and consultative turns at speaking are highlighted by an arrow to the left).

Dyad 1 (FRAP94, S22): Lorraine (6;11) and Rashia (6;7)
```
92    Rashia:→   But don't you think we need a step?
93               (0.5)
94    Lorraine:  Uh huh.
95               (0.5)
96    Rashia:→   So how will we make our step?
97    Lorraine:  We'll put i:t (0.2) two off the ground. (0.2) >The
98          →    door will be two off the grou:nd< (0.2) >and the
99               step will be like< (0.2) (Ik!)
```

Dyad 2 (FRAP94, F3): Luke (5;1) and Rick (5;2)
```
150   Rick:→     Lu:ke, we're not makin' a house.
151              (0.5) ((R puts a piece into box))
152   Luke:      °Oh! (.) mm:: hm::°
153              (0.5)
154   Rick:→     We're makin' a heli°copter° ((R points to
155              instruction booklet))
156              (1.2)
157   Luke:→     Yup- see:, (.) we have to do that- (.) that- (.)
158              that- (.) that- ((L is pointing in the booklet with
                 each 'that'))
```

Dyad 3: (FRAP94, S13) Lucy: (6;1) and Ruthie (5;10)
```
83    Ruthie:→   Well I guess we'll have t' use little ones.
84               (2.5) ((both dig in box))
85    Lucy:→     Oh goodness- ((giggles)) here- let's just make
86               anything.
87    Ruthie:    No::: ((leans over to booklet on floor)) (That!
88               Please)=((R points at picture))
89    Lucy:→     = >How c'n we< make that?
```

However, based on what the children seemed to anticipate and adjust for in producing turns neo-rhetorically, each dyad displayed an orientation to a different issue as being pivotal in whether they achieved the joint effort we asked for. For Lorraine and Rashia, the pivotal issue seemed to be the potential for conflict, but this was tied to cognate concerns with the potential to be relegated to a subordinate role, for competition, and for separation of effort. For Luke and Rick, it seemed to be the potential for either to be judged and treated by the other as not being of equal competence in making objects with this Lego set. For Lucy and especially Ruthie, the pivotal issue seemed to be the way in which Lucy's activity was in fact marginalizing Ruthie.

An analysis of neo-rhetorical participation in each of the three interactions follows. As has been noted, in analyzing the neo-rhetorical 'artfulness' and rationality of the way some of the children's interactional turns were fashioned, we are not making any claims that the children consciously thought matters through in the way we have represented them, and then spoke and behaved accordingly. Our claim is simply that these interactional turns were fashioned *as if* such calculations were being made, and it is a quite separate consideration what the actual cognitive events are that actually occur and have this result.

Dyad 1, FRAP94, S22: Lorraine (6;11) and Rashia (6;7)

Lorraine and Rashia generally pursued a division of labor, each assembling components to be added to what they had agreed to make, but interacting continuously as they did so about what they were each doing, consulting the other, etc. Of the two, Rashia was more likely to produce interactional turns that created a potential for conflict or independent effort. Lorraine generally fashioned interactional turns that countered such potential consequences when they arose without directly confronting Rashia about them. For that reason, we consider Lorraine to have taken the neo-rhetorical lead in much of the interaction. However, at times Rashia too fashioned both talk and behaviour that were intricately adjusted to offset the potential in local moments for unwanted consequences. We analyze two specific instances here, one produced by Lorraine (also see Sanders, forthcoming b), the other by Rashia.

Lorraine. The greater part of the sequence we examine here involved the positioning of the green Lego base which provides a stabilizing (but not essential) foundation on which to assemble objects. As they were getting organized, while talking about what to make, Lorraine had put the green Lego base at the back of the table. On agreeing what to make, Rashia took the green base and repositioned it where they could use it to build on, at the front of the table between them. Lorraine then promptly pulled the base out from under Rashia's hand. (The most equivocal matter in this sequence is why Lorraine did this, but our analysis does not depend on what we surmise: Our focus is on how Lorraine went about it, and what ensued.)

Consider that to take the base away from Rashia in that way created a potential for conflict — which would jeopardize their success in complying with our instruction that they work together — something that the non-verbal and linguistic particulars of Lorraine's move seem to anticipate, and to be fashioned to mitigate. First, when Lorraine picked the green base back up, she did not immediately reposition it, she held it in midair to her side as she surveyed the table. At the same time she self-narrated her action (lines 23–24: 'And this (.) i:s (0.2) aroun:d' . . .) so as to implicate that the placement of the green base had not already been attended to by Rashia, but was a new issue, by omitting any phrasing that indicated otherwise (such as *and this would be better around* . . .). Lorraine followed through on repositioning of the base just when the potential for actual conflict became salient, when Rashia uttered a protest (line 25: 'Hey:::'). Finally, in re-repositioning it, she did not return it to where Rashia had placed it (which would give in to Rashia, and thus make it relevant for Rashia to treat Lorraine as malleable and submissive) or place it nearer herself where it would be easier for her to reach it than Rashia (which would make confrontation relevant). Instead, she placed it at the back of the table again, away from both of them, thus preventing either of those consequences from being relevant. In addition, she appended to her self-narration of this move (lines 23–24, 26) a marker that it was temporary ('f'r now:').

```
17  Lorraine:  Well, how 'bout just- a plain old- (0.2) house?
18  Rashia:    °Okay.°
19  Lorraine:  (With) flowers.
20  Rashia:    Okay. ⌈That'll be easy.  ((R picks up the green
                                          base, sets it down right
                                          next to her;
21  Lorraine:         ⌊°mmm::hm!°
22             (2.1)                      R thumps twice on the base,
                                          L pulls it from under R's
                                          hand, and holds it in mid-
                                          air, self-narrating;
23  Lorraine:  And this (.) i:s (0.2)
24             aro⌈un:d
25  Rashia:       ⌊Hey:::                 after R's 'Hey,' L moves it
26             (0.2)                       to the back of the table on
                                           her side))
27  Lorraine:  ('at!) f'r now:.  Okay.
```

However, Rashia followed her initial protest (line 25: 'Hey:::') with a second, upgraded protest (line 30 below: 'We need that') that effectively increased the potential for the interaction to take a course towards conflict, despite Lorraine's steps to avoid it. Lorraine countered this potential by reversing herself and returning the base to where it had been, in front next to Rashia.

However, in avoiding this unwanted consequence by reversing herself, Lorraine created the potential for another consequence that jeopardized their ability to work together; by 'giving in' to Rashia, she made it relevant for Rashia to continue asserting her wants over Lorraine's. Lorraine functionally weakened the potential for this by returning the green base in a way fashioned to not seem to be 'giving in'. Rather than put the base back in a single movement, Lorraine returned it in three steps that seem fashioned to make her self-reversal appear to be based on her own decisions, not Rashia's protest. First, after Rashia provided a reason for objecting (line 30), Lorraine did not immediately pick the base up. First she stated that she already knew they needed the base (and therefore that Rashia was not telling her anything):

```
30  Rashia:    We need that.
31             (0.5)
32  Lorraine:  Yes, I know.
33             (0.5)            ((L picks green base back up))
```

Second, after picking the base up, Lorraine did not return it directly, but held it suspended above the table, and produced a statement of why they 'need that' as a formulation of Rashia's objection (line 34: 'We need to be able to reach it?'). To produce this formulation at all, especially in the midst of already acting on it, seems gratuitous except to underscore that Lorraine was self-directed and not simply compliant, that she did in fact already 'know' they needed the base, and why. Third, Rashia reached to take the base after Lorraine formulated why they needed it, but Lorraine prevented it with an exaggerated movement of the base up and over Rashia's hand even though Rashia would probably have placed it exactly where Lorraine then placed it herself. This was accompanied by self-narration that arguably implicates that this positioning was one Lorraine just then selected, in that her phrasing omitted any indication that it was a restoration (line 36: 'Put this down right here' instead of for example, *put this back right here*).

```
34  Lorraine:  We need to be able to reach it?
35  Rashia:    Yeah.                      ((R reaches for base,
                                           L evades her))
36  Lorraine:  Put this down right here.  ((L puts base in
                                           front of R))
```

The final segment of this sequence starts with a turn in which Rashia asserted her own agenda exactly as Lorraine evidently anticipated and tried to avert. As soon as Lorraine put the green base down, Rashia (line 37), in a rare use of the first person singular pronoun in their interaction, stated the *she*, not *they*, would now build the house. Rashia's stated intent to work on her own obviously created a potential for the interaction to take an unwanted course, either towards conflict, or individual rather than joint effort. (Note that while it is equivocal whether it was expressive or neo-rhetorical, Rashia mitigated this to a degree by stating that her intention was to build 'the' house, not *a* house — this use of the definite article indexed her continued involvement in the project she and Lorraine had decided on jointly, to build a house.)

After a pause, Lorraine agreed rather than objected (albeit in a qualified form, 'Okay then', rather than just *Okay*), thereby avoiding conflict but arguably at the expense of her personal wants. However, Lorraine then formulated an utterance that, in the intricacies of its design, offset Rashia's move towards individual effort by incorporating Rashia's statement in an elaboration that functionally reconstructed it as initiating a division of effort on a joint project instead of an individual effort on a joint project she had usurped:

```
36  Lorraine:  Put this down right here.=  ((L put base in front
                                            of R))
37  Rashia:    =(And now) I'm going to make the house (on it).
38             (1.5)
39  Lorraine:  Okay °then°, you make the house. (.) And I'll get
40             the flowers ready.
```

Lorraine's response to Rashia (lines 39–40) is noteworthy in several respects. First, by using the definite article, as Rashia had, to state her intention to get *the* flowers ready, Lorraine marked her activity as also part of the same previously adopted plan. Second, Lorraine stated her own intention by creating a parallel structure incorporating Rashia's — parallel both syntactically (you do X and I'll do Y) and vocally (with stress on the first person singular pronouns in each clause, and stress on the objects they would respectively assemble).

Rashia. In the initial turns of the interaction, Lorraine had proposed and Rashia agreed to 'just make- (0.5) our own thing.' (line 8). Several minutes later, Rashia picked up the instructions booklet, a possible breach of this agreement, and Lorraine objected (line 126) by reminding her that they were not making something from the booklet. Rashia had already oriented to picking up the booklet as a potential breach of their agreement, however, perhaps anticipating that Lorraine might object, because she produced an account or disclaimer as she reached to pick up the booklet (line 123), before she actually committed the breach and before Lorraine objected (line 126).

```
122  Lorraine:  °No the door ⌐goes like (   )°      ((spoken to
                              ⌊                      herself))
123  Rashia:                   I need to copy
124             something.                           ((picks up
                                                     booklet))
125             (0.5) ((R is leafing through the instructions
                    booklet))
126  Lorraine:  Ah, >we're not making the house in the book,
                remember.<
```

What is also noteworthy is not only that Rashia did not promptly put the booklet back down when Lorraine objected, but what she also did while she held onto it. First, she did not make actual use of it: she kept flipping pages as if looking through it, yet did not stop anywhere or (visibly) settle her gaze on anything. At the same time, she twice started (but did not complete) formulating a justification for using the booklet (in the form *I know [we agreed not to use it] but ...*), even though Lorraine had already shifted her attention back to what she was assembling. And she interrupted both of her own starts at formulating a justification with exclamations that indicated she had just then found something noteworthy even though her gaze had not settled on anything: 'look!' (line 127) and '>Oh yeah! (.) I forgot.<' (line 131).

```
127  Rashia:   I know but I need to do some-=look!
128            (2.2) ((R continues flipping pages))
129  Rashia:   I know we're not copying something in the house,
               but-=
130  Lorraine: =Ah, let's see:: ((Spoken to herself about her
                                  next step))
131  Rashia:   ((R closes up booklet)) >Oh yeah! (.) I forgot.<
132            ((R turns back to table and gathers pieces))
```

The internal incongruities of Rashia's talk and behavior make it implausible that any of it was expressive of her own wants or subjective reactions. She professed to have an acceptable reason for looking in the booklet (lines 127, 129: *I know but . . .*) yet evidently did not, considering her two self-interrupted starts at stating one. Moreover, as she energetically flipped back and forth through pages of the booklet, without looking at anything, she produced two exclamations as if reacting to something in the booklet. Her second such exclamation (line 131: 'Oh yeah! (.) I forgot.') seems to express that she found what she was looking for, but because this came after she closed the booklet and was putting it down, it was not produced in spontaneous reaction to seeing what she was looking for.

However, these details of Rashia's interactional turns can be rationalized in terms of anticipating and compensating for two unwanted consequences. Given that the sub-goals of avoiding conflict and achieving equity as participants are tied to the instruction we gave the children to work together to make something, Rashia was in a bind once Lorraine admonished her. To have put the booklet down when Lorraine objected would have had the potential consequence of producing an inequity between Lorraine and herself, subordinating herself to Lorraine by tacitly admitting that Lorraine was in the right and Rashia in the wrong. On the other hand, without a justification for using the booklet, to go ahead and make some application of something in the booklet would markedly disregard both their agreement and Lorraine's objection, thus risking conflict.

Rashia's interactional turns were fashioned so that she effectively did neither of those (did not make direct use of the booklet nor put it down). She did this by 'pantomiming' an examination of the booklet without actually consulting it. In that way, she made no direct use of the booklet for which she could be faulted, but delayed putting the booklet down when Lorraine objected, so that when she did — because it came after a delay and was accompanied with the exclamation that she had gotten what she wanted — she made it seem as if she put it down for her own reasons, not because Lorraine objected. Of course, had she been able to justify using the booklet, she could have gone ahead and actually got something from it, so it is congruent with the rationale for having 'pantomimed' consulting the booklet that she also made two tries to justify using it.

Dyad 2, FRAP94, F3: Luke (5;1) and Rick (5;2)

After the first few turns of this interaction, Rick took physical control of the Lego set: he took possession of the instructions booklet, he alone assembled the object they were making (at first a helicopter, then a car), and he gave Luke the job of finding pieces he needed. Besides finding parts that Rick asked for, Luke actively participated by making suggestions, corrections, and objections. The boys talked throughout the interaction, mostly about their activity, for example, about what parts were needed or why Rick couldn't get a piece attached. (Some of their turns are equivocal, however, as to whether they were in response to the other, or were 'thinking aloud' in the manner of egocentric speech.) In addition, the boys evidently had the social competence not only to be aware of the sharpness of their division of labor, but to be able to abstract it to the enactment of exchangeable roles they respectively termed the 'creator' and the 'giver' (lines 815 and 818):

```
812  Luke:  ((half laugh)) Rick you're havin' a (0.7) a really
813         rough time, don't ya?
814         (0.5)
815  Rick:  How w'd you like to be the creator?
816         (3.2) ((L pauses activity, gazes into space with
817               a thoughtful expression))
818  Luke:  And you (w'd) be the giver?
```

Despite Rick's physical domination of their activity, we consider that it was Luke who took the neo-rhetorical lead: Luke monitored and tried to direct the way Rick assembled the pieces they found and corrected his mistakes, but in indirect, mitigated, forms that on the surface deferred to Rick and avoided overtly challenging Rick's competence or his physical control of their activity. For his part, though Rick sustained an engaged interaction with Luke, and displayed the pragmatic competence to produce and respond to indirect as well as direct forms of expression, he did relatively little to fashion his turns in anticipation of interactional consequences beyond the local moment, except sometimes to mitigate the way he expressed rejections of Luke's suggestions (for example, by saying *sorry*). Our analysis here thus focuses on Luke alone.

Luke: As noted, Luke often fashioned turns that 'told' Rick what he should do, but indirectly, fashioning his utterances in the form of questions that provided candidate answers. He thus avoided the unwanted consequence of making it relevant to be responded to for having challenged Rick's competence or his physical control of the activity. Such responses could involve conflict and jeopardize their achievement of 'joint effort.' One example is that Luke corrected Rick in one instance indirectly by asking about the matter in question rather than 'telling' Rick directly that he needed to put a piece in some particular spot:

```
179  Luke:  Hey >Rick. Isn't this?< supposed t' go: on that?
180         (0.2)
181  Luke:  Isn't ⌈it?
182  Rick:        ⌊Oh: Yeah, °I fergot.°
```

In the example below, Luke again employed a question form, this one of considerable logical and syntactic complexity (line 222), to indirectly challenge Rick's conclusion (lines 215–220) that Luke had given him a wrong part:

```
215  Rick:  Oh:: Luke, (0.5) this is what it's: 'posed t', see?
216         (1.0)
217  Rick:  That's what it's supposed t' connect on.
218         (1.5) ((Manipulates object in hand while L
219               looks on))
```

```
220  Rick:  °I'm sorry.°
221         (0.5)
222  Luke:  But- what're these two for?  ((pushes a couple
223                                        of pieces toward R))
```

Note that Luke's question in line 222 overtly defers to Rick and presupposes that Luke trusts him to have an answer, but at the same time it puts the burden on Rick to justify his prior judgment and it is marked as a challenge by being prefaced with the counter-factual 'But-'. The substance of this challenge is expressed by the question in the form of a truncated if-then argument that identifies an incongruity between what the facts are and what Rick's judgment implies, and 'asks' Rick to resolve it or concede his error: *But- [if you're right that ~p ∥ (~p → ~q), then] what are these q's for?* Rick acknowledged the question without evidently being able to answer it, and thus made it relevant for Luke to pursue his case, which he promptly did (lines 226 and 230):

```
222  Luke:  But- what're these two for?      ((Pushes a couple
223                                            of pieces toward R))
224         (1.0)
225  Rick:  Those two?
226  Luke:  I see 'em on there=      ((L is leaning across in
227                                    front of R to study the
                                      instruction booklet lying
                                      to the right of R))
229  Rick:  =(Yea:h), ┌(right off) the top.
230  Luke:            └See?
```

However, in a few instances Luke participated in the interaction in a way that created a potential for the interaction to take an unwanted course, and then seemed to realize it and 'reverse' himself. The following episode involves the most visible such case. The episode came late in the interaction, and involved a disagreement where Luke exclaimed (line 528) that he figured out something they needed to do, and Rick rebuffed this (lines 531–533). Unlike much of their prior interaction, Luke then flatly rejected Rick's reason for disagreeing and Rick (qualifiedly) conceded (line 536).

```
528  Luke:  °Ooh!° hhh (0.2) >Rick.= ((pointing in book))
529         =See:, look! < That's tha:t. (.) >So we< nee:d it.
530  Rick:  Oh yea:h, oh that's (.) <f'r the front,> though.
531         (1.0)
532  Rick:  Sorry Luke. I don't have enuff roo:m for it.
533         (1.7)
534  Luke:  °Yes you do::.°
535         (0.5)
536  Rick:  >I guess I do.<
```

Luke did not end the matter there, however, even though for all practical purposes he could have. He may have pursued it because of the tentativeness of

Rick's concession in line 536, or because it was an opportunity to further display his competence on top of his success in combating Rick, or because he could append a further directive to this follow-up (line 542) — but in any case he went on to give reasons why he was right.

```
538   Rick:   (we┌ll I'll)
539   Luke:       └It has t' be bigger than that, ((points in
                                                     book))
540   Luke:   See?
541           (0.2)
542   Luke:   So ya make it with tho:se two.
543           (0.7)
544   Luke:   But the:n, (0.2) how d'we gonna- (0.2) hhh (.)
545           >hook it together (on the thing)?<
```

What is of particular interest here is that after this series of turns in which Luke more and more aggressively dictated to Rick what they should do and why, he ended the episode with a question about what the next step should be (though it is unclear whether he was speaking to Rick or talking to himself). The question is in marked contrast to what preceded it, shifting from certainty to uncertainty and from directiveness to deference (lines 544–545). Of course, Luke's question could simply have been expressive, he might have just got confused about what they should do at that juncture. But it has to be considered that if Luke had not expressed uncertainty just then, the course of the interaction that his own directiveness produced left him with little he could relevantly do next except overtly try taking control of the activity away from Rick. Luke had fashioned other turns at other junctures to avert that same consequence, and the potential for this was similarly averted in this instance by Luke's shift from assertion to question. There is thus a warrant for taking seriously that this turn too was fashioned in anticipation of potential interactional consequences.

In another instance, when there seemed to be an impasse about what they should do, Luke averted the direct conflict that had become relevant by simply making an abrupt topic change. This occurred after Rick remained stolidly nonresponsive to Luke's repeated efforts to show him — relatively directly — that he was making a mistake. Luke's efforts consisted first of an objection (lines 466–467), then he tried to take the part from Rick to show him what should be done (lines 466–469), then he cited the instruction booklet (lines 471–472), and then he directly specified what needed to be done (lines 474–475). When Rick continued to be unresponsive, Luke shifted attention/topic to 'pants' he found for a toy figure (line 479):

```
462   Rick:   We jus' need one more, Luke.
463           (0.7)
464   Luke:   One more? ((leans over to look at book))
465   Rick:   Yih, where's all::? (.) Wh┌ere's
466   Luke:                             └No- (.) See
```

```
467            ┌how ya <make it?>
468            └((L is trying to take piece from R's hand,
469            R prevents it))
470            (0.5)
471   Luke:    Ya make it like-
472            (1.2) ((L makes click, gestures towards book))
473   Rick:    ┌(Naa:)
474   Luke:    └Rick. Ya take tha:t, 'n >put it on the other<
475            si:de, like that.
476            (1.7)
477   Rick:    No: (.) what.      ((looking at book, possibly not
478                                responding to L))
479   Luke:    I got some pa:nts.((referring to pants for a toy
                                   figure))
```

Although Luke's neo-rhetorical participation was consistently more extensive and complex than Rick's, Rick's participation did not indicate he necessarily had less developed pragmatic and social competencies: he seemed as able as Luke was to produce and understand indirect as well as direct forms of expression, and deployed them as needed to avert threats to the other's 'face' wants (Goffman, 1967; Brown and Levinson, 1987). It is possible that Rick did not participate neo-rhetorically more than he did simply because he did not have to: Luke's way of participating consistently made it possible for Rick to sustain his physical control of the activity without engendering conflict or preventing them from working together to make something.

Dyad 3, FRAP94, S13: Lucy (6;1) and Ruthie (5;10)

Although these girls too sustained interaction throughout, neither Lucy or Ruthie seemed to fashion turns in response to local exigencies that seemed at the same time to anticipate the potential consequences of current utterances or behaviors for the future interaction. Compared to both Lorraine and Rashia, and Luke, they were comparatively more reactive and self-expressive in their turns, and at cross purposes more often than happened in the other interactions (for example, brief episodes of exchange when one girl responded to the other with *no* and a *yes-no-yes-no* exchange ensued). In the first several minutes of the interaction in particular, when Ruthie was actively trying to participate in making the house they agreed on, Lucy consistently rebuffed Ruthie's suggestions with little mitigation. When Ruthie was rebuffed, she did little more about it than plead with Lucy to let her have her way. Both tendencies are evident in the following example, where the issue they address is what colour bricks to use:

```
196   Ruthie:  (Let's make- ) red things aroun::d (red things)
197            (4.0) ((R grabs box and jerks it toward her; L
198                   reaches into box and digs around; R takes
199                   box as L works on floor))
```

```
200  Ruthie:  Let's. Let's. Let's. Hey ┌(let's      )
201  Lucy:                             └(          ) put all
202           different color things around.
203  Ruthie:  No (please)
204  Lucy:    YES.
205  Ruthie:  No!
206           (5.0) ((Both are working assembling pieces, R
207                 presses one down on board))
208  Lucy:    ((whispers)) °Yes yes yes°
```

However, at times after the interaction had already taken an unwanted course, one girl or the other responded by fashioning one or more interactional turns so as to constrain future participation and thus change the interaction's course, instead of (or in addition to) directly confronting her partner about what she just then said or did, and appealing to her to change it. Each girl can thus be said to have occasionally participated in the interaction neo-rhetorically. Further, while both girls participated neo-rhetorically to about the same extent, it was Ruthie who seemed to do so with an orientation to the goal of achieving joint effort, whereas Lucy seemed more concerned with finding ways for Ruthie to participate in specific instances without interfering with Lucy's wants about the house 'they' were making. We thus consider that Ruthie took the neo-rhetorical lead.

Ruthie. Lucy's way of being engaged in the activity of building a house consistently marginalized Ruthie, but Ruthie did not respond by withdrawing and engaging in a separate activity. However, unlike the children in the other two dyads, she also did not fashion turns proactively to counter the unwanted effects on the interaction of Lucy's turns whenever they occurred. She fashioned turns proactively at two principal junctures. In each case, Ruthie fashioned turns that had the potential to divert Lucy from the activity of making a house, in which she consistently opposed any but a menial role for Ruthie. Ruthie's first attempt to do this was to introduce an alternate activity the two girls could engage in jointly with the Lego set. When that failed, she initiated a campaign to subvert Lucy's activity.

The first of these efforts to divert Lucy can be characterized as making a bid to shift their activity from 'work' (the effort to make a house) towards undirected play with the Lego pieces. Admittedly, taking just the episode into account in which Ruthie introduced this new agenda, it is a matter of interpretation whether Ruthie's turns were fashioned (as we contend) to change the course of the interaction to favor a more active role for herself, or whether Ruthie's attention and interest simply began to wander after becoming bored by Lucy's absorption in the activity of making a house and her exclusion from it. However, the matter is less equivocal when the episode's sequential placement is considered. It came after an extended series of efforts by Ruthie to participate that were all rebuffed (as in the example above in lines 196–208), and just after Ruthie displayed a new playfulness about their activity by making an exaggerated display of excitement at finding a piece for Lucy (in the example in lines 264–269 below).

Moreover, when Ruthie then introduced this new agenda more markedly and it failed, she did not withdraw or shift her attention to other irrelevancies (as one would expect if she had simply become bored with the activity of making a house). Rather, she resumed her efforts to 'seriously' participate with Lucy in the activity of making a house (again without success — see the examples in the section below on Lucy, lines 318–327 and 388–395). In any event, as noted, the new agenda was first introduced indirectly by an exaggerated performance of excitement (lines 264–269) whose extensiveness and pitch contours give it a playful aspect:

```
260  Ruthie:  Here you go, here's something (f'you/new).
261  Lucy:    Ah ye┌ah
262  Ruthie:       └(I) got ┌one ((takes piece from box, looks at
                             │     it as L in stalls pieces))
263  Lucy:                  └>(There is, there is, got it)<
264  Ruthie:  oh! >oo!oo!oo!oo!< ah! ah! ((falsetto)) >Lucy.
265           Lucy. Lucy.< (0.2) Lucy. (0.2) Lucy.
266           (0.5) ((R is leafing through the book))
267  Ruthie:  Lu::cy
268  Lucy:    What!
269  Ruthie:  °Lu::cy:° (0.2) Lucy! (0.2) Lucy! (0.2) Lucy!
270           ((slowly raising piece upward, drawing L's gaze))
```

Ruthie followed this performance, which got little response or reciprocation from Lucy, with a more marked introduction of a shift from 'work' to 'play'. This was accomplished by first indirectly making it relevant to put an end to trying to make a house by making a woeful assessment of the enormity of 'their' project (line 278). After Lucy responded to this by countering it, Ruthie changed the focus of her talk to Lego pieces that were irrelevant to the project of making a house but potentially fun or funny in their own right. She expressed a playful attitude towards these pieces both by announcing discovery of an irrelevant toy figure's 'broken hea:d' and especially by prefacing this with an assessment that was both enthusiastic and sardonic — 'Oh::: (goody)' (line 282):

```
278  Ruthie:  Oh. God, we're gonna make- all: this? Oh:::
279  Lucy:    No >we're not gonna make that,< we're just gonna
280           make a plain ordinary house.
281           (2.8)
282  Ruthie:  ((falsetto)) Oh::: (goody) a broken hea:d ((L
283           laughs, then R joins in))
284  Ruthie:  Or a broken body, whatever (it)
285           (0.8)
286  Lucy:    Broken head.
287  Ruthie:  Broken body.
```

Ruthie's playfulness was again only minimally responded to by Lucy (with laughter in line 282, and a correction response in line 286). Ruthie seems to have tried to elicit more from Lucy by pressing an otherwise inconsequential disagreement about whether the part she found was a broken body or a broken head (lines 286–287).

Several minutes after Ruthie seemed to abandon the agenda of undirected playfulness with the Lego pieces and resumed trying to participate in making a house, she introduced a second new agenda. We characterize this agenda as being to sabotage Lucy in a playful rather than hostile manner, as exemplified by her initial attempt at this (lines 406–407 below). Although the introduction of this agenda had the potential to create conflict — and in fact the girls moved closer to actual conflict at that point than happened in any of the other dyads we analyzed — it is noteworthy that both girls fashioned their turns during this exchange so as to keep this conflict from becoming serious:

```
406   Ruthie:  Oooo (0.2) (eh!)      ((R takes piece from structure
                                        Lucy is making, and
407                                     holds it up close to L's face))
408   Ruthie:  ((sings)) I'm fucking you (up), I'm fuck⌐ing you (up)
409   Lucy:                    ((singsong)) └We'r:e gonna
410            (sleep) over at, (E::rin's) hou:se.
411   Ruthie:  (Ye⌐ah)?
412   Lucy:       └Yeah (      ) ((chortles))
413   Ruthie:  (NOW/WELL) I DON'T HAVE TO GO TO YOUR HOUSE. ('CUZ
414            >I'M SLEEPING OVER) AT< (.) ERIN'S HOUSE.
415   Lucy:    >So am I< (heh) ((L continues working on structure))
416   Ruthie:  >SO AM I. SO AM I, SO IS DANI⌐ELLE. So is Danielle.<
417   Lucy:                                └Shhhh
```

Note that Ruthie and then Lucy relied initially on singing and singsong to aggress and counter, thus avoiding overtly hostile displays and preventing more serious conflict from being relevant. Second, more serious conflict was kept from being relevant through Lucy's shifting the topic away from their present activity (lines 409–410), and Ruthie followed suit, to more ritualized combat regarding their respective friendship, social alliances and opportunities. When Ruthie raised her voice and the potential for serious conflict seemed greater, Lucy responded with 'Shhhh' and Lucy promptly complied.

Ruthie's shift in lines 406 and 409 to 'mocking' Lucy's activity and interfering with it was not an isolated moment in the interaction, but marked a shift to that way of participating in much of the remaining interaction. This escalated through various intermediate levels of mocking or interfering with Lucy's activity until it reached its most extreme form, shortly before the interaction was ended — when Ruthie began play-threatening Lucy and physically 'molesting' her:

```
608   Ruthie:  Oohh here, I'm gonna hammer your knee. (0.2) Ah!
609            (1.5) ((R sits up, slowly raises left arm holding
610                piece above her head, L watches R's hand))
611   Lucy:    ((chortles))
612            (4.5) ((R brings hand holding Lego piece down in
613                slow motion to 'hit' L's knee; L rolls back))
```

```
614   Lucy:     ((chortles; sits up))
615   Ruthie:   I'm gonna hammer you agai::n
616             (1.0) ((raises piece to inspect it, L sits back))
617   Ruthie:   Ah- haahhh. ooh. ooh. oh. (0.2) Look.
618             (1.5) ((R waves a small piece over her head, brings
619                   it to L's face as L works on structure, then
620                   pulls it back and inspects it))
621   Ruthie:   (I'll get you:::) (.) ((reaches towards L's ear))
622             (Let me look in your ear).
```

Lucy. Lucy's recurrent way of responding to Ruthie's marginalization and the potential that created for conflict was either to 'humor' Ruthie when Ruthie was involved with something that did not interfere with Lucy, or to distract her attention away from Lucy's efforts if Ruthie was actually or potentially getting involved. These forms of response occurred primarily in the middle portion of the interaction (when Ruthie was no longer pleading as in the first portion, but had not begun actively trying to interfere as in the third). In the following example Ruthie tried installing a piece that Lucy did not want, and persisted despite Lucy's objection. Instead of pursuing the argument, Lucy produced a play on words (lines 323–324). This had the potential and actual effect of deflecting Ruthie's attention from the substance of their dispute to the wordplay. It is noteworthy that Lucy produced this wordplay shortly after Ruthie tried to shift the activity (as discussed above) from goal-oriented to undirected play. It thus made it seem that Lucy was cooperating in that shift by becoming playful, possibly increasing the chances that Ruthie would shift her attention to this, away from the substantive issue:

```
318   Lucy:     That's the- THESE are chai:┌::rs
319   Ruthie:                               └Lu:cy:: ((R tries
320             installing piece on structure))
321   Lucy:     Wait. Those are for the (.) inside.
322             (0.8)
323   Ruthie:   No:: these are not chai:rs=
324   Lucy:     =Hair? You need hair? ((chor┌tles))
325   Ruthie:                               └Oh yeah, I need hair
326             (0.8)
327   Ruthie:   I need hair, (      ).
```

In a later example, Ruthie was evidently experimenting with attaching a piece for making flowers (line 390). Lucy baldly objected to the installation of flowers at that juncture as something that *she* (first person singular) did not want, then produced a slight laugh as if trying to soften that (lines 391–392). After Ruthie began an account that she was not actually trying to install flowers (line 394), Lucy interrupted with a directive that Ruthie try to find more flowers (line 395).

```
388             (2.5) ((Each girl brings pieces to green base.
389                   working on separate parts))
390   Ruthie:   (Then how do you put that on: there)=
```

```
391   Lucy:     =I don't WANT a flower yet.
392             (0.8)
393   Lucy:     ((chortles))
394   Ruthie:   (No, I'm just trying to see    )
395   Lucy:     Find all the flowers you can.
```

Neither Lucy's chortling (line 393) nor her directive to Ruthie to find 'all the flowers you can' (line 395) are relevant to what was then taking place. But both can be viewed as anticipating unwanted consequences. Lucy's unqualified, ego-centered expression of an objection to Ruthie's placement of a flower on the green base implicated hostility and made conflict relevant: Lucy's chortle cancels the implicature of hostility and to that extent cancels the relevance of conflict. However, Ruthie's response, to justify placing a piece for making flowers on the board, made it relevant, if agreed to, for Ruthie to resume. For Lucy to respond to this by directing Ruthie to find more flowers avoids rebuffing her again and instead endorses Ruthie's interest in the flowers, thus avoiding a renewed potential for conflict, but makes it relevant for Ruthie to pursue her interest in the flowers without continuing to interfere with what Lucy wanted.

Some Concluding Observations

The most prominent question that arises from comparing the neo-rhetorical participation of the children in these three dyads is how to account for the considerable differences among them. There is obviously no justification for attributing it to the children's age or gender, and thus developmental issues do not seem to be involved. Even if we consider some of these children to have interacted in ways that are exceptional for their age and gender, the fact would remain that (for children above 5) age and gender are not good predictors of children's neo-rhetorical participation in interactions.

There are several other possibilities, but first we should also rule out that it was an artifact of the situation in which the interactions were recorded, or the interpersonal relationships between the children in each dyad. The situations were equivalent (the interactions took place in a space apart from their usual play areas, in front of a video camera, in the presence of adults). The interpersonal relationships involved seem to have an inverse relationship, if there is one at all, to the extent and complexity of the children's neo-rhetorical participation: the more established the children's friendship, the less coordinated in their interaction, and less likely to fashion their interactional turns to avoid confrontation and constrain the interaction to take a favoured course they were. Lucy and Ruthie were in the same friendship network, and from references they made to sleeping over at a mutual friend's house, this evidently included time apart from their daycare attendance. Lorraine and Rashia may have interacted previously in the school environment but were not in the same friendship network. The coordination and harmoniousness of the interaction between Luke and Rick, who were also in the same friendship network, complicates matters, but the differences among these dyads suggests that children with an established relationship are less concerned about what happens in their interactions than more causal acquaintances. Hartup et al. (1993) did in fact find that conflict occurred more frequently and lasted longer between friends than non-friends. However, even if the special circumstances in which these results were induced apply here, it does not account for individual differences among these children, just dyadic differences.

One possible reason for differences in the extent and complexity of these children's neo-rhetorical participation is that there may be individual differences among these children in what O'Keefe (1991) refers to as 'message design logic'. O'Keefe noted that situations typically pose multiple interactional concerns, not single ones — especially 'task' versus 'face' concerns — and that individuals differ in terms of their cognitive capacity to process and integrate these distinct concerns. Individuals may also differ in regard to which concerns they habitually give priority.

O'Keefe identified three generic 'methods' for processing and responding to these concerns, one or another of which individuals characteristically employ. One is when turns at speaking are oriented 'selectively' to one or another from among the larger set of concerns the situation presents. The second is when sub-parts of turns at speaking are oriented 'separately' to different interactional concerns, each in turn. The third is to fashion turns at speaking 'integratively' so that they are oriented simultaneously to different interactional concerns. From this perspective, both Lorraine's and Rashia's turns at speaking, and also Luke's, seem to have characteristically been fashioned 'integratively' (oriented at the same time to moving forward on their project, maintaining parity, avoiding conflict, being respectful of the other, and so forth), whereas Rick's, and both Lucy's and Ruthie's, turns at speaking seem to have been oriented 'selectively' to one or another among several possible concerns at the expense of the others. The dyad that was most effective and co-ordinated in complying with our instruction that they work together to make one thing was then Lorraine's and Rashia's, the one in which both children tended to fashion turns at speaking 'integratively'. The dyad that achieved an intermediate level of compliance with our instruction was then Luke's and Rick's, where one of the children (who also most markedly took the neo-rhetorical lead) tended to fashion turns at speaking integratively. The dyad that responded to our instruction with least coordination and effectiveness was Lucy's and Ruthie's, where both children tended to fashion their turns at speaking with an emphasis on 'separate' concerns and where each gave priority to different concerns (Lucy's priority was evidently to get something made, Ruthie's was evidently that whatever they do with the Lego set, it be done jointly).

Another possibility is that there may have been differences between the three dyads in terms of the social attitudes or priorities, one might even say the moral codes, the children had acquired. Lorraine in particular, and to some extent Rashia as well, seemed to have placed a premium on achieving harmony and finding compromises, even if that called on them to sacrifice (to some extent) getting their own way on the matter at hand. Lucy and Ruthie, in contrast, seemed to have placed a premium on their individual agendas, and to have expected full compliance by the other with that. Luke and Rick differed from each other in this regard, Luke more closely resembling Lorraine and Rashia, Rick more closely resembling Lucy and Ruthie.

A final possibility is that the pairings themselves were consequential. Although this has not received attention in studies of interaction that we know of, a case can be made that the functional adequacy of one's turns at speaking (and perhaps their cleverness, originality, and the like) depend on who one's partner is, i.e., how the partner characteristically participates. Daly (1983) proposed that communicative competence is not a property of individuals but of dyads: the same person may produce elaborated turns at speaking or minimal ones, be funny or dull, combative or accommodating, and so forth, in interactions with one partner versus another. Sanders (forthcoming a) characterized this as a form of compatibility that attracts persons to each other, and when it is absent interferes with their ability to form and sustain a personal relationship.

Thus, rather than attribute interpersonal compatibility to such matters as the congruity of each person's attitudes, one has to consider that it also or instead involves the congruity of their interactional styles. In terms of the analysis above, 'compatibility' would be a matter of each person consistently fashioning interactional turns that make relevant what the other wants to say or do, and what the other can say or do effectively; 'incompatibility' would thus involve the reverse, for example, when each person consistently fashions turns that make relevant what the other does not want to say or do, or do not make relevant what the other can say or do well.

Despite their friendship, therefore, Lucy and Ruthie may not have been compatible in that interactional sense, whereas despite their relative social distance, Lorraine and Rashia evidently were. It is conceivable that Ruthie was accustomed to being accommodated, or to negotiating, when she contributed something to an ongoing activity, not to being recurrently and flatly rebuffed as she was by Lucy, so that Ruthie was taken off guard in this interaction and perhaps disoriented in considering how she might fashion turns at speaking to compensate. It may also be that Lucy was sufficiently task-oriented that once they had agreed on what to build, she expected that they would proceed according to the illustration in the instructions booklet (to which she referred on a few occasions when she and Ruthie disputed how to proceed). When Ruthie made contributions that were 'arbitrary' or 'wrong' from this perspective, Lucy too might have been taken off guard.

Of course, these various possibilities are not mutually exclusive, and it is not difficult to conceive how they might combine to explain in detail the differences between the neo-rhetorical participation in the interactions of each dyad. It is worth noting in closing, however, that all of these considerations (except the developmental one, but we have provisionally discarded that) are ones that apply equally to the interactions of adults and the ways in which they vary. One can readily imagine adult counterparts of each of these three interactions, such that it is the content much more than the manner of participation that marks them as childish or not. This is a quite different picture of the social world of children of this age than one tends to get from research and theory on children's interactions, and it arises simply from attending to the contribution of turns at speaking to the course of the interaction, and not the expressive and social qualities of turns at speaking in and of themselves.

Notes

1 Earlier versions of this report were presented at the Convention of the Speech Communication Association, November 1994, and at the Conference on Children and Social Competence, University of Surrey, July 1995. Some transcript material and analysis in the current version draws on the work of a data group at the University at Albany composed of the authors and Shiao-Yun (John) Chiang, Thomas Hoey, Cathleen Rizziello and Tara Seaman. We are indebted to Marjorie Harness Goodwin for her comments on an early draft.

2 In general, the circumstances under which this occurs are when the interaction is not routinized, so that its future course is uncertain, and one or more participants have preferences about how the interaction concludes or what is included in it.

3 Lego System building sets comprise plastic building bricks, along with specialized pieces, such as human figures, windows and shutters, plants, wheels, propeller hubs, and the like. The particular set we provided the children was no. 535, and seemed among the most gender-neutral of the sets available. It did not support making more gender-biased objects for boys than for girls, and it supported making some gender-neutral objects as well. The instructions booklet that was provided illustrated in the following order how to make a helicopter, a car, a house with a yard and plants with a car in front, a dog, the interior of a room in a house, a seaplane, and a 'high-rise' building/windmill. The children were free to make other objects than those depicted in the instructions booklet, of course, and whether they were trying to match something in the booklet (as to what they made, or such details as the colours they used) or be innovative was sometimes a matter of contention between children.

4 The term '*neo*-rhetorical' is preferred to simply 'rhetorical' even though the phenomenon of interest is essentially rhetoric — discourse that is artfully fashioned to secure others' cooperation and thus promote (or discourage) certain social consequences. However, there are important differences between classical rhetoric and rhetoric in the give-and-take of social interaction that change what 'artfulness' consists of and what it is based on. Traditional writing about the practice of rhetoric principally involves oratory (and other suasory and didactic discursive forms): discourse that is relatively self-standing, composed well in advance of having to actually communicate, usually by a single author in unhurried, conscious, reflection about the occasion, audience, and issues. Speakers in social interaction have only micro-seconds in which to formulate and produce their turns at speaking, the occasion and issues often emerge in the local moment rather than being known in advance, little may be known about the audience before the fact, and the (ratified) audience is entitled and expected to participate during and as part of one's speaking. Speakers in social interaction also differ from traditional orators in that the discourse they produce in any interactional turn is not self-standing, but only a fragment of what they may want to communicate overall, and a fragment of the present interaction. Because each turn combines with the other such fragments of an interaction produced by self and others to form the whole, what one eventually communicates across turns and what the consequences are is unavoidably a joint construction, giving individual agency considerably less force than it is considered to have in traditional oratory (see Sanders,

forthcoming a). Finally, because of the speed with which turns have to be fashioned, rhetoric in social interaction does not admit of due reflection except after the fact, and may not be something about which the person is even conscious — but it is not a prerequisite for producing rational, strategic discourse that persons do it knowingly, as long as one can specify a systemic basis for the discourse so produced (see Grice, 1975; Brown and Levinson, 1987; Sanders, 1987).

5   Hartup et al. (1993) explained that they analyzed conflicts as beginning when 'a child objected to the actions of the other . . . (b)ecause the actions instigating these conflicts were often innocuous or difficult to determine. . . .' (p. 448)

6   Robinson's findings (Robinson, 1981; Robinson, Goelman and Olson, 1983) indicate that children seem relatively insensitive to semantic intricacies, and more oriented to the pragmatics of utterances, until relatively late (around the seventh year). This is hard to explain in terms of the sentence processing involved, unless we consider it a matter of the child's interactional priorities rather than sentence processing abilities, and endorse what is being proposed here — to subordinate the information-centered premise to a neo-rhetorical one. Then one can surmise that until a child encounters the demands of formal education, when semantic intricacies and the truth conditions of linguistic forms become increasingly consequential, attending to the pragmatics of an utterance and its interactional consequences would be far more useful in interactions with adults and peers alike.

7   The children's names have been changed to preserve their anonymity: names were devised that began with L or R, to indicate whether the child was positioned on the left or right of the video picture, with an effort to preserve the phonological and ethnic qualities of their given names.

References

ATKINSON, J.M. and HERITAGE, J. (1984) *Structures of Social Action: Studies in Conversation Analysis*, Cambridge: Cambridge University Press.

BARNES, M.K. and VANGELISTI, A.L. (1995) 'Speaking in a double-voice: Role-making as influence in preschoolers' fantasy play situations', *Research on Language and Social Interaction*, **28**, pp. 351–89.

BLOOM, L. (1973) *One Word at a Time: The Use of Single Word Utterances Before Syntax*, The Hague: Mouton.

BROWN, P. and LEVINSON, S. (1987) *Politeness*, Cambridge: Cambridge University Press.

BRUNER, J. (1975) 'The ontogenesis of speech acts', *Journal of Child Language*, **2**, pp. 1–19.

DALY, J. (1983) 'Participant comment', seminar on communicative competence, Speech Communication Association Convention, Washington, D.C.

DAVIDSON, J. (1984) 'Subsequent versions of invitations, offers, requests and proposals dealing with actual or potential rejection', in ATKINSON, J.M. and HERITAGE, J. (eds) *Structures of Social Action*, Cambridge: Cambridge University Press.

DORVAL, B. and ECKERMAN, C.O. (1984) *Developmental Trends in the Quality of Conversation Achieved by Small Groups of Acquainted Peers*, monographs of the Society for Research in Child Development, vol. 49 (Serial no. 206), Chicago, IL: University of Chicago Press.

EISENBERG, A.R. and GARVEY, C. (1981) 'Children's use of verbal strategies in resolving conflicts', *Discourse Processes*, **4**, pp. 149–70.

FREEMAN, K.E. (1996) 'Tag questions can be used strategically, right?: Power hidden in "powerless" forms', paper presented at the International Communication Association convention, Chicago.

GOFFMAN, E. (1959) *The Presentation of Self in Everyday Life*, Garden City, NY: Doubleday.

GOFFMAN, E. (1967) *Interaction Ritual: Essays on Face-to-Face Behavior*, New York: Anchor Books.

GOODWIN, C. (1995) 'Co-constructing meaning in conversations with an aphasic man', in JACOBY, S. and OCHS, E. (eds) *Special Issue: Co-construction. Research on Language and Social Interaction*, **28**, pp. 233–60.

GOODWIN, M.H. (1990) 'Tactical uses of stories: Participation frameworks within boys' and girls' disputes', *Discourse Processes*, **13**, pp. 33–71.

GRICE, H.P. (1975) 'Logic and conversation', in COLE, P. and MORGAN, J.L. (eds) *Syntax and Semantics 3: Speech Acts*, New York: Academic Press.

HARTUP, W.W., FRENCH, D.C., LAURSEN, B., JOHNSTON, M.K. and OGAWA, J.R. (1993) 'Conflict and friendship relations in middle childhood: Behavior in a closed-field situation', *Child Development*, **64**, pp. 445–54.

HERITAGE, J. (1990/91) 'Intention, meaning, and strategy: Observations on constraints on interaction analysis', *Research on Language and Social Interaction*, **24**, pp. 311–32.

HOBBS, J.R. (1990) 'Topic drift', in DORVAL, B. (ed.) *Conversational Organization and its Development*, Norwood, NJ: Ablex.

HYMES, D. (1974) *Foundations of Sociolinguistics: An Ethnographic Approach*, Philadelphia, PA: University of Pennsylvania Press.

JACOBY, S. and OCHS, E. (1995) 'Special issue: Co-construction', *Research on Language and Social Interaction*, **28**.

JEFFERSON, G. (1993) 'Caveat speaker: Preliminary notes on recipient topic-shift implicature', *Research on Language and Social Interaction*, **26**, pp. 1–30.

MCTEAR, M. (1985) *Children's Conversation*, Oxford: Basil Blackwell.

O'KEEFE, B.J. (1991) 'Message design logic and the management of multiple goals', in TRACY, K. (ed.) *Understanding Face-to-Face Interaction: Issues Linking Goals and Discourse*, Hillsdale, NJ: Erlbaum.

POMERANTZ, A. (1984) 'Agreeing and disagreeing with assessments: Some features of preferred/dispreferred turn shapes', in ATKINSON, J.M. and HERITAGE, J. (eds) *Structures of Social Action*, Cambridge: Cambridge University Press.

ROBERTS, R.J. and PETERSON, C.J. (1983) 'Perspective taking and referential communication: The question of correspondence reconsidered', *Child Development*, **54**, pp. 1005–14.

ROBINSON, E.J. (1981) 'The child's understanding of inadequate messages and communication failure: A problem of ignorance or egocentrism', in DICKSON, W.P. (ed.) *Children's Oral Communication Skills*, New York: Academic Press.

ROBINSON, E.J., GOELMAN, H. and OLSON, D.R. (1983) 'Children's understanding of the relation between expressions (what was said) and intentions (what was meant)', *British Journal of Developmental Psychology*. **1**, pp. 75–8.

SACKS, H. (1988/89) 'On members' measurement systems', *Research on Language and Social Interaction*, **22**, pp. 45–60.

SANDERS, R.E. (1983) 'Tools for cohering discourse and their strategic utilization: Markers of structural connections and meaning relations', in CRAIG, R.T. and TRACY, K. (eds) *Conversational Coherence: Form, Structure, and Strategy*, Beverly Hills, CA: Sage.

SANDERS, R.E. (1984) 'Style, meaning and message effects', *Communication Monographs*, **51**, pp. 154–67.

SANDERS, R.E. (1985) 'The interpretation of non-verbals', *Semiotica*, **55**, pp. 195–216.

SANDERS, R.E. (1987) *Cognitive Foundations of Calculated Speech: Controlling Understandings in Conversation and Persuasion*, Albany, NY: SUNY Press.

SANDERS, R.E. (1991) 'The two-way relationship between talk in social interaction and actors' goals and plans', in TRACY, K. (ed.) *Understanding Face-to-Face Interaction: Issues Linking Goals and Discourse*, Hillsdale, NJ: Erlbaum.

SANDERS, R.E. (1995a) 'A neo-rhetorical perspective: The enactment of role-identities as interactive and strategic', in SIGMAN, S.J. (ed.) *The Consequentiality of Communication*, Hillsdale, NJ: Erlbaum.

SANDERS, R.E. (1995b) 'The sequential inferential theories of Sanders and Gottman', in CUSHMAN, D.P. and KOVACIC, B. (eds) *Watershed Research Traditions in Human Communication Theory*, Albany, NY: SUNY Press.

SANDERS, R.E. (forthcoming a) 'Find your partner and do-si-do: The formation of personal relationships between social beings', *Journal of Social and Personal Relationships*.

SANDERS, R.E. (forthcoming b) 'The production of symbolic objects as components of larger wholes', in GREENE, J.O. (ed.) *Message Production: Advances in Communication Theory*, Mahwah, NJ: Erlbaum.

SCHEGLOFF, E.A. (1991) 'With half a mind: Interaction with commissurotomies', paper presented at the First Rector's Colloquium, Tel Aviv University.

SCHEGLOFF, E.A. (1995) 'Discourse as an interactional achievement III: The omnirelevance of action', in JACOBY, S. and OCHS, E. (eds) *Special Issue: Co-construction. Research on Language and Social Interaction*, **28**, pp. 185–211.

SEARLE, J.R. (1969) *Speech Acts: An Essay in the Philosophy of Language*, London: Cambridge University Press.

SHELDON, A. (1992) 'Conflict talk: Sociolinguistic challenges to self-assertion and how young girls meet them', *Merrill-Palmer Quarterly*, **38**, pp. 95–117.

SHELDON, A. (1996) 'You can be the baby brother, but you aren't born yet: Preschool girls' negotiation for power and access in pretend play', in SHELDON, A. (ed.) *Special Issue: Constituting Gender Through Talk in Childhood, Research on Language and Social Interaction*, **29**, pp. 57–80.

Chapter 6

Social and Cognitive Competencies in Learning: Which is Which?

Hilary Gardner

Introduction

In this chapter I will be looking at how 4-year-old, preschool children function in a novel learning situation, namely that of speech therapy tasks in a clinical setting. Whilst this may appear to be a very specialized field of study there are parallels to be drawn between therapy tasks and other institutional learning contexts and it also gives a valuable insight into children's social functioning.

Using Conversation Analytic (CA) techniques (after Schegloff, 1972; Sacks, Schegloff and Jefferson, 1974) I will show that children are not simply passive respondees in the therapy dyad, as has often been portrayed in the past, but rather have an active role, using their developed interactional skills to display their level of understanding of the therapist's talk and work cooperatively towards an acceptable resolution of a supposed miscommunication. The role of social competence in handling therapy contexts has been acknowledged but the use of CA to detail how this is made explicit at the interactional level is a new approach to the subject. This work gives a far more positive picture of specifically language impaired children than is sometimes the case. The inclination of much research is to describe the deficits in social competence that arise from their communication difficulties rather than acknowledge that such children can have considerable capability in interactional terms.

The children involved in this research have a language disorder that predominantly affects their ability to produce intelligible speech (i.e. 'phonologically disordered'), despite having adequate comprehension and sentence structure. The aim of speech therapy is to break down the faulty output rules for certain speech sounds (phones) that the children have in their mental lexicon and move them toward a more 'normal' pattern. The phonemic components of language are presented in a fairly artificial way as therapists routinely present the child with isolated phones and words, describe explicitly how the articulations are produced and state where the sounds occur sequentially. There is a general belief that, although it is often not

Editors' Note

Because the present volume is directed at a non-specialist audience, phonetic transcriptions have not been used in this chapter. Rather, the phonetic and phonological details have been 'glossed' in order to provide an accessible account for readers not familiar with the relevant linguistic literature.

explicitly taught, 'metalinguistic' knowledge (conscious awareness of the structure of words) is enhanced by therapy and, if the child is at a stage to cope with this type of material, that better intelligibility results from this. These 'meta' conceptual skills generally develop between 5–7 years and children learning language normally appear to do so without these explicit skills.

A number of researchers suggest that the contribution of meta-awareness to success in therapy should not be overemphasized as maturing social and pragmatic skills make an equal contribution, with children treating therapy as a social encounter. For instance Ripich and Panagos (1985) found that their phonologically disordered subjects, when questioned about the instructional process, said that they asked themselves 'What is this place, who is this lady and what do I have to say for her to get along?' They argued that the children may be focussing on the pragmatic components of the session whereas clinicians focus on linguistic structures which the children are barely aware of. They additionally noted how children viewed their role in therapy as 'error-makers' as this was how the therapist cast them. McTear and King (1991) agree with the above statements and describe how good pragmatic skills can carry a child through language therapy without necessarily coming to grips with the conceptual content. They claim that the therapist is likely to be guided overridingly by global theoretical goals yet a child can provide responses that attend only to the local coherence of the conversation. For example they can give an appropriate 'yes' response to a yes/no question or imitate a given model, but in the context of the whole conversation topic or global plan, these responses prove inadequate. In other words the child can cope at the local level of conversation without ever being aware of what therapy is aimed at.

In line with the above research certain studies show that children may not be as aware of the 'metalinguistic' content of the sessions as the adult may assume. Some phonology disorders may have their roots in poor internal representations of phonological detail (Chiat, 1983; Stackhouse and Wells, 1993; Dodd, 1995) and many speech disordered children have problems processing and manipulating linguistic information. Therefore it would seem rather counterintuitive for therapists to presume that such children should easily pick up on the underlying 'meta' content. Indeed Howell (1991) found phonologically disordered, preliterate children only improved after therapy aimed explicitly at metalinguistic skills, not the kind of therapy described in this study which does not target these skills specifically.

This chapter will further substantiate claims as to the significance of social competence in therapy by showing, through detailed interactional analysis, the delicate interplay between the child's emerging conceptual knowledge and maturing social skills. Schegloff (1987) talked about how interactants can not only display trouble with possible intended referents but with the sequential import (implicativeness) of the prior turn i.e. what action is being done by the turn and what is an appropriate next. In this data it is the child's interpretation of the adult's prior that is of import. By looking specifically at repair strategies it will be shown that, although a child's initial speech error may be due to internal cognitive mechanisms, an apparent subsequent failure to correct the error phonetically (the therapist's goal) can be brought about interactionally through the construction of the therapist's repair request and how the child treats that request. Basically children can deal with a miscommunication as they would any other in more mundane talk and repair it in what seems the most appropriate and effective way. The interactional patterns that divert the child from the therapist's goal of initiating phonetic repair will be looked at in detail.

The final part of the data presentation will consider how individual children reveal different patterns of response. As therapy progresses certain moves suggest that learning has indeed taken place, as much in interactional as in cognitive terms. Individual strategies form part of behaviour patterns that display an understanding of goals in therapy that use of routine conversational practice may not meet.

The Aims of Therapy

The global aims of the therapist are to make the child change the phonetic content of his or her speech. The theoretical foundation from which therapeutic methods are derived is that of a postulated underlying system of natural processes by which children form simplification rules to govern their phonological output (Stampe, 1969; Grunwell, 1992). In children developing 'normally', immature patterns resolve but phonologically disordered children have unusual and idiosyncratic processes that are resistant to change. The therapist has to assess the child's system and decide which processes and phone substitutions are contributing significantly to poor intelligibility.

In the type of phonology therapy used in this data the therapist working with phonologically disordered children first ensures that the child can discriminate targeted speech sounds auditorily. It is especially important that they should be able to distinguish between the target phone and their own version used in error. For instance if a child is substituting [b] for [f] so saying 'feather' as 'beaber', 'fan' as 'ban' etc. then the contrast 'b'/'f' will be presented. The tasks will then involve modelling sounds and words for imitation followed by spontaneous production. The therapist will look for signs that the child is coming to terms with the target of therapy when they start making extra displayed efforts with the target phone involved. For instance they may divide the target phone off from the word or preform the articulatory shape in anticipation of a try, as well as more obviously giving a spontaneously correct version of a target word. Even if they make an error initially it is considered a significant step if they can produce a phonetic correction spontaneously, following a request for self-repair, rather than the therapist having to provide a further model for imitation. It is eventually hoped that the child will generalize new skills to all words with the targeted phone and this is an important sign that their phonological rules have undergone radical realignment.

Data Presentation

In this paper I predominantly use data taken from a longitudinal study of two 4-year-old children involved in therapy sessions over six months. Other examples come from individual sessions from a cross section of children videoed at various stages of their therapy programme. In the following extract, taken from the first months of Stuart's programme, the therapist is targeting the contrast 'sp' and 'p', the latter supposedly being the child's substitution for the former. It illustrates a typical error repair sequence where the child is providing locally appropriate answers but does not provide the phonetic correction the therapist is seeking.

The target word is 'spots' presented in the form of a picture (following discussion about measles etc.) and the therapist is hoping for a correct articulation of 'sp'. At first the child is expected to self-repair his error and when this does not happen modelling and imitation are introduced in the pursuit of an acceptable child try. Where imitation is involved the child is obviously pointed in the direction of a phonetic repair but the same is not true where a request for self-repair occurs and this is where the child has to realize, first, that a phonetic error is the root of the problem and, secondly, display a move in the right direction in his repair.

```
(1)   Stuart and Therapist. [First presentation of
      /sp/ in 'spot' (picture of spotty face).]
1. Th.        s:pots.
2. St.        bots.
              ((looking at picture))
3. Th.        pots?
4. St.        bots.
              ((looking at therapist, then away))
5. Th.        Are they pots?
              ((St. looks to therapist again))
6. St.        ((shakes head))
7. Th.        Let's hear the Sammy snake sound at the
              beginning then.
              (.)
8. Th.        .h s:pot.
9. St.        bots.
```

The therapist at line 1 models a new word exemplifying [sp] and the child imitates it inaccurately in his first try. There then follows a repair sequence in which the therapist attempts to initiate self repair on the part of the child through the use of an understanding check (line 3), incorporating an inaccurate 'redoing' (a form of repeat) of the child's prior. This utterance 'pots?' forms an alternative lexical referent apparently suggesting the child is referring to cooking utensils. The child's repeat of the target word (line 4) is actually a restatement of his first try 'bots' with no phonetic work being done on it. It will be established through the analysis that the child's reply is legitimate and is implicitly rejecting the adult's version as equivalent to his own. The ambiguous nature of the therapist turn means it could be taken literally, simply to query content. The therapist displays her wish for phonetic revision to take place with increasing explicitness after this repeat by describing which phone ('the Sammy snake sound') is missing (line 7).

The above extract also illustrates how such instructional talk differs from most mundane interaction in that the adult routinely displays they have the solution to their query in mind. This is revealed by their use of cues, prompts and modal verbs ('what should it be?') in the repair sequence and this is a factor that the child is seen to take into account through their actions. For instance by simply rejecting the adult's version of their try (with a shake of the head at line 6) the onus is passed back to the adult to initiate appropriate repair. It will be illustrated at a later stage, through several extracts, that this child rarely addresses the phonetic issue spontaneously following adult redoings of child error until explicitly directed by modelling or phonetic comments by the therapist.

It would be neat to put the lack of phonetic repair down to the early stage of therapy involved in much of this data, suggesting the children are not yet ready to recognize the phonetic errors for themselves and correct them appropriately. However McCartney (1989) also found little phonetic repair following understanding checks when she investigated the final carryover stage of therapy some months on. The data presented in this chapter corroborates her findings and more specifically bring requests for self-repair into question as a technique for gaining phonetic repair or even stimulating the child to address phonetic issues at all without more explicit direction. This discussion will show precisely why this is so.

In the following sections I will first consider how the therapist's global phonetic goals are expressed interactionally. The discussion will then move on to consider the interactional experience of repair that young children have in the course of mundane talk with their mothers, specifically looking at how lexical and phonetic repair are handled and comparing the evidence from mundane talk to that of therapy. Basically these areas of repair are more clearly defined in mundane than in therapy talk. Especially significant in the discussion is the adult's use of certain repeats of the child's prior utterance called 'redoings' (Tarplee, 1993).

Evidence of the Therapist's Global Phonetic Goals

First of all we will consider the adult's viewpoint and the nature of the conceptual knowledge she hopes to impart to the child, the therapist's overall theoretical goals being reflected in the organization of her turns at talk. The therapist routinely breaks language down into units and thereby distorts the speech signal in ways that reflect the theoretical basis of her therapy programme. She is wanting to teach the child how to use 's' blends such as 'sp' as he produces only a version of the plosive 'p' with no 's' component. It is hoped he will generalize this production to all words with these initial 's' blends. Her initial presentation of the target is 's:pots' where the [s] is extended and 'sp' is not really presented as one unit. She is using 'spots' and 'pots' (sp/p) in contrast as this fits neatly into a system of presenting meaningful minimal pair words. However this does not actually bear any relation to the system of contrasts which the child is consistently using, namely 'pots' and 'bots': the first is here used correctly while in the second, an unaspirated allophone which actually sounds more like a 'b' is used for 'sp'. The consistency of the child's system and of the therapist's presentation can be seen across all target words in this phone group and in other 's' blends as illustrated below.

For example, with a target word 'spade' the therapist uses the contrast 'sp'/'p' and produces the redoing 'pade' (not a viable alternative referent, as was 'pots') whilst the child is using his consistent contrast, hence his version which sounds like 'bade'.

```
(2)   Stuart/Therapist. [Target word 'spade'
      (picture).]
1. Th.        You dig the garden with a:
2. St.        bade.
3. Th.        a pade?
              (.)
4. Th.        It's not a pade, what is it?
5. St.        bade.
```

Stuart's response to the therapist's inaccurate redoing is similar to that with 'spots'. Thus at line 2 the child uses [bade] for 'spade' and the therapist uses a redoing 'pade' at lines 3 and 4, clearly different to his version and rejecting line 2 as unacceptable. The child then repeats his own original try, but now in contrast to the therapist's version (line 5).

Similar features occur with the contrast [st/t]. The therapist contrasts the target 'stick' with 'tick' but the child is saying something that sounds a bit more like 'dick' with [d] substituted for 'st'. He displays that he knows it is not a walking 'tick' (as the therapist says at line 3) and then reiterates his own version of 'stick' (line 6), a different thing entirely.

```
(3)   Stuart/Therapist. [Target word 'stick'. First
      presentation. (picture)]
1. Th.        What is it?
2. St.        (walkin) dick.
3. Th.        Mmm, is it a walking tick?
4. St.        ((single firm shake))
5. Th.        It's a walking:
6. St.        dick.
```

The same occurs with 'steps' where the therapist redoes the child's version 'deps' as 'teps' and Stuart knows they are not so called, shaking his head (line 2–3) and repeating 'deps'.

```
(4)   Stuart/Therapist. [Target word 'stairs' ('What
      you go up to get to bed').]
1. St.        deps
2. Th.        Are they teps?
3. St.        ((shakes))
4. Th.        What are they?
5. St.        deps
6. Th.        Snakey sound first.
```

Thus in these extracts the adult and child turns follow very similar patterns. The consistency of the therapist's inaccurate redoings is presented as evidence for this being a deliberate policy on her part. Although it does not always produce a meaningful word contrast as with spots/pots it does produce a neat dichotomy between the target sound and another English phone. However the child is producing something different, specifically allophonic variants of 't' and 'p', and he responds equally consistently by rejecting the therapist's redoings as being equivalent to his own.

The overall goal of phonetic repair is made clear by the therapist as she moves on through the repair sequence and is forced into giving him phonetic cues and, ultimately, models for imitation.

Why the Child doesn't Repair his 'Error' Phonetically: Contributing Factors

I will now consider the variable contribution of social and metalinguistic competence in the child's apparent 'failure' to produce the repair the therapist requires. Whilst the therapist aims specifically at the phonetic content of speech the child will be seen to use his considerable interactional skills to deal with each adult turn as it arises and to repair breakdown in communication in a way justified at that interactional juncture. In the therapist's terms he may have 'failed' to produce a phonetically correct version but he is making appropriate moves in his turn at talk according to the information available.

It is particularly important to disentangle what is going on for the child when the therapist produces an understanding check such as 'pots?' which appears to question the lexical reference rather than any phonetic content. How is the child to know it is phonetic change that will clarify what he means? For a start any trouble with lexical reference is routinely dealt with first in talk and the position of 'pots?' as an initial understanding check is in accord with this and could justify the child dealing with lexical matters. The crucial argument put forward in this paper is that the child in therapy is having to cope with a blurring of the division between phonetic and lexical repair which is routinely more clearly constituted in the mundane adult/child talk commonly experienced. This division is outlined below.

The most significant piece of recent research for comparative normative data for this paper is Tarplee's (1993) work on mother/child interaction in which she describes the characteristics of repair work in picturebook labelling episodes and mundane mother/child talk. The children in her study are considerably younger [1,7–2,3 years] than those presented in this chapter but valuable comparisons are still possible and her findings have been reinforced by those of Cresswell (1994), working with 3–4-year-olds.

In conversation adults typically do not orient so much towards correcting linguistic features of the child's talk but rather to affirming ones where there is little problem. Tarplee finds that phonetic teaching episodes are easily identifiable as different to those dealing with lexical matters on a number of parameters. Looking simply at redoings occurring in one sequential position, following a child's attempt at a label, Tarplee states that they can be distinguished in terms of their prosodic design and interactional accomplishment. A dispreference for overt phonetic other-correction exists (where the listener provides the repair) and this affects turn design, whereas other-correction commonly occurs when factual/lexical knowledge is being dealt with. Adult repeats of the child's prior are seen as a form of disguised or 'embedded' phonetic correction (after Jefferson, 1987). There is no explicit rejection and the lexical (word) accuracy has to be confirmed prior to phonetic work taking place. Rarely is this explicitly done. Part of Tarplee's argument identifies certain redoings as having a complex role, initiating phonetic repair at the same time as confirming the child's lexical choice. She finds one single case of overt (or in Jefferson's terms 'exposed') correction in mundane talk which dealt with articulatory aspects of the child's prior turn in an undisguised fashion. In this instance it deals with the teaching of a new word and Tarplee suggests this could constitute a special case. Unlike her data, both direct and indirect styles are found in therapy talk dealing with phonetics.

Frequent other-repair initiations mean the child's opportunity for self-initiation of repair is rare, and Tarplee (1993) suggests these features are characteristic of talk involved in 'doing instructing' as she found during picture labelling with books. Activities of adult repair initiation and affirmation: 'reduce the responsibilities left with the child for a self-monitoring of the adequacy of the talk produced' (p. 330). Therefore self-repair would seem to be a little required skill that is given far more emphasis in the type of therapy talk in my data.

It would be surprising if talk in therapy were to share all the characteristics of mundane talk outlined above when the phonetic details are what is central to therapy. In fact structures more commonly associated with lexical matters are hijacked in therapy to be used for phonetic talk. For instance Tarplee (*ibid.*) finds that mothers do not contrast two phonetically different versions of the same word (for example, 'It's not gourteen it's fourteen') but they do use such contrastivity for two different words (for example, 'it's not a goat, it's a cow'). However in the present author's work (1989 and this corpus) this is exactly the type of structure that occurs frequently in the therapy data dealing with phonetic matters and is taken up by the mother when undertaking supportive therapy work at home.

Because factual matters do have to be addressed the child in therapy is constantly having to judge what level of language (either phonetic or lexical) is being questioned. Another feature of the special nature of therapy talk is the unusually frequent use of understanding checks when compared to those routinely used by adults talking to children. Tarplee (*ibid.*) found only 2 per cent of repair sequences from picture book talk included such clarification requests. Thus repair requests in the form of a query (for example, child: 'x' Adult: 'x?': as in extract [1], 'pots?') are unusual for a lexical or phonetic query. However we know that Stuart can cope with this style of query in mundane talk with the therapist, and that he will routinely make revisions of a lexical nature and could have been expected to treat 'pots?' in the same way. For example:

```
(5)  Stuart/Therapist. [Talking about home, no
     props.]
1. Th.      What sort of toys have you got?
            (4.0)
2. St.      {t}ars and stuff.
3. Th.      Tarzan?
            (2.0) ((Stuart looks away, down and then
            up))
4. St.      ((looks down)) {tars}
5. Th.      Cars, I see.
```

In this extract, at line 3, the therapist makes an attempt at interpreting only a portion of the child's utterance, with an exaggerated surprised rising pitch. In response the child contracts his repair down to the key word 'cars', a repeat of the first portion of his initial utterance with no significant phonetic change. The therapist makes another repeat of the child's repair at line 5 with unexaggerated falling pitch and confirms mutual comprehension through 'I see'. The phonetic shortcomings of the child utterance ({tars}) are not taken further.

In the following similar example, at lines 2–3, the therapist actually makes two attempts at interpreting Stuart's word, the hesitancy at the beginning of the line intimating a lack of confidence — after all one shoe would be an unlikely present! That her second interpretation is more definite is marked by the falling, conclusive pitch and the question frame that limits the child's options. The child's answer is interpretable as rejecting both these attempts as it reiterates his first try, and it is the mother's intervention ('suit', line 5) that confirms he is saying something different to either of the therapist's versions.

```
(6)  Stuart/Therapist/Mother. [Discussing birthday
     presents. (no props)]
1. St.      And a {shu}
2. Th.      a,a sh-, a shoe?
            (.)
3. Th.      or a shoot.
4. St.      A {shu}
5. M.       A suit!
6. St.      What my Aunty Kath brought me.
```

So Stuart can be seen to be seen to be capable of dealing with these queries at a lexical level.

Therefore, as therapists, we are setting a hard task in expecting a phonetic rather than lexical repair following an understanding check, since this does not occur routinely even in 'normally developing' children. Nor do phonologically disordered children undergoing therapy choose to repair phonetically following understanding checks whilst they are engaged in mundane conversation. For instance whilst playing and looking at books with their mothers such children (3–5 yrs) made 50 per cent structural/lexical repairs following understanding checks and only 30 per cent phonetic revisions (Gardner, 1989). So it would seem phonologically disordered children do not predominantly seek to repair their speech phonetically unless it is clearly required by the prior utterance or context. Clarification requests (understanding checks) do not routinely make that specific requirement explicit.

Another confounding factor which helps to blur the distinction between lexical and phonetic matters is the type of redoing which the adult employs. Looking at the overall use of redoings in the present data corpus a consistent pattern emerges. With the adult's query 'pots?' (extract 1) it has already been established that this is an inaccurate redoing of his initial try that produces not only a phonetic but a lexical contrast. The therapist is testing the fragility of the child's knowledge by introducing a lexical red herring, based on her theoretical knowledge of phonological patterning. The child subsequently does not make any phonetic change as he does not relate his error automatically to the therapist's overriding goal of phonetic improvement but rather seeks to clarify that he really is talking about 'spots'. Precisely because he was not calling the spots 'pots' he is justified in repeating his answer 'bots'. In contrast to what happens in extracts (1) and (3) (walking 'tick') where inaccurate redoings occur, if an accurate redoing of the child error is used which does not take the form of an alternative lexical referent (but maintains an element of nonsense), the child is far more likely to produce a phonetic repair.

There are numerous examples of the children making phonetic corrections following accurate redoings, even when they occur in the unusual form of understanding checks found so rarely in mother/child talk. In the following example the simple query 'two deet?' (line 5) follows an initial model (line 1) and then a slot filler query ('Two what?', line 3) when Elizabeth fails to repeat the model as the therapist expected.

(7) Elizabeth/Therapist. [Target 'feet' (picture).]

```
1. Th.        Feet.
2. E.         erf (.) two.
3. Th.        Yeh. Two what?
4. E.         two {dit}.
5. Th.        two {dit}?
6. E.         feet.
7. Th.        oh yeh, nearly thought you said it wrong
              then!
```

At line 5 the therapist makes an accurate redoing 'dit?' of the child's prior try. No alternative referent exists and the child corrects something other than the lexical content by correcting the initial consonant to [f] in 'feet'. This is instantly confirmed as an appropriate repair and the therapist makes direct reference to her saying it wrong.

Accurate redoings also produce change in the next extract where the therapist repeats back the child's 'thampoo'. The sequence also shares the feature of the simple redoing as understanding check.

(8) **Elizabeth/Therapist. [Target 'shampoo' (no picture).]**

1. E.	thampoo.
2. Th.	Pardon?
3. E.	thampoo.
4. Th.	thampoo?
	(0.5)
5. E.	shampoo

The first query 'pardon' here receives no repair but is treated as a failure to hear and answered with a straight repeat. The second query 'thampoo?' [line 4] is followed by a phonetically corrected response 'shampoo' (line 5). The query 'thampoo?' is less ambiguous for the child than 'pots?' because the wordlike structure that the therapist repeats back is unlikely to be recognizable as a potential alternative referent. A straight repeat of her original try has already been shown to be inadequate as far as the listener is concerned and phonetic revision occurs instead.

Thus, accurate redoings of a child try, especially those forming nonsense rather than real words, are more likely to be followed by an accurate phonetic repair. So with less distractors the child can display a realization that the error can be repaired phonetically, in line with the therapist's overall goal.

There are other cases that make it even clearer that the child (Stuart again) is working at the word level rather than phonetically. In the following two extracts, instead of simply repeating his first try following the repair request, he actually changes the lexical content to an alternative.

(9) **Stuart/Therapist. [Target 'nurse'.]**

1. Th.	And who's this? She helps you when you go to hospital.
2. St.	Nurt.
3. Th.	The nurt?
	(.)
4. Th.	What, what should it be?
	(.)
5. Th.	Not the nurt, the:
6. St.	doctor.
7. Th.	No. You were right but you said it wrong. You forgot the snakey sound at the end.

In this extract the child offers a semantically appropriate response 'nurse' to the first question. However it is queried by the therapist, who produces an accurate repeat: 'nurt?'. This query is closely followed by another question (line 4) that shows clearly, through the emphatic use of the word 'should', that the therapist had no problem with hearing his response but that the content is inappropriate at some level. Therefore confirmation of his first try would be inappropriate, especially as she then says 'not the nurt', a clear rejection. Stuart therefore completes the procedure with the alternative 'doctor' (line 6). Again the therapist's repetition of the

child's inaccurate attempt 'nurt' has involved a nonword with no alternative referent, unlike 'pots'. The child may not have perceived this mispronunciation, or does
not treat it as relevant as it does not affect meaning, and thus responds at the lexical
level, replacing the rejected 'nurse' with another possibility. After gaining a lexical
repair 'doctor' the therapist adjusts her repair request and goes on to state that it
was his pronunciation that held the fault and exactly what the fault was.

In the following extract there is a similar occurrence, the child beginning to
replace 'spoon' with 'needle' following a clear rejection of his initial try.

```
(10)   Stuart/Therapist. [Target 'spoon' (picture).]
1. St.        boo(m).
2. Th.        not a poon.
              (.)
3. Th.        Was it a poon or a:?
4. St.        nee:=
5. Th.        =s:poon.
```

Stuart produces a version of 'spoon' that is consistent with his production rules and
features the same version of 'sp' ({b}) as occurred with 'spots'. The therapist at
line 2 uses a tidied up redoing 'poon' (not a possible alternative referent) that again
fits in with the idealized minimal pair she has planned therapy round and again is
not what the child actually said. However she clearly rejects this nonsense version
with 'It's not a poon' and at line 3 explicitly requests something as an alternative.
It is not possible to know whether the child perceives the mispronunciation but he
clearly understands that the referent 'spoon' has been rejected and tries to offer
another word with 'nee-' (established later as 'needle'). At line 5 the therapist
cuts across him to bring him back to the phonetic content with an extended [s]
on 's:poon'.

The above extracts clearly show that working at the lexical level is seen as a
viable option by the child when engaged in repair sequences during therapy but that
phonetic repair is an option in defined circumstances.

Coming to Terms with a Goal other than Successful Communication

I would like to finish by showing some preliminary evidence from the data that
children do begin to use individual strategies that show they become aware that phonetic repair is of paramount importance in therapy rather than an optional activity.
These are not one off instances but a pattern of response in each case although
there is little space to illustrate that here. Each child in this section was filmed at
a time when they were well established in therapy.

In the first case the child repairs phonetically at almost any breakdown in
communication, at the expense of the meaningful content of the therapy session. In
this extract the child, Chris, makes a decision to repair phonetically in circumstances where a lexical repair would be appropriate and is expected by the therapist.

She has used the type of direct rejection that routinely deals with lexical repair in mundane talk.

```
(11)   Chris/Therapist. [Target word 'gnomes'.]
1. C.          hamster
2. Th.         They're not hamsters=
3. C.          =hansters
4. Th.         They're not hamsters, they're gnomes.
5. C.          gnomes ((tries to get cards))
6. Th.         look ((holds onto cards))
7. C.          ((fleeting gaze)) gnomes
8. Th.         gn:ome
```

Chris is being taught the contrast [n] and [m] as at the moment he produces them both as 'n'. At line 1 Chris has just picked up a game card featuring the target picture 'gnomes' but confuses it with another new label 'hamsters' that he has also learnt during the course of the game. He actually says the [m] appropriately in his try but, of course, the label is inappropriate so the therapist rejects it at line 2. However, instead of producing a version of the target, Chris actually repairs the phonetics of his *first* try, changing [m] to [n] and appending the plural (line 3). The therapist then gives him the correct label herself and they move on to the phonetics from there.

A more subtle approach is taken up by the next child, Elizabeth (doing therapy tasks with her mother), who is keen to cover all possibilities, repairing both phonetically and lexically in the same turn in a very skilful fashion. In the first extract Elizabeth is counting the zoo animals she is playing with and her mother rejects the number she ends up with:

```
(12)   Elizabeth/Mother. [Counting toy animals]
1. E.          girteen gourteen, .h now.
2. M.          No, no it's not gourteen, what is it?
3. E.          fifteen.
```

Elizabeth is using her standard substitution of [g] for [f] and her mother does an accurate redoing 'gourteen' (fourteen) at line 2, embedded in a clear rejection and followed by a request for a repair. Elizabeth in her response changes fourteen to 'fifteen', which is factually incorrect, but in addition executes an appropriate phonetic repair. Her mother has to correct the factual side of this response but acknowledges the phonetic correction.

Whilst this example took place in a learning context prior to a therapy task Elizabeth also uses the same tactic in talk during play, a time when she might be expected to be less aware of the phonetic aspect of her talk.

```
(13)   Elizabeth/Mother. [Talking during play re.
       Nursery.]
1. M.              And what did Mrs Edgar say to you when you
                   were crying and she was cross with you?
```

```
2. E.        Her- her gaid.
3. M.        Sh:e:
4. E.        shaid. 'what is the matter?' .hn me gaid-,
5. M.        I.
             (0.3)
6. E.        shaid, 'That boy hit me'.
7. M.        said. Then what did she say?
8. E.        Naughty boy!
```

At line 2 Elizabeth makes two errors, using an inappropriate pronoun ('her' for 'she') but also using her standard substitution of [g] for [s]. Her mother provides a wealth of information in her utterance at line 3. She directly repairs the prior pronoun but at the same time prolongs the 'sh' drawing attention to the pronunciation. Additionally she simultaneously uses a turn shape that prolongs the vowel (with monotonic pitch) in a way that cues the child to complete the phrase. Elizabeth does just that at line 4 but also substitutes a 'sh' initially in 'said' hence 'shaid'. She then carries on directly with her story and makes similar errors again, using 'me' for 'I' and mispronouncing 'said' again. Once again the mother chooses to directly correct the pronoun. Although it is not set up as a cue Elizabeth again completes the repair with 'shaid' (line 6) and continues her tale. Only at line 7 does her mother directly repair the pronunciation herself to 'said', and she does not wait for an imitation but shows interest in the punchline instead.

Working Towards Collaborative Repair

Norrick (1991) states that repair is negotiated between the participants based on their differing states of knowledge. As evidence he describes how 'accountings' of errors by participants frequently address issues of differences in knowledge or competence between speaker and listener regarding the matter in hand. Who does the correcting of an error is based on the interactants' respective ability to carry out this task. Langford (1981) showed that certain turn designs lead to cooperative correction instead of self-correction. When self-correction is projected there may be a belief by the second speaker (seeking clarification) that the initial speaker can put it right, and this is what the therapists appear to be testing out. However, the child also has an equal role in deciding the direction that any repair sequence may go.

Children can also use certain behaviours in the next turn that delay the provision of any sort of repair, putting the onus on the adult to give more information, rather than providing a possible inappropriate repair themselves. This was a detectable trend over the sessions where Stuart was filmed. He would appear to take a yes/no query literally and simply deny or confirm the therapist's interpretation. This strategy more often than not resulted in further information being proffered by the therapist. This type of behaviour displays an awareness that the adult routinely has the solution to their query in mind, which is indeed routinely displayed by their handling of the subsequent repair sequences. By simply rejecting the adult interpretation of his initial version of the target word the onus is passed back to the adult to initiate the appropriate repair. In much of mundane talk, when a potential misunderstanding arises, the knowledge of the intended word may lie solely with the child who initiated the topic; thus such a minimal response would not be appropriate as collaborative repair would not be feasible.

If we return to the original data for instance, at line 6 of extract (1), the child simply rejects the therapist's version 'pots?' but does not provide further clarification himself.

```
(1)  Stuart and Therapist. [First presentation of
     /sp/ in 'spot' (picture of spotty face).]
1. Th.          s:pots.
2. St.          bots.
                ((looking at picture))
3. Th.          pots?
4. St.          bots.
                ((looking at therapist, then away))
5. Th.          Are they pots?
                ((St. looks to therapist again))
6. St.          ((shakes head))
7. Th.          Lets hear the Sammy snake sound at the
                beginning then.
                (.)
8. Th.          .h s:pot.
9. St.          bots.
```

However, in examples from mundane talk we know that in similar circumstances Stuart can produce a further repeat or expansion. The follow up to this turn is that the adult provides the acceptable answer and the process of repair becomes collaborative. Other children exhibit similar propensities and there follow two extracts in which a child, Bernice, appears to be having difficulty with the implicativeness of the adult's prior turn. Yet we know from evidence in mundane talk taken from the same session that she can cope with the type of query the therapist uses, as is displayed in this extract:

```
(14)  Bernice/Therapist. [Discussing place of
      birthday party (no props).]
1. B.           Near {yor}.
2. Th.          Near York?
3. B.           No, near your house.
```

Here Bernice has initiated the topic and the subject is known only to her. When the therapist (line 2) queries what Bernice has said, using a redoing of the child's prior, Bernice promptly expands her first utterance, repairing at the lexical level.

In the following two extracts the picture is a shared referent for both participants.

```
(15)   Therapist/Bernice. [Looking at birthday card.]
1. Th.          What's that?
2. B.           A {thard}.
3. Th.          It isn't a tard is it?
                (1.0)
4. Th.          .hh
                (0.2)
5. B.           ((nods + smile))
6. Th.          What's it start with?
```

In the above Bernice names the picture as a 'card', (sounding like 'thard'). The therapist uses an unusual request for clarification at line 2 which incorporates 'tard', an inaccurate redoing of the child's prior. There is a long pause and the child makes no move to take up the turn so there is an opportunity for the other speaker to do so. The therapist only draws breath and continues to smile at Bernice during the pause and does not appear to be about to offer further help at this stage. Only after 1.2 seconds (cf. Jefferson, 1989) does Bernice nod slowly and acknowledge the therapist's apparent joke with a smile. This minimal response does not acknowledge any error. That confirmation was not what the therapist required is displayed by her pursuance of a phonetic repair in the following turns. If Bernice was looking for help with her response she has to wait a long time for a direct clue as to what the therapist is expecting.

In the final extract the child is even more non-commital, making neither confirmation or denial but simply smiling and looking to the therapist to fill the gap.

```
(16)   Bernice/Therapist. [Target: fur coat
       (picture).]
1. B.           a {hur} coat.
2. Th.          a which coat?
3. B.           P{hur}P coat.
4. Th.          a {hur} coat?
                (0.8) ((child smiles and looks at Th.))
5. Th.          I don't think so!
                (1.0) ((child smiles more broadly and looks
                around room))
6. Th.          What sound have we got at the beginning?
```

Here Bernice is expected to produce [f] on 'fur' but instead produces her standard substitution [h]. Her first try is queried in a way that isolates which word the listener has apparently not understood and Bernice treats it as simply needing a repeat (although not confidently as the decreased volume shows). When her quiet repetition is again queried (line 4) with a question that can be answered with simple confirmation, she does not answer straight away. The turn is then taken up by the therapist who at least displays that this is definitely what it is called. Bernice still makes no move to repair her try and the therapist again comes in with clues as to the direction the repair should take. So it can be seen in the last two extracts that the therapist is manoeuvred into having to take responsibility for the way the repair sequence continues. She chooses not to give a direct solution straight away but still works on getting the child to self correct at some level through more explicitly directing Bernice to phonetic issues ('what's it start with?' etc.).

Summary

This chapter has provided a specific illustration of children's social competence and adaptability in action. Using the example of the didactic talk involved in speech therapy with speech disordered children it has been shown that from the outset of therapy preschool children use great interactional skill in actively managing the course of repair. Their ability to explicitly display a grasp of therapeutic goals and concepts is closely interwoven with their social understanding.

Providing the child with the wealth of phonetic information in the way therapists do is no guarantee that the child will grasp the overall conceptual aim, even if superficially the child is providing appropriately articulated responses. However in this chapter I argue that the opposite case is also true; that the lack of a phonetic repair following an error doesn't mean that the child is necessarily unaware that therapy is aimed at altering his phonetic output. Simply it means that in certain individual cases the adult's reaction to his error does not lead him to see that phonetics is the source of the trouble.

This work has begun to illustrate how individuals learn to adapt interactionally to cope with the unusual demands placed on them in the clinical setting. From the evidence presented it would seem that the accuracy of a child's first try at a target word can depend on their internalized phonological system but after that, the ability to phonetically repair an error depends more on their reading of the local interactional context. As their understanding of the therapist's motivations grow then the likelihood of a phonetic repair being done rather than a lexical one may become greater. The accuracy of that repair may again be due to the stability of their phonetic 'knowledge'.

From a professional standpoint this chapter should heighten the need for therapists to address their traditional way of designing therapy programmes. Therapists must be aware of the complexity of skills such as that labelled 'metalinguistic awareness', and the need to control the interactional aspects of therapy as well as the cognitive ones is clear. Specifically, for instance, these findings bring requests for self-repair into question as techniques for gaining phonetic repair except as a carefully directed target behaviour at a specific stage in therapy.

Note on Transcription

Where indication of volume accompanies a phonetic transcription the following will be used after the style of Kelly and Local (1989):

Ch. ᶠ[ ]ᶠ indicates 'forte' i.e. loud.
Ch. ᵖ[ ]ᵖ indicates 'piano' i.e. quiet.
{ } indicates a 'hearing' of what the child said.

References

CHIAT, S. (1983) 'Why Mikey's right and my key's wrong: The significance of stress and word boundaries in a child's output system', *Cognition*, **14**, pp. 275–300.

CRESSWELL, A. (1994) 'Correction in adult/child conversation', unpublished MA dissertation, Language Centre, University of Newcastle upon Tyne.

DODD, B. (1995) *Differential Diagnosis and Treatment of Children with Speech Disorders*, London: Whurr.

GARDNER, H. (1989) 'An investigation of maternal interaction with phonologically disordered children as compared to two groups of normally developing children', *British Journal of Disorders of Communication*, **24**, pp. 41–61.

GRUNWELL, P. (1992) 'Principled decision making in the remediation of children with phonological disability', in FLETCHER, P. and HALL, D. (eds) *Specific Speech and Language Disorders in Children*, London: Whurr.

HOWELL, J. (1991) 'The phonological awareness of phonologically disordered children and normally developing children: A comparative study', paper presented at the Second International Symposium, Specific Speech and Language Disorders in Children, Harrogate.

JEFFERSON, G. (1987) 'On exposed and embedded correction', in BUTTON, G. and LEE, J.R.E. (eds) *Talk and Social Organisation*, Clevedon: Multilingual Matters.

JEFFERSON, G. (1989) 'Preliminary notes on a "standard maximum" silence of approximately one second in conversation', in ROGER, D. and BULL, P. (eds) *Conversation: An Interdisciplinary Perspective*, Clevedon: Multilingual Matters.

LANGFORD, D. (1981) 'The clarification request sequence in conversation between mothers and children', in FRENCH, P. and McCLURE, M. (eds) *Adult-Child Conversation*, London: Croom Helm.

McCARTNEY, E. (1989) 'Speech teaching strategies', in GRUNWELL, P. and JAMES, A. (eds) *The Functional Evaluation of Language Disorders*, London: Croom Helm.

McTEAR, M. and KING, F. (1991) 'Miscommunication in clinical contexts: The speech therapy interview', in COUPLAND, N., GILES, H. and WIEMANN, J.M. (eds) *Miscommunication and Problematic Talk*, London: Sage.

NORRICK, N.R. (1991) 'On the organization of corrective exchanges in conversation', *Journal of Pragmatics*, **16**, pp. 59–83.

RIPICH, D.N. and PANAGOS, J.M. (1985) 'Accessing children's knowledge of sociolinguistic rules for speech therapy lessons', *Journal of Speech and Hearing Disorders*, **50**, pp. 335–46.

SACKS, H., SCHEGLOFF, E.A. and JEFFERSON, G. (1974) 'A simplest systematics for the organisation of turn-taking for conversation', *Language*, **50**, pp. 696–735.

SCHEGLOFF, E.A. (1972) 'Sequencing in conversational openings', in GUMPERZ, J. and HYMES, D. (eds) *Directions in Sociolinguistics*, New York: Holt, Rinehart and Winston.

SCHEGLOFF, E.A. (1987) 'Some sources of misunderstanding in talk-in-interaction', *Linguistics*, **25**, pp. 201–18.

STACKHOUSE, J. and WELLS, B. (1993) 'Psycholinguistic assessment of speech disorders', *European Journal of Disorders of Communication*, **28**, pp. 331–47.

STAMPE, D. (1969) 'The acquisition of phonetic representation', *Chicago Linguistic Society Papers*, pp. 443–5.

TARPLEE, C. (1993) 'Working on talk: The collaborative shaping of linguistic skills within child-adult interaction', unpublished PhD thesis, University of York.

Chapter 7

Children's Participation in the Discourse of Children's Television

Joanna Thornborrow

Introduction

The broad aim of this chapter is to begin to examine the discourse of children's television from a linguistic point of view, and more specifically, to analyse the structures of participation that are available for children when they take part in these programmes. Although there is a body of work within media studies which addresses the relationship between children and television (Brown, 1976; Cullingford, 1984; Hodge and Tripp, 1986) none of this work really deals with the *language* of children's television, while work in the field of language, interaction and the media (see for example Heritage, 1985; Montgomery, 1986; Scannell, 1991; Hutchby, 1996) has mainly been concerned with the study of broadcast talk which is produced by adults for adult audiences. The discourse of children's television, and the role that children themselves may play in the production of that discourse, has so far been relatively unexplored. My intention here is to look at children's involvement and participation in those speaking practices which take place within the context of programmes made specifically for child audiences, and analyse their status as participants in this kind of talk.

Before looking at the data, I briefly outline the background to some of the issues relating to children's conversational competence within the field of discourse analysis and sociolinguistics, and to some of the existing research on children's television. I then move on to an analysis of extracts from the programmes *Blue Peter*, *Live and Kicking*, and *Why Don't You?* in order to explore children's participation in interviews, phone-ins and finally, in an episode where no adults are present, a 'cookery demonstration'. I will draw on Goffman's (1981) concept of participation frameworks for utterances in my analysis of the sequences of verbal interaction involving children in these contexts.

Children's Conversational Competence

Sociolinguistic research into children's patterns of conversational competence has been based for the most part on the developmental aspects of children's language.

The main interest has been in the stages at which children acquire communicative competence in the Hymesian sense of an awareness of socially appropriate forms of speech (Hymes, 1972). This work has focused on three distinct, though sometimes overlapping, areas of language use: grammatical and phonological variation, discursive or conversational competence, and the development of an awareness of social norms of interaction.

Since Labov's (1964) claim that children were largely monostylistic until adolescence, at which time adult stylistic patterns became established, there has been a concern to discover how far children may be aware of social constraints on language use. Subsequent research has shown that children are not only aware of, but actively engage in stylistic variation on both grammatical and discursive levels of language use at a much earlier stage than Labov had believed (Reid, 1976; Cheshire, 1982; Slosberg-Andersen, 1990).

Research into children's conversational or 'discursive' competence has explored issues such as children's patterns of turn-taking and their use of directives and cohesive devices (Ervin-Tripp and Mitchell-Kernan, 1977; McTear, 1985), while a further body of work has focused on the socialization of children into adult norms of interaction in specific social and cultural settings (Ochs and Schieffelin, 1979). These modes of socialization may vary according to different cultural traditions and views of childhood (Ochs and Schieffelin, 1983; Schieffelin, 1990) but the principal focus of these studies has been the same, i.e. the developmental stages of progression towards adult norms of communicative competence. Similarly, the research on style shifting has been concerned with comparing children's patterns of variation with those of adults in relation to social variables such as class or gender.

In contrast to this attention to the developmental aspects of children's discursive competence, there has also been some research into those domains of their language use which constitute an oral culture in which adults play little or no part, and in which the norms of interaction are clearly very different from those in play within adult social settings and speech events. The use of linguistic 'routines' by children has been studied by Labov (1972) in his analysis of the use of ritual insults, as well as by Corsaro (1986) and Katriel (1987). Maynard (1985) has looked at the structure of children's arguments, and Goodwin (1990) has conducted a highly detailed study of the role of language and interaction in the social organization of a group of black children in Philadelphia. All these studies show how language interaction plays a central role in shaping the social worlds in which children exist to a large extent independently of adults. In these settings, children demonstrate communicative skills which have much more to do with being proficient participants within their own culture, than with learning how to become competent members of an adult speech community.

In this chapter I look at the status of children as participants in children's television, a domain of discourse which engages them in interaction with adults. However, the context for this interaction is unlike other areas of adult/child interaction (in the classroom, within the family), which have been previously researched in so far as it is designed primarily to entertain an absent audience as well as in some cases to inform and educate. I am interested therefore in how this specific context affects their participation, and what kind of discursive positions are available for children to take up in these programmes.

Children, Discourse and Television

The world of broadcasting is obviously enough an adult world, but within the domain of children's television, there are a growing number of programmes which involve children as participants in various ways, including phone-ins, quiz shows and games, and in some cases, whole programmes are presented entirely by children. However, when the interactive frameworks of some of these broadcasts are studied more closely, it can be shown that children are involved in what are essentially adult-centred discourses, where their participatory role is constrained not only by the type of speech events or genres they are taking part in, but also by the interactive organization of the talk itself. Thus, despite the apparent intention of broadcasting institutions to involve children in programmes designed specifically for them, in practice this involvement is restricted to a set of limited actions, particularly in relation to the talk that children produce.

Before taking this claim further, in the following section I want to contextualize it within the broader framework of current research into children and television, which provides a starting point for the analysis of children's participation in the domain of media discourse.

Research into Children and Television

There has been a substantial amount of work within sociology and media studies which has addressed the relationship between children and television, but none of this work specifically deals with the language of children's television as a form of 'public' discourse, nor with the role of children in its production. Instead, this work tends to focus either on how children watch television and what they do with what they watch, or on a largely content-based approach to programming for children.[1]

Cullingford (1984) has looked at what children expect from television, what they 'see' in it, learn from it and what they take from it (in terms of how watching television becomes part of the social texture of their lives), but his only mention of the *language* of children's television is that 'there is an implicitly friendly private voice speaking personally and intimately to the single individuals of a vast anonymous public', and that this language 'must be personal, the tone chatty, in contrast to the formality of news readers and politicians' (p. 82). In the light of recent research into the centrality of language in the media,[2] this now seems a rather limited description of the multiplicity of voices that constitute many children's programmes, which like their adult counterparts, draw on a range of speaker types from presenters to interviewers to 'guest personalities' and 'experts' (particularly in programmes like *Blue Peter* or the live Saturday morning broadcasts such as BBC 1's *Live and Kicking*).

Through a combined approach which draws on semiotics, psychology and theories of social agency, Hodge and Tripp (1986) aimed to investigate the interpretative systems that children bring to meanings on television, and to demonstrate that 'a television show is not a single stimulus (but) a vast meaning-potential complex, an interrelated set of verbal and visual meanings' (p. 7). They claim that researchers' preoccupations with the (often undesirable) effects of children's viewing habits has been misguided, and argue that we should be more interested in how television produces meanings which children, as social agents, then interpret and act upon.[3] Language is, of course, crucially involved in the production of those meanings, but Hodge and Tripp focus essentially on children's television programmes as *narrative* structures, so there is still no account of the wide variety of discursive genres and forms of interaction which make up these programmes, nor of children's roles as active participants in the talk.

Buckingham's (1993) study of the way that children talk about television, their understanding of what they watch, the complex ways that they make sense of their viewing practices, and the wider role of television in constructing peer-group and family relationships, moves closer to a more critical discursive account of what children are doing with what they watch on TV. Drawing on theories from discourse analysis (particularly Fairclough, 1989) as well as from cultural and media studies, he analyzes children's talk *about* television rather than focus on the talking they do *on* television. He does however provide some insights into the nature of the discourse of children's television and its 'cultivated appearance of spontaneity' (p. 51), which he attributes to an anxiety about the distance between the adult programme presenters and the child viewers. Children's programmes are often constructed as haphazardly amateurish and anarchic, with the presenters getting things wrong and appearing to be out of control, as well as dressing like children. In my data, Emma Forbes, the presenter in *Live and Kicking*, often dresses in schoolgirl outfits, and Andy Peters from the same programme wears a tracksuit and baseball cap. Timothy Mallett dresses as a clown; even the dress of *Blue Peter* presenters has apparently changed over the years to bring them closer to the dress codes of their audience. Most significantly of all, Buckingham comments that this essentially adult construction of the child as wild and anarchistic[4] contrasts with the highly circumscribed role of children on the programmes (*ibid.*, p. 52). Real children are frequently onlookers rather than participants in this discourse.

There are, however, a number of occasions when children do become involved as active speaking participants in some programmes, for example Saturday morning television and programmes made for school holiday entertainment, as well those programmes designed to inform and entertain such as the long-running *Blue Peter* on BBC 1. The role of children on these occasions is often to take part in specific media 'genres' or activity-types, such as games, quizzes and phone-ins, as well as participating as members of the studio audience. Children's participation in programmes like *Blue Peter* is often within the context of an interview, where children are engaged in some activity in the studio and are then questioned about what they are doing by one of the presenters. Saturday morning programmes like *Live and Kicking* or *Going Live* consist of a juxtaposition of these genres, each possessing its own distinctive discursive framework, which is reproduced through familiar parameters and structures. As well as their team of presenters, these programmes regularly include other media figures and personalities such as pop singers, actors and entertainers, with music, interviews, chat and phone-ins interspersed with comic sketches and cartoons. These programmes then provide a site where the children who take part in them enter into a discursive role as members of a heterogeneous media community. What interests me here is how that role is interactively constructed and managed through the participatory frameworks available for the children, and this is the question I address in the following analysis.

Analysis: Children's Participant Roles

In order to explore the ways in which children participate in specific interactive situations, I have selected three different media genres, or speech events, from the data: a phone-in, an interview, and a 'cookery' demonstration. In the first two events, the children are involved in interactive settings with other adult participants, (a phone-in and two *Blue Peter* interviews), and in the last one, the children interact with each other without the (obvious, on screen) presence of adults.

It is of course difficult to establish how much of the talk in these extracts is scripted, or at least partly scripted, but it does seem likely that most of the exchanges, with the exception of the phone-in, have been rehearsed to some extent prior to the broadcast. The type of talk we are dealing with here can be characterized as relatively 'planned spoken discourse' (Ochs, 1983). Both *Blue Peter* and *Live and Kicking* are broadcast live, whereas *Why Don't You?* is not. It is also worth noting that the age of the group of children in the studio audience for *Live and Kicking* is between 10 and 15 (although we have no access to the age of the callers in the phone-in sequences), while the participants on *Blue Peter* are slightly younger.

Goffman's Participation Roles and Frameworks

In his (1981) essay on the relationship between speakers and their utterances, Goffman shows how the 'conduit' model of communication, where a speaker (S) encodes a message for a hearer (H), who then receives that message, is inadequate as a description of the complexity of spoken interaction. Rather, he analyses the web of interactive relationships between speakers, hearers, and their utterances in terms of participant roles and frameworks, and he describes this concept of participation frameworks in talk events in the following way:

> An utterance does not carve up the world beyond the speaker into precisely two parts, recipients and non-recipients, but rather opens up an array of structurally differentiated possibilities, establishing the participation framework in which the speaker will be guiding his delivery. (*ibid.*, p. 137)

Thus, rather than having a single category of 'hearer', Goffman suggests that there are different types of hearers: those who are 'ratified' participants in the speech event, the direct addressee(s) and the unaddressed, but nevertheless 'official' recipients of the utterance, and those who are 'unratified' participants, who may be unintentional overhearers or intentional eavesdroppers. In mediated discourse, ratified recipients of the talk include members of the viewing or listening audience, the studio audience, and all other participants who may be involved in the programme. Individuals or groups of individuals from all of these categories may at any stage become direct addressees. For instance chat show hosts may occasionally address an utterance to the studio audience or the viewing audience at home; radio DJ's may address a specific group of listeners (see Montgomery, 1986; and Hutchby, 1995, for detailed accounts of how these shifts in address are accomplished). Furthermore, it is possible for speakers to address one participant, while at the same time designing their utterance to be heard by another co-present participant, who then becomes the indirect target or recipient of that utterance (see Levinson, 1988, for a critical account and development of Goffman's concept of footing and participant roles).

The three types of mediated speech events I analyse here mostly share the same basic discursive framework of ratified participants: studio speakers, (including presenters, guests and children) the viewing audience, and in one case (*Live and Kicking*) a studio audience. In each data extract, children occupy what Levinson (*ibid.*) terms 'productive' speech roles, as questioners and answerers, as well as recipient roles of direct addressees and audience. In the following sections, I will focus on each of these roles in turn, and examine how children take up those roles and what kind of talk they produce within those discursive positions.

Productive Participant Roles: Children as Questioners

The first category of participant role I focus on is that of 'productive' participant in the talk. What do children do when they take an active part in the speech event, and how does that participation come about? One of the contexts where children take up a productive role as speakers is in the TV phone-in, when they can ask questions either as a member of the studio audience, or as an outside caller in to the programme.

The first data extract is taken from BBC 1's *Live and Kicking*, and consists of a sequence from the phone-in slot in this programme entitled 'The Hot Seat'. Outside callers and members of a small group of children on screen ask questions to a guest personality (in this instance the actor Chris Barrie, well known for his roles in the television series *Red Dwarf* and *The Brittas Empire*) who then has to 'tell all'. This initial staging appears to place the questioners in a potentially strong position, and the answerer in a potentially uncomfortable one, where the studio guest is under obligation to answer even the most embarrassing questions. In the event, the studio questions are prepared and outside calls selected, and the phone-in guest knows in advance more or less what he is likely to be talking about (near the beginning of this particular phone-in, Barrie mentions 'one of the questions we may have coming soon', indicating that he is aware of the questions and the order in which they are being placed).

As a mediated speech event, the television phone-in has a complex framework of participation which involves different categories of participants taking up different roles at various points in the talk. The participants in the studio are the presenter and 'host' of the phone-in, Emma Forbes; the phone-in guest; a small group of children seated near the host and guest who provide some of the questions, and the studio audience (who can be heard but are 'off screen'). Outside the studio is the viewing audience and also the caller, whose talk can be heard not only by the host and the guest (who hold the phones) but also by the rest of the people in the studio as well as the viewing audience. The caller is of course at the same time a member of the viewing audience as he/she has access to the screen sound and image of the television set.

The telephone link is established between the caller and the phone-in guest through the mediation of the host, as in the following examples of opening exchanges:

(1)
```
1  EF:      ---let's get straight onto the phones and hello
2            line one who's there
3  Caller:  Emma Jones from Leicester
4  EF:      Good morning Emma how are you
5  Caller:  ok
6  EF:      yeah (.) ok (.) what's your question for Chris
```

(2)
```
1  EF:      Let's get back onto those phones hello line two
2            who's there
3  CB:      Hello
4  Caller:  Hello it's Sarah from Plymouth=
5  CB:      =Hi [Sarah
6  EF:          [Hi Sarah from Plymouth what-
```

The host invites the caller to identify her/himself in the first turn, then moves through a greeting turn to a specific cue for the caller to ask a question (for example, line 6 in extract 1). Typically, the opening exchanges in calls to radio phone-in programmes with a guest speaker present follow this pattern. The extract below, taken from a 1987 BBC Radio One phone-in to Margaret Thatcher which specifically targeted a young audience, contained similar patterns of exchanges between the caller and host:

(3)
```
Host:    Ned in York you're on line to Mrs Thatcher hi
Caller:  Hello Mrs Thatcher
MT:      Hello
```

```
(4)
Host:    Elliot you're on line to Mrs Thatcher
Caller:  Good evening
MT:      Hello Elliot good evening
```

This pattern sets up the host in a mediating position between the caller and the guest, and callers do not normally interact directly with the guest until given a signal to proceed by the host. In the above examples, these take the form of a 'channel opener'[5] such as 'you're on line to Mrs Thatcher' or 'what is your question to Chris'. After this channel opener has been supplied by the host, there is normally a greetings sequence, before callers ask their question. In a phone-in of this type, unlike other forms of call-in radio, asking the question can be the only time that a caller gets to speak.[6] Their status as a participant in the talk consequently shifts from being actively engaged in the opening sequences of the call, to becoming one of a set of ratified hearers, which includes all those currently in the studio as well as the viewing audience, until the call gets terminated by the host. At that point they become, briefly, the direct addressee of the host's closing utterance:

```
Host:  thanks very much for that question Emma (.)
       let's take a question from Miles.
```

In some calls, they may be addressed by the host at a later stage in the sequence, often shortly before the closing exchange, as in the following example:

```
(5)
1  Host:    Sarah you sound like a big fan of Chris's are
2           you
3  Caller:  very=
4  Host:    =very much so (.) [thanks
5  Caller:                    [Red Dwarf=
6  Host:    =thanks very much
```

This brings the caller back into the talk as a productive participant, but also tends to signal that the call is approaching its close. Sarah's attempt to take another turn after the pause (line 5) overlaps with the host, who closes the call without giving Sarah the possibility of finishing her comment on *Red Dwarf*. At no point, then, do callers get to take the floor without being specifically addressed and selected as next speaker by the host. Indeed, most of callers' actions tend to be elicited by the host, and when callers try to initiate a 'next action' without waiting for the host's eliciting utterance, as happens above and in the following two extracts, that leads to overlapping talk and the sequence has to be repaired so that the host eliciting turn is taken:

```
(6)
Host:    Oliver have you got an impression you could do for us
Caller:  yeah [one of my favourites
Host:         [do you want to have a big break right now=
```

```
Caller:   =thank you very much one of my favourites is
          actually..
```

(7)
```
Host:     Hi Sarah from Plymouth [what
Caller:                          [can I=
Host:     =you're through to Chris
Caller:   can I be really cheeky first of all and ask if I can
          have your autograph
```

In (6), the caller stops talking and waits for the host's invitation to 'have a big break right now', and similarly in (7), the overlap is repaired by the caller relinquishing her turn, and the host producing her mediating utterance 'you're through to Chris'. It is worth noting here that the host changes from the initial 'what' of 'what is your question', to 'you're through to Chris' thereby acknowledging that this caller has disrupted the normal sequence and proceeded to ask a question without waiting for the host's channel opening utterance. The caller, in her next turn, completes her question, and indicates that she is aware of the normal procedure for call openings by explicitly marking her action as being prior to the real business of the call, 'really cheeky first', and that her request is an inappropriate one in this context.

If we now relate this interactional structure to an analysis of the participant framework in play between the host, guest and callers, we can see that callers occupy the position of productive 'speaker' in a way which is highly circumscribed. Their role as a participant in the talk (in Levinson's (1988) categorization a participant is a party with a ratified channel-link to other parties (p. 170)) is established by the host, who explicitly opens that link and thereby ratifies the status of the caller. As we have seen, any subsequent turn taken by the caller follows a host utterance which selects them as next speaker, so callers do not take the floor by self-selecting in this context.

The children in the on-screen audience have an even more limited role as participant speakers. They are selected as questioners by the host in what is likely to be a pre-established order, with predetermined questions, as the following examples show:

(8)
```
Host:     thank you very much for that question Emma (.) let's
          take a question from Miles
Miles:    Do you ever fall into funny voices by accident and
          find yourself in embarrassing situations?
```

(9)
```
Host:     thanks very much for that question let's take a
          question from Rachel
Rachel:   Who and what makes you laugh?
```

Although it may occur in other programmes, in the phone-in data I have recorded there is no instance of a child who has asked a question from within the studio audience being directly addressed by the host in a subsequent turn, nor of their being given the opportunity to take up an active participant role in the ensuing talk.

Address and Recipiency

While the children in the studio who ask questions, in these data at least, are not addressed directly by either host or guest during the ensuing talk, a momentary shift in status of telephone callers from speaker to direct addressee of the answer to their question is identifiable in the talk. This generally occurs at the beginning of the answer turn where the guest sometimes uses first name direct address, as Chris Barrie does in the two extracts below:

```
(10)
CB:  well to be honest with you (.) Sarah (.) it's just er
     the roles
```

```
(11)
CB:  well Oliver I- I first started doing impersonations of
     the teachers at school
```

Yet in the following extract, we can see how in studio questions the sequence develops to become essentially an exchange between the host and the guest, where the child who has briefly taken up a role as a participant producer quickly rejoins the category of audience rather than continuing in the role of addressee.

```
(12)
1    Host:   thank you very much for that question Emma (.) let's
2            take a question from Miles
3    Child:  Do you ever fall into funny voices by accident and
4            find yourself in embarrassing situations
5    Guest:  Occasionally yes erm (.) I mean when I'm out with
6            friends for example I might sort of just do (.) the
7            odd impersonation or I might if I'm sort of loo- you
8            know (.) loose I was going to say if I'm really sort
9            of happy and joyful I might erm [ha ha
10   Host:                                   [(laughs -----------)
11   Guest:  Hello good afternoon I might sort of do Brittas for
12           example
13   Host:   what's the easiest voice though for you to fall into
14           and will you fall into it for us right now in the hot
15           seat
```

After a question like this from a child in the studio, it is not clear whether at any point Chris Barrie can be seen to be targeting the children (Rachel or Miles in these extracts) as direct addressees of his talk. Rather, he seems to be addressing the collective range of recipients, including the host and the studio audience as well as the individual questioners. What can be identified in the transcript above is a shift in address when the ambiguities arising from the specific participatory framework in this context becomes manifest in his talk (see lines 7–10). Barrie starts to use the word 'loose' (line 7), which then becomes the object of some quite complex repair work, as he not only substitutes it with a longer adjective phrase 'really sort of happy and joyful', but he also draws attention to the fact that he was going to say it, thereby indicating that this use is in some way inappropriate, or the wrong register, for this particular context. His following utterance, the 'aside': 'hello (.) good afternoon' maintains this shift as Barrie continues to display his apparent unease with the situation, which appears to result from the diverse range of recipients of his talk.

In the remainder of this particular sequence, initiated by a question from a child in the studio, the main participant roles of speaker and primary addressee are taken up by Barrie and Forbes, with the children as the studio audience recipients. In the phone-in sequences, although the talk develops in a similar way as an exchange between the host and guest, the maintenance of the absent caller as a recipient of the talk is achieved by both speakers continuing to talk to each other through the phone sets, while retaining eye-contact with each other, (which also produces an amusing on-screen image of a conversation between two co-present participants where the telephone would normally be redundant).

To summarize the points made so far then, we have seen that in this programme, despite the presence and involvement of children as questioners in the studio phone-in, the participant role available for them is principally that of audience. They are only rarely in the position of direct addressee, and when they do produce their questions, their participation as speakers is always framed by the mediating work of the host. If we return to Levinson's (1988) observation that 'a participant role is, from the point of view of participants, not something that is unilaterally assigned, but rather jointly negotiated' (p. 176), by looking at the organization of the talk in these contexts it seems that this negotiation is essentially asymmetrical, in so far as the children's participant roles are defined through the actions of the adults, rather than by the children as equal status interactants. Although this may be partly due to the context of the talk, (and adult participants in similar media speech events may be constrained in the same kind of ways) it is nevertheless significant for the purpose of this analysis that the participation of children in these programmes is from a discursive point of view, highly controlled and circumscribed. This contrasts strongly with the prevailing effect of apparent chaos and lack of control created by the presenters that has been noted by Buckingham (see discussion above), and which is also present in the apparent potential embarrassment of the 'Hot Seat' interview.

Productive Participant Roles: Children as Answerers

So far, I have looked at what children can do in the productive speaking role of *questioner* on a phone-in programme, and how adult answerers deal with them as addressees in interactive sequences of talk. In this section I want to focus on how children participate as *answerers*, this time in a different type of speech event: the interview. The following two extracts are taken from *Blue Peter*, and take place in the studio where the children have been engaged in a specific activity or task, which then forms the basis of an interview with one of the presenters. In the first extract, members of a boys' choir are interviewed after performing their song which has just been released into the charts, and in the second, a group of children who have been taking part in a beauty experiment are asked for their opinions on the treatments.

(13) Transcript: Blue Peter, 5 June 1995
Presenter Tim Vincent

```
1    Pres:  it's like five Take Thats squeezed into one Darren
2           you're the soloist (.) who wrote this beautiful song
3    Ch.1:  oh it was our producer (.) Bob Prizeman
4    Pres:  'n he's also involved with the choir as well isn't he
5    Ch.1:  oh yeah he teaches us music like a choirmaster and he
6           produced the song
7    Pres:  yeah very talented guy now Michael what other kind of
8           songs do you sing in the choir
9    Ch.2:  we'll sing all different types from hymns to this sort
10          of music
11   Pres:  and that's because you're actually a church choir
12          aren't you
13   Ch.2:  yeah=
14   Pres:  =now the two stars (.) or two of the stars of all of
15          them are these whisperers over here Lee and Liam (.)
16          Lee did you enjoy singing this song
17   Ch.3:  yeah I really enjoyed it cos it's got quite a loop (.)
18          quite a lot of movement in this song
19   Pres:  and you like a bit of funky movement do [you
20   Ch.3:                                          [yep=
21   Pres:  =now Liam obviously this is gonna go straight to
22          number one(.) when the call comes through to go on to
23          Top of the Pops whatya gonna say
24   Ch.4:  yeah hi hi
25   Pres:  why though you wanna meet somebody don't you
26   Ch.4:  erm East 17 and Meatloaf ha
27   Pres:  Meatloaf (.) unusual combination well I'm sure it is
28          going to go to number one (.) n'well done
```

In this interview with the choir, individual children in turn are brought into a productive speaking role as they each get asked a question by the presenter. However, these questions are often framed in such a way that the possible responses to them are limited. Four of the questions in this extract are declarative tag questions, which consist of a complete proposition followed by the tag, and which tend to elicit either affirmations, or affirmations followed by an elaboration, in the response:

```
Pres:  that's because you're a church choir aren't you?
Ch:    yeah

Pres:  you like a bit of funky movement do you?
Ch:    yeah

Pres:  he's also involved with the choir as well isn't
       he?
Ch:    oh yeah he teaches us music like a choirmaster
       and he produced the song

Pres:  why though you wanna meet somebody don't you?
Ch:    erm (.) East 17 and Meatloaf
```

In framing the questions in this way, the interviewer is able either to provide a piece of information which then is confirmed by the child interviewee, or in some cases, to prompt the child to respond with some additional information as in the last example. It is worth noting that *Blue Peter* is broadcast live, and although it is likely that this sequence will have been prepared, and that the content of the questions is predetermined, one of the consequences of this framing is to ensure either that the relevant information to be elicited from the children is *already* provided in the presenter's question turn, or that children are cued into providing appropriate answers, thereby minimizing the risk involved for the participants (particularly the adults). Another consequence however, is that this practice undermines the position of the children as answerers, in so far as it limits the type of responses they are able to produce in an interview situation.

The selection of next speaker provides a further constraint on the extent of children's participation in the discourse. The presenter clearly indicates when he is moving on to nominate the next speaker by using the transition marker 'now' as in the following examples:

```
now Michael
now the two stars
now Liam
```

He does this immediately after the answer turn of the previous speaker, or immediately after his third turn acknowledgement of their response, clearly signalling the end of one child's participation and bringing a new speaker into the frame as next answerer. Once again, we find that the children's access to a productive role in the talk is strongly bounded by the framing work of the adult presenter's talk.

In the second *Blue Peter* interview, a similar pattern of nominating next speakers can be identified, as well as a question format which tends to produce short, one word answers from the children. Here is the transcript of the 'beauty treatment' interview:

(14) Transcript: Blue Peter, 7 June 1995
Presenter: Diane Louise Jordan

```
1   Pres:  time travelled ten minutes since we last saw our
2          beauty treatment volunteers so how do they look and
```

```
3              feel now hh David and Lisa had the strawberry face
4              mask (.) Jerome and Emma were treated with the
5              porridge mask (.) David (.) what do you think would
6              you do it again
7    Ch.1:     yeah=
8    Pres:     =how does it feel then
9    Ch.1:     softer and smoother
10   Pres:     Excellent what about you Emma
11   Ch.2:     I feel a lot better and my skin is softer and smoother
12   Pres:     would you do it again
13   Ch.2:     yeah=
14   Pres:     =hundred per cent so far (.) I know that Lloyd and
15             Victoria you had the tea bags and the potato slices on
16             your eyes (.) Lloyd (.) you don't look too happy
17   Ch.3:     mm no (.) I wouldn't use it again
18   Pres:     why's that
19   Ch.3:     sticky
20   Pres:     aah (.) but don't you think your eyes have gone less
21             puffy (.) no (.) ok well swiftly moving on to the
22             people who had the erm hair treatment (.) George do
23             you think your hair's more soft and manageable now
24             would you do it again
25   Ch.4:     probly
26   Pres:     and your hair's looking nice and shiny as well
27             hh well I just wanted to say that you've all been
28             brilliant sports thank you whether you think these
29             natural beauty treatments work or not if you don't
30             want to use them (.) you can always eat them
```

The clear nomination of 'next speaker' can be seen in these sequences as the presenter opens and closes the children's access to the role of answerer:

```
David (.)   what do you think
what about you Emma
Lloyd (.)   you don't look too happy
George (.)  do you think your hair's more soft and manageable
            now
```

Although the information being elicited here is the children's opinions about the beauty treatments they have been experimenting with, rather than the more factual type of information in the first interview above, there is still a tendency to elicit these opinions through polar interrogatives, which prompt a yes/no answer rather than an open 'wh' question. In the first presenter turn below, both question forms are used, but the open question is immediately followed by a more restricting polar interrogative:

```
Pres:  David (.) what do you think would you do it again
Ch.1:  yeah
```

```
Pres:  George do you think your hair's more soft and
       manageable now
Ch.4:  yeah (.) I can move my fingers through it a lot
       more
Pres:  would you do it again
Ch.4:  probably
```

The only exception to this pattern is the declarative 'you don't look too happy', which produces an agreement response, followed by a declarative similar in form to the presenter's initial question, 'I wouldn't use it again'.

```
Pres:  Lloyd (.) you don't look too happy
Ch.3:  mm no (.) I wouldn't use it again
Pres:  why's that
Ch.3:  sticky
```

The structure of these question/answer exchanges is very similar to the question/ answer sequences of certain types of classroom talk (Coulthard, 1985 and 1993). The clear nomination of next speaker, and the presence of an evaluation or follow-up question in the third turn receipt of the answer, is distinctive of classroom interaction which is strongly teacher-centred:

```
T:     Let's see what you think Martin
P:     Heeroglyphs
T:     Yes you're pronouncing it almost right
(Coulthard, 1985, p. 127)
```

Here, it is the teacher who nominates who goes next, and who evaluates the pupil's response, while the child is clearly in the position of having to provide an answer. The presence of a similar interactive structure in the *Blue Peter* interviews indicates a comparable relationship between questioners and answerers, as in the following sequence:

```
5    Pres:  David (.) what do you think would
6           you do it again
7    Ch.1:  yeah=
8    Pres:  =how does it feel then
9    Ch.1:  softer and smoother
10   Pres:  Excellent what about you Emma
11   Ch.2:  I feel a lot better and my skin is softer and smoother
```

The participation status of children in these two extracts is limited. They are never really in a position to do more than provide answers which are then subject to an interviewer assessment or follow-up comment, and within this interactive framework, the talk of the adult interviewers sets up strong constraints on the type of possible actions available for the children.

Interaction Between Children

In the data I have looked at so far, the interaction has taken place between children and adults, where the children have occupied the participant roles of questioners and answerers respectively. I now want to turn to some data where the talk is between two children, with no adult on screen presence (although I take it that adults are necessarily involved in the production of this programme) and examine how the participatory framework is managed by the children without any participating adults. The context is a programme from a series called *Why Don't You?*, (BBC 1) broadcast during school holidays, and presented entirely by children. This particular extract consists of a cookery demonstration (again a genre 'borrowed' from adult television), where one girl (Cathy) shows the other (Ingrid) how to make 'Hedgehog Bread'. The extract given below is taken from the beginning of the sequences, apparently filmed at home in Cathy's kitchen.

```
(15)  Transcript: Why Don't You?*
1    I:  why do you need the yeast
2    C:  um it's to help them double in size and (.) to rise in the
3        oven
4    I:  hmm (.) [ . . . ] start then
5        (6.0)
6    I:  do you just dash em in all at once
7    C:  no you put the dry ingredients in first
8    I:  why
9        (3.0)
10   C:  well it just helps them (.) n' then (.) you add the water to
11       it
12   I:  why do you need warm·water
13   C:  um I think it really just helps the yeast begin to work
14       (2.0)
15   I:  do you just add (.) water bit by bit or do you just put it in
16       all at once
17   C:  you just put it in a little bit at a time or else it all
18       sticks together
19   I:  oh (1.0) how long does it usually take to mix
20   C:  just (.) normally about two or three minutes
21       (2.0)
22   I:  looks disgusting
23   C:  (laughs) (2.0) think maybe that's just about done now
24   I:  what next
25   C:  well I just need to dust the board so it doesn't stick
26   I:  has it stuck on before
27   C:  yeah (.) it's stuck quite a few times before this and (0.5)
28       it really did make a mess
29   I:  right wha' we gonna do now
30   C:  I jus' (1.0) flour my hands=
31   I:  =why (.) why've you [put flour
32   C:                      [so that it doesn't stick
```

Apart from Ingrid's comment at line 22, 'looks disgusting' and Cathy's following turn 'think maybe that's just about done now', the whole sequence consists of a series of question and answer pairs. The participation structure is asymmetrical in as much as one child is always in the position of questioner and the other in the position of answerer. The sequence also contains some rather long pauses: during the six second gap at line 5 Cathy is mixing various ingredients in a bowl, and most of the other long pauses occur as she moves through the various stages of making the bread. Listening to this sequence, one gets the impression that it has been largely scripted, as it shows little trace of the features typically found in naturally occurring, spontaneous talk. There is only one instance of overlapping speech, very little repetition or disfluency, and the high proportion of question/answer pairs would be unusual in other more informal speech contexts. The children seem to a large extent to be role playing, rather than producing 'fresh' talk in Goffman's (1981) sense. There are no third turn receipts of the information supplied by Cathy, apart from the 'oh' in line 19, and the questions are produced very baldly, with no framing or other mitigating forms.

What is revealed in this extract, however, is how the children engage with the work of reproducing a specific media genre through their talk: TV shows about food and cooking.[7] One of the girls asks all the questions, which are either procedural, such as 'what next' and 'do you just add water bit by bit', or to do with getting reasons for the specific actions involved, such as 'why do you need warm water', 'why do you need the yeast'. The other provides the answers as she prepares the food, so that each stage in the recipe is displayed within these question/answer sequences. There is only one point in the extract where a different type of conversational action is evident, which is the sequence at lines 22–24 beginning with Ingrid's assessment 'looks disgusting'. The overall effect of this question/answer display is to produce a very 'staged' piece of interaction.

Some problems occur too, as can be seen at various moments in the sequence. For example, the talk is not always synchronized with the actions. The question at line 6 is produced *after* Cathy has mixed her ingredients, and at line 10, Cathy is uncertain of the 'right' answer to Ingrid's question about why the dry ingredients should go in first: she pauses for three seconds before responding 'well it just helps them'. The only example of overlapping speech in the data also seems to be a case of mistiming, rather than a shift towards more spontaneous, unplanned speech. Cathy doesn't respond to Ingrid's 'why' question at the predictable moment straight after the first 'why':

```
I:  why (.) why've you [put flour
K:                      [so that it doesn't stick
```

Instead, she waits for Ingrid to repeat her question, but then starts to talk before Ingrid has supplied its full propositional content, anticipating the appropriate moment to take her next turn. She seems simply to have missed her cue and mistimed her response to this particular question.

Even in a programme which is free of the on-screen presence of adults, the children are still attempting to reproduce the discourse of adult TV genres. The interactive 'goal' of the recipe sequence is clearly to educate the viewers, focusing on the informative 'why' and 'what next' aspects of the process, rather than what the children may have to say about the experience itself. As noted above, there is only one third turn receipt of the information that is being supplied, and interestingly, this lack of third turn receipt of 'news' markers is a typical feature of mediated interviews where the information is produced not for the benefit of the interviewer, but for the listening or viewing audience (see Heritage, 1985). The fact that the sequence is predominantly accomplished through question–answer pairs again limits the interactive roles available for the children in this particular context. Negotiation of participatory roles is not an issue here, since these are necessarily predetermined by the format and distribution of the turn types, which the children rigidly adhere to. In this extract then the children are engaged in what appears to be a scripted role play of adult interaction, rather than producing what could be recognized as talk between children despite the fact that there are no adults involved in the discursive framework here.

Discussion: Children and Media Discourse Competence

The aim of this chapter has been to begin to explore the type of discursive frameworks within which children can participate as active producers of talk in children's TV programmes. Through an analysis of the participant roles available to children in three different programmes, I have tried to show how these frameworks are highly circumscribed, with children taking up restricted participatory roles when interacting with adults, and reproducing an adult media genre through a largely scripted role-play when there were no adults present on screen. The phone-in sequences from *Live and Kicking* contained limited occasions for children to ask questions, while the interview questions on *Blue Peter* were constructed so as to restrict the kinds of answers that children could provide in response. In the extract from *Why Don't You?*, the talk appeared largely planned, leaving little opportunity for the children to interact in more spontaneous ways. From the analysis of these three examples of mediated speech events involving children, I have claimed that their talk is constrained by the generic structures and format of the events themselves, as well as by some specific discursive actions of the adults who are acting as hosts and presenters. The media represent a discursive domain where children are participating very much on adult terms, both with regard to the activities they are involved in, and what they can get to say.

To return to the issue of children's discursive competence within the context of mediated speech events, from the evidence in these data it would seem that this competence is being developed and at the same time firmly controlled within the parameters of adult-centred discourse, and according to adult conceptions of what children should be able to say and do, which constrasts strongly with the evidence of children's skills in negotiating participation in peer-group interaction. Children are learning to participate in this form of public discourse through engaging in the production of generically specific forms of interaction, in phone-ins and interviews and their highly constrained question/answer routines, without there being any space for negotiation of what that participation could or should be, nor any move towards more child-centred discourse. Despite the appearance of chaos and lack of control in the production of programmes like *Live and Kicking*, and the challenge to the established order in features like 'The Hot Seat', the discursive organization of children's television is overwhelmingly to do with the maintenance of established interactive norms within a mediated context, and of the adult's position of authority. The actions of the children themselves are strikingly restrained and controlled in all the interactive sequences analyzed here, while the presentation of children's worlds as wild, uncontrollable and disorganized remains by and large an adult construction of what childhood is about. There is little evidence in these programmes of children being given the space to display discursive competence in anything other than their ability to participate in adult forms of mediated talk, and the discourse of children's television has yet to evolve a framework in which children can participate outside of the highly adult-controlled configurations described in this chapter.

Notes

1 There seems to be little evidence that children actually prefer those programmes which are ostensibly designed for them. Cullingford (1984) states that research has indicated that children's favourite programmes are very close to the viewing preferences of adults, and in one of the early surveys carried out in this area, less than 18 per cent of children said that they specially liked any of the programmes designed with them in mind. One of the reasons he suggests for this is that children's programmes don't offer the same type of viewing pleasure, in terms of their style and content, that is manifested by programmes designed for their parents, and that children see the function of television as primarily to entertain rather than to inform.

2 See, for example, Scannell (1991) for an overview of the centrality of language in the study of the media.

3 Again, Hodge and Tripp (1986) make the point that 'almost invariably, children's shows are made by adults, and children's television viewing equally invariably includes shows that were made for adults' (p. 7).

4 This view of the child as anarchistic and uncontrollable when removed from the sanctions of contact with adults has literary precedents in the work of Golding, Sendak etc.

5 See Levinson (1988) for a discussion of 'channel' and 'channel-linkage' in interaction (p. 177).

6 See for example Hutchby (1996) for an account of arguments on talk radio.

7 BBC2's programme *Ready Steady Cook* is an example of this genre, where there is a presenter who relays information about what is happening to the viewing audience.

References

BROWN, R. (1976) *Children and Television*, London: Collier Macmillan.

BUCKINGHAM, D. (1993) *Children Talking Television*, London: Falmer Press.

BUCKINGHAM, D. (1995) 'On the impossibility of children's television: the case of Timmy Mallett', in BAZALGETTE, C. and BUCKINGHAM, D. (eds) *In Front of the Children*, London: British Film Institute.

CHESHIRE, J. (1982) *Variation in an English Dialect*, Cambridge: Cambridge University Press.

CORSARO, W. (1986) 'Routines in peer culture', in COOK-GUMPERZ, J., CORSARO, W. and STREECK, J. (eds) *Children's Worlds and Children's Language*, Berlin: Mouton de Gruyter.

COULTHARD, M. (1985) *An Introduction to Discourse Analysis*, London: Longman.

COULTHARD, M. (1993) *Advances in Spoken Discourse Analysis*, London: Routledge.

CULLINGFORD, C. (1984) *Children and Television*, Aldershot: Gower.

ERVIN-TRIPP, S. and MITCHELL-KERNAN, C. (1977) *Child Discourse*, London: Academic Press.

FAIRCLOUGH, N. (1989) *Language and Power*, London: Longman.

GOFFMAN, E. (1981) *Forms of Talk*, Oxford: Blackwell.

GOODWIN, M. (1990) *He-Said-She-Said*, Bloomington, IN: Indiana University Press.

HERITAGE, J. (1985) 'Analyzing news interviews: Aspects of the production of talk for an overhearing audience', in VAN DIJK, T.A. (ed.) *Handbook of Discourse Analysis, Volume 3*, London: Academic Press.

HODGE, B. and TRIPP, D. (1986) *Children and Television*, Cambridge: Polity Press.

HUTCHBY, I. (1995) 'Aspects of recipient design in expert advice-giving on call-in radio', *Discourse Processes*, **19**, pp. 219–38.

HUTCHBY, I. (1996) *Confrontation Talk*, Hillsdale NJ: Erlbaum.

HYMES, D. (1972) 'On conversational competence', in PRIDE, J.B. and HOLMES, J. (eds) *Sociolinguistics*, London: Penguin.

KATRIEL, T. (1987) ' "Bexibudim": Ritualised sharing among Israeli children', *Language and Society*, **16**, pp. 305–20.

LABOV, W. (1964) 'Stages in the acquisition of standard English', in SHUY, R. (ed.) *Social Dialect and Language Learning*, Illinois: National Council for Teachers of English.

LABOV, W. (1972) 'Rules for ritual insults', in SUDNOW, D. (ed.) *Studies in Social Interaction*, New York: Free Press.

LEVINSON, S. (1988) 'Putting linguistics on a proper footing', in DREW, P. and WOOTTON, T. (eds) *Erving Goffman: Exploring the Interaction Order*, Cambridge: Polity Press.

McTEAR, M. (1985) *Children's Conversation*, Oxford: Blackwell.

MAYNARD, D. (1985) 'How children start arguments', *Language and Society*, **14**, pp. 1–29.

MONTGOMERY, M. (1986) 'DJ talk', *Media, Culture and Society*, **8**, pp. 421–40.

OCHS, E. (1983) 'Planned and unplanned discourse', in OCHS, E. and SCHIEFFELIN, B. (eds) *Acquiring Conversational Competence*, London: Routledge and Kegan Paul.

OCHS, E. and SCHIEFFELIN, B. (1979) *Developmental Pragmatics*, London: Academic Press.

OCHS, E. and SCHIEFFELIN, B. (eds) (1983) *Acquiring Conversational Competence*, London: Routledge and Kegan Paul.

REID, E. (1976) 'Social and stylistic variation in the speech of children', in TRUDGILL, P. (ed.) *Sociolinguistic Patterns in British English*, Cambridge: Cambridge University Press.

SCANNELL, P. (1991) *Broadcast Talk*, London: Sage.

SCHIEFFELIN, B. (1990) *The Give and Take of Everyday Life*, Cambridge: Cambridge University Press.

SLOSBERG-ANDERSEN, E. (1990) *Speaking with Style*, London: Routledge.

Part III

Competence and Institutional Knowledge

Chapter 8

'What's the Problem?' Restoring Social Order in the Preschool Classroom

Susan Danby and Carolyn Baker

Introduction

Early childhood settings present children with many opportunities to engage in inter-actions with each other and with the teachers in their classrooms and playgrounds. Young children are routinely propelled into play situations where they are sometimes out of sight and out of earshot of the teachers. What goes on in those play situations is the very serious work of constructing social order (Denzin, 1982; Goodwin, 1985 and 1990). On close inspection, this work turns out to be intricate and itself ori-ented to a recognition that there is more than one social order to manage. One of the themes of this volume is that children's achievements are bounded by structural features (especially in this case, a potentially overhearing teacher). This chapter also shows how children make use of such structural features (the possibility and the fact of teacher intervention) as material for their work of social organization.

This chapter examines the relation between social orders by studying two instances of conflict in play that attracted teacher intervention in a preschool class-room. These episodes were videotaped. The first episode involves three girls in home corner area; the second shows boys in block area. In each episode, the teacher responds to a crying child, seeing the situation as both the product of a conflict to be settled and the cause of a problem to be solved. In each episode, she intervenes to repair the situation and to restore order to her classroom. Our analysis of each episode tracks the work of the children before, during and after the appearance and disappearance of the teacher around a 'problem'.

Our initial reading of the teacher's intervention suggested that teacher and children shared a common construction of events as they attempt to resolve the conflict. But close analysis shows that the teacher's solution absolutely misses how the children operate within their social worlds. As she intervenes, she replaces their social order with her own version, one prescribed by early childhood pedagogy for dealing with conflict. The children momentarily operate within the teacher's social order but when she departs, they return to their own social orders to effect their own repairs. This suggests that the children in each episode treat the teacher's intervention pragmatically, as an interruption to their ongoing arenas of action.

Our analysis reveals two central themes in the process of the teacher managing the conflict. Our first theme explores the diverse discourses in which the children and teacher can operate while appearing to be constructing common meaning. The problem identified in each episode by the teacher and addressed to the participants in the group suggests that the teacher understands that there is a commonly agreed problem — that of hurting another child's feelings. Yet, in each episode the participants deal with this differently. This leads to our second theme, that of the gendered work of the participants' responses. In both episodes, the conflict and the teacher's intervention serve to enable participants to practise and consolidate discourses of gender. The boys' response, upon the teacher's departure, highlights how the boys resolve the problem according to the dominant masculine practices of this classroom which dismiss the teacher's version of events. The teacher's assessment and resolution of the problem of hurt feelings, however, becomes accepted by the girls. They take on the problem originally constructed by the teacher and displayed through the teacher's intervention in the conflict. In their private repair, they use the same notions of care and condolence as did the teacher. These examples serve to show evidence of the gendered membership work of the preschool classroom, in which the teacher's brief appearance and disappearance becomes material with which the children work to restore their social orders.

Children are Competent Players in their Social Worlds

Traditional early childhood pedagogy has as its focus the importance of play in developing the individual child (cf. Bredekamp, 1987; National Childcare Accreditation Council, 1993). However, this emphasis upon the observation and development of the individual child misses the power of peer culture and how children work to shape and reconstruct one another. The dynamic and fluid nature of children's engagement in their everyday work of communicating with each other and with the teachers is subsumed by an approach that sees individual children moving through developmental phases (Corsaro, 1997; Jenks, 1989; Speier, 1982). Both Speier (1982) and Jenks (1989) argue that the concept of development is not a natural process but a socially constructed one. Jenks (1989) suggests that the idea of development is designed through 'an appearance of care' to enforce dependence. Such a view of 'the child' has led to the conception that children are immature, incomplete, and consequently, incompetent, in their dealings with each other and with adults (Mackay, 1991).

While there is a significant body of contemporary research that shows otherwise (Corsaro, 1997; Corsaro and Streeck, 1986; Danby, 1996; Davies, 1982 and 1989; Goodwin, 1985; Goodwin and Goodwin, 1987; Kantor, Elgas and Fernie, 1993; Sheldon, 1990, 1992 and 1996; Waksler, 1991), traditional early childhood pedagogy has been slow in considering the view that children are competent social agents. This study recognizes and builds on this prior work to show that children are competent practitioners of multiple social orders in their relationships with each other as well as with teachers and other adults.

Mackay (1991) notes the paradox that adults and teachers 'simultaneously assume and interactionally den(y)' the competence of the child (p.27). This paradox is evident in the two episodes here. Analysis shows that the teacher relies upon the children's competence to enact her discourse of care and consolation, but her intervention implies incompetence suggesting that children are viewed as unable or incompetent in maintaining their social orders. This view of children's 'precompetence', as Speier (1976) puts it, is one that is largely supported in the literature on traditional early childhood pedagogy, albeit under the guise of development (p. 98).

A number of studies have examined gender differences in preschool-aged children (Davies, 1989; Paley, 1984; Sachs, 1987; Sheldon, 1990, 1992 and 1996) and school-aged children (Davies, 1993; Goodwin, 1985, 1990 and 1995; Goodwin and Goodwin, 1987; Kamler, Maclean, Reid and Simpson, 1994; Thorne, 1993). These studies show that even before school-age, girls and boys already show understandings of gendered social orders. Girls and boys use the structural features of talk and action differently, boys' interactions appearing to be more highly aggravated, with more physical action and contact, than that of girls.

The concept of children's incompetence implies that adults can make judgements for/over children without regard to their value systems (Goode, 1994). Goode portrays adults in a missionary-like role where they are 'culturally in the position of domination and conversion . . . not hav(ing) to acknowledge or concern (them)selves with the natives' beliefs in order to get the job of conversion . . . done' (p. 168). In the two episodes presented in this chapter, our analysis shows girls appearing to be converted to the teacher's moral order which she imposes through the care and consolation discourse. The boys are not converted, but actually use her discourse as a foil for their practice of dominant masculinity. Our analysis of these gendered practices indicates support for Sacks' (1974) suggestion that children are not only competent to use adult rules, but to use them to accomplish their own agendas.

Methodology and Procedures

The Study

Data reported in this chapter are part of a larger study exploring how children, as members of a preschool childcare room, produce their everyday interactions, displaying to each other their locally accomplished order. This study utilizes the methodological approaches of applied ethnomethodology (Garfinkel, 1967) and conversation analysis (Psathas, 1995; Sacks, 1974, 1984b and 1995). This requires paying close and detailed attention to the production of locally accomplished order (Silverman, 1994). The 'how' of the talk and action reveal 'the practices by which social order is accomplished' (*ibid.*, p. 180). By explicating sequences of talk and interaction by the children in their everyday interactions in the preschool room, we reduce the context for the study 'to interactional units of *occasioned and situated activity*' (Speier, 1982, p. 184). The focus is on observing children 'in real settings with real children' (Corsaro, 1997, p. 172) engaged in their everyday interactions and social practices. Sequences of interactions are analysed for how the children build their talk and action together to make sense of their social orders. Underlying this approach is the demonstrated competence of children as they routinely employ conversational procedures and resources. Disputes and conflict are not seen as reflecting children's incompetence, but rather as part of their efforts in discovering how social orders are accomplished. The work by Corsaro (1985), Goodwin (1985) and Evaldsson (1993) are examples of situated activity studies.

The Setting

The setting is a preschool room in a childcare centre in an Australian inner city area. The children are aged between 3 and 5 years. Some of these children are new to the 3–5-year-old room and some have been there the previous year. Some children attend every day whereas some attend only on some days. Many of these children have been in the childcare centre for one to three years. On any day, there were two teachers and up to sixteen children in the preschool room.

Method of Data Collection

Videotaped observations were taken of the social interactions of the children during the first three weeks of the school year. This entailed approximately two hours of video data each day. Videotape was used to capture the complexity and interconnectedness of the talk and action in this classroom (Jacob, 1987; Mehan, 1979). Baker (1997) and Denzin (1989) note that this method examines 'natural' talk in everyday life, preserving the data in a way that most closely resembles the original form. Mehan (1979 and 1993) and Denzin (1989) both suggest this type of approach allows careful observation through retrieval of videotape materials for data analysis, and a critical reexamination of the event many times which facilitates many possible interpretations of the same data.

The video data focused on the children participating in their everyday play activities. These activities occurred in a period of play known as 'free play', where a number of learning experiences, activities and play materials are available from which the children self-select, individually and with others. The two teachers organize and oversee this environment and may participate in the activities of the children, but more often, attempt to extend children's learning through interactive questions and comments. Another important role was to mediate to settle disputes. As the focus of this study is children's construction of their social orders in their everyday world, our purpose was to collect video data of the children interacting in these free play activities.

In discussing the difficulties of undertaking ethnographic studies in preschool settings, Corsaro (1985) considers the assumed power of the researcher to be one of the problems of gaining access to young informants. In his work, he used a reactive strategy to minimize his perceived power as an adult: he responded to the children rather than initiating contact with them. Similarly, in this study, responses by the researcher to the children were mostly confined to affirming their initiations. For example, questions would be answered but conversations would not be initiated. The children and teachers appeared to take little notice of either the camera or the researcher's presence after the first few days; however we cannot assume that the researcher's presence was not part of the scenes being filmed.

Transcription and Analysis

Particular segments of video data were chosen for closer analysis because they were of initial interest. Sacks (1984a) explains the choice of particular data in the following way:

> Now people often ask me why I choose the particular data I choose. Is it some problem that I have in mind that caused me to pick this corpus or this segment? And I am insistent that I just happened to have it, it became fascinating, and I spent some time at it. (p. 27)

The segment of aggravated action involving the boys was initially selected because the event appeared very frightening for Connell and highly charged with emotion. The girls' segment was chosen later for comparative analysis because their talk and physical action in this segment is the only example of aggravated action in the videotape data, thus making it a departure from the norm and opening it up for scrutiny (Heritage, 1984). Because both segments had the teacher intervening, this common element became the focus for further analysis.

The production of the transcript is more than a technical exercise. It involves close and careful listenings to reveal the detailed features of the talk and action (Baker, 1997; Silverman, 1993). Bloom (in Baker, 1997) suggests that transcribers of videotape data, to avoid being overwhelmed by the details, see themselves as interpreters of the event, rather than providers of descriptions. What is transcribed and what is left out by the transcriber means that the transcription process and outcomes are not neutral but reflect the transcriber's theoretical interests. Reid, Kamler, Simpson and MacLean (1996) demonstrate this point very clearly when they describe how researcher positionings influence what is seen (or not seen). The transcription process, and most notably, the notation used by ethnomethodologists and conversation analysts, has been described as messy, fragmented and difficult to read (Atkinson, 1981), but the close and detailed work of transcription provides the following advantages, as described by Heritage (1984):

> the use of recorded data is an essential corrective to the limitations of intuition and recollection. In enabling repeated and detailed examination of the events of interaction, the use of recordings extends the range and precision of the observations which can be made. . . . the original data are neither idealized nor constrained by a specific research design or by reference to some particular theory or hypothesis. (p. 238)

The Two Episodes

Each episode involves three phases: play which builds to conflict and the crying of a child, the teacher's intervention to restore the problem of hurt feelings and class-room order, and the participants' subsequent work to repair their problem of unsettled social order. The transcripts are first presented in full, and later, extracts are analysed more closely. An explanation of the transcript notation is provided in Appendix 1 (p. 183).

In Transcript 1, Amelia and Elana are at the play computers. Portia joins them and the three begin a new game involving three chairs placed one behind the other. These chairs represent a car. They play cars and ballerinas (for approximately 10 minutes) and then Portia instructs Elana to remain at the car while she and Amelia 'go home'. Elana announces that she is going to play in home corner, walks into the area and picks up some plates. Amelia accepts this new storyline, knocking at the door and declaring that she is home. Portia, however, tells Elana that she is not her friend and seeks confirmation from Amelia. Amelia pretends to lock Elana into jail and Portia continues this new move. Amelia then stands nearby, watching. The reader of the transcript should be aware that there is no actual door, there is no actual lock, and there is no actual key. Yet the door, lock and key are real to the participants and Elana's opening of the door with the key unleashes a swift physical response from Portia.

Transcript 1

Amelia and Portia are 4 years old, Elana is 3; Amelia attends the centre four times a week, Elana attends three days and Portia, two days.

1	Portia	((Portia moves closer to Elana, but is still outside the home corner area.)) No you can't have locks on it locks( )
2	Amelia	((Amelia, with a book under her arm, moves closer to home corner to rest her arms on the stove.))
3	Elana	(1.0) ((Elana pushes open an imaginary door with a flourish of the right arm and walks out the home corner away from Portia. At this time, she is looking at Portia.)) the keys
4	Portia	No you can't ((Portia, biting her lip, grabs Elana's right arm and vigorously tries to pull her back towards home corner)) the police [will get you]
5	Elana	((Elana resists while Portia continues to pull her arm.)) [NO:O], NO:O NO:O ((crying louder and looks at researcher. Elana grabs onto researcher.))

6	Portia	(2.0) ((Portia, standing very still, looks solemnly at researcher and then at Elana, then looks down, then looks back to researcher and then down.))
7		(2.0) ((Amelia moves close to Portia and Elana while John walks past and then goes into home corner picking up pots but looking at Elana and Portia.))
8	Elana	Uhhh ((A quiet whimper and then Elana is silent.))
9		(1.0)
10	Teacher	((from a distance)) What's the problem Portia? (1.0) Amelia what's the problem Amelia why is Elana upset why is she sad? ((Portia, with a solemn expression, walks quietly towards home corner, turns around, gives a sideways glance to Amelia, and then walks away while giving a sideways glance at the teacher. At this point, Amelia joins her and they start to walk away together. Elana is silent.))
11	Teacher	((Teacher is now at the scene.)) No Amelia Portia back here and you talk to Elana please ((Amelia and Portia turn around and come back. John is now standing as part of the group. Elana remains silent.)) what's the problem (1.0) why is she crying (1.0) why is she she crying? ((softer voice)) (1.0) Did you hurt her feeling
12	Portia	No? ((Amelia looks at Portia.))
13	Teacher	Who hurt her feelings then Amelia did you hurt Elana's feelings then
14		((Amelia shakes her head and Portia looks at her.))
15	John	[She did] ((pointing to Portia))
16	Teacher	[Then why] is she sad Portia why is she sad?
17	John	She did she she she pulled her hand ((pointing to Portia and then Elana))
18	Teacher	Did you pull her hand Portia but why is Elana crying yu'you have to tell me so we can solve the problem (2.0) Do you think you can talk to Elana and make her feel better? (1.0) Can you make her feel better? because she's feeling a bit sad at the moment. ((Elana remains silent.))
19		((Portia starts to walk away, turns, goes to Elana and gives her a hug; Elana looks down and remains silent; Amelia watches.))

20   Teacher   Thank you Portia I think that makes her feel much better

21   ((Portia, Amelia and John walk away towards book corner. Portia looks at the book display; Amelia, still clutching a book, stands and looks at the teacher and Elana.))

22   Teacher   You right there Elana? ((Elana nods briefly.)) Go and play again? ( ) ((The teacher walks away and Elana walks over to stand near to the puzzle table.))

23   (4.0) ((Amelia then moves to be near Portia.))

24   Portia   ((to Amelia)) (   ) Go and make Elana feel better (1.0) go and make her ((nodding towards Elana)) [feel better]

25   Amelia   [I I didn't] do (anything)

26   Portia   Yes you did

27   Amelia   No:o ((shaking her head))

28   (5.0) ((Amelia and Portia look at each other; Portia looks away and back again.))

29   Portia   (   ) ((in a very quiet voice))

30   ((Amelia immediately walks over to the puzzle table, the other side of the room, where Elana is standing with a book. Amelia sits down and glances briefly as Elana walks away.))

31   ((Elana walks away looking at the book until she stands in front of book corner, but facing away from Portia, looks up, and swings arms and book from side to side, looks briefly at researcher.))

32   ((Portia walks out of book corner, past Elana on her way to her locker, and pulls out something from her locker and then replaces it.))

33   ((Amelia leaves the puzzle table and brushes past Elana towards the preparation room.)) whe whe whe (in a rhythmic fashion)

34   ((John brushes past Elana)) (   ) ((says something to Amelia))

35   ((Portia brushes past Elana, giving her a brief glance, and goes to the preparation room, meeting the teacher as she comes out)) ( )

```
36                ((Teacher acknowledges Portia by a look and
                  weaves around her as she keeps walking; Portia
                  stops and holds her dress.))

37                ((Amelia and Elana talk briefly to each other.
                  Amelia then walks into home corner and Elana
                  follows.))

38                ((Portia goes to sit beside the teacher assistant
                  in manipulative area.))
```

In Transcript 2, a group of boys aged between 3 and 5 years are playing on a carpeted area surrounded by two shelves storing large wooden blocks. There are three main participants in this episode: David, John and Connell. David is the oldest boy and has been in this classroom for the longest time, almost two years. John has been in this classroom for almost a year, and Connell is new to this classroom, having recently come from the 2–3-year-old classroom. Colin and Andrew are also playing in the block area and while they do not participate in the interactions with the teacher, they are nearby and within hearing range of the exchange.

Connell and John are using large blocks to make a road for their cars. They are side-by-side but playing independently of each other. Connell engages in a discussion about who is bigger by challenging John, one of the older boys. David (also an older boy) and John use this to launch into a lesson for Connell on the discursive practices of masculinity in the block area (see Danby, 1996). They act in concert to educate Connell about how to act as a hegemonic masculine member in the block area. When the dispute escalates so that Connell begins to cry, the teacher intervenes in an attempt to resolve the conflict. The transcript begins where David and John threaten Connell with terrible consequences if he says that he's bigger.

<u>Transcript 2</u>

David is 4 years old; John, Colin and Andrew are 3, and Connell had just recently had his third birthday. David, John, Connell and Andrew attend the centre full-time (five days) and Andrew attends four times a week.

```
12  Connell  And I'm bigger

13  David    No we'll just BASH YOU RIGHT off the (  ) ((David
             swings fists; Connell turns to look at David))

14  John     ((pointing towards Connell)) (  ) in jail

15  David    (Well)=

16  Connell  =No

17  David    Yes, (well) you just (we just) if you punch John,
             well I'll just THROW you ((making throwing
             movements)) through that television (1.0) that's
             standing right over there.
```

18 John   (3.0) And then I'll kick ya ((Connell looks at
                John))

19 David   ((now beside Connell)) And I'll kick you right
                through the [(window)]

20 John   ((leans towards Connell)) [And then] I'll get
                Batman.

21 David   ((pats John on the head)) Will you stop talking
                John? ((Connell looks away towards floor and then
                at David)) ( ) ((a short sentence)) square bum
                ((smiles at John))

22 John   ((to David)) And I'll get the police ((Connell
                looks at John and then the floor))

23 David   And all the ( ) will come out

24 John   And I'll and I'll piss on 'im ((points to
                Connell) and and then the police will (get) it

25 David   Yeah, and then you'll ((points to Connell)) be
                going to jail. Rmmp Rmmp, [Rmmp ((David starts to
                make car noises, claps hands close to Connell's
                face, jumping up and down, making play sounds
                that are high and song-like.))]

26 Connell   ((starts to cry out)) [NO:O NO:O] ((to David))
                I want to go home with mummy and my daddy.
                ((Connell crying, looks up briefly at the teacher
                when she arrives.))

27 Teacher   ((touching David)) David, what's the problem with
                Connell. ((Connell is still crying loudly, looks
                up briefly at the teacher and then John, who is
                still standing nearly and is now swinging a small
                plastic car towards Connell.))

28 David   ((turning away from Connell towards the teacher,
                but looking at the block shelf and touching the
                blocks))=We're just talking to him. ((John looks
                on, standing a little away.))

29 Teacher   Well, he looks very sad. Look at his face.
                ((Connell appears to be crying more loudly with
                his mouth wide open, almost a wail.)) (1.0) Does
                he look happy? ((David looks up at the teacher.))
                Well, can you make him feel better please?

30 David   ((David is standing on the bottom shelf of the
                block shelves, he starts to swing away from the
                teacher and Connell; Connell is now crying more
                loudly.))

31	Teacher	No:o ((takes David's arm and pulls him back to standing on the floor near Connell)) come back and make him feel better please. ((David puts hand tentatively on Connell's chest; Connell is now crying quietly.)) How are you going to make him feel better? ((Andrew looks on briefly.))
32	David	Give him a cuddle?
33	Teacher	O-Okay, give him a cuddle. ((David leans across for a fleeting moment to put an arm around Connell.)) (and) what else did you say could you say make him feel better?
34	David	( ) ((a short utterance))
35	Teacher	Is that are you feeling okay now Connell? ((Connell shakes his head and continues crying.)) We get you a tissue? Wipe the tears away? ((Teacher leaves for a tissue.))
36	John	((steps closer and swings the plastic car close to Connell's body))
37	David	((Connell is still crying quietly; David looks at the teacher leaving and then puts his finger gently under Connell's chin, talking in a cajoling tone. Andrew, who has been playing nearby, stands beside Connell and looks at David.)) ( ) it was a joke ((turns towards John)) ( ) a joke
38	Teacher	((Teacher returns; Connell starts crying more loudly; teacher wipes Connell's nose.)) Wipe the tissues away?
39	David	((to teacher)) We were just tricking him.
40	Teacher	Now (1.0) well, maybe he doesn't like being tricked, David. Did you think of that?
41	David	No, [we were just tricking]
42	Teacher	[You're right Connell.] ((rubbing Connell's head; Connell now stops crying and walks away from the teacher to the edge of block area.)) It's okay. Are you going to build with the blocks now?
43	David	Bpp, bpp, bpp ((a play sound rising in tone)) they should(n't) even be (here) ((David is leaning against the block shelf, facing away from the teacher.))

```
44  Teacher  Well Dave, if you can't co-operate with the
             little ones in the group, you'll have to find
             something for you to play with away from
             them=((David walks away with his back towards
             the teacher as she talks.))

45  John     ((standing nearby then starts to play with blocks))

46  David    ((jumps over blocks, makes a play sound))=They're
             not even four.

47  Connell  ((Connell crouches, pushing a small car on the
             block road.))

48  Colin    ((Colin and Andrew are near the block shelves.))
             I'm bigger than you Andrew.

49  Andrew   ((jumps up and stands tall beside Colin, then
             puts foot on shelf) I'm bigger I'm bigger
```

The Division of Social Order Between the Teacher and Children

Our analysis is intended to foreground the distance between the teacher's work of restoring order through the discourses of caring and consolation and the children's work, as we see it, of using conflict in other domains altogether. Put more simply, the adult notion of children's conflict as a problem to be solved or an interaction to be stopped by adults would appear to run contrary to how children actually use conflict to pursue their own agendas. As Maynard (1985) proposes, conflict is not dysfunctional, rather 'the occurrence of a single episode of dispute may represent the precise moment during which a small group's social organization is fundamentally negotiated' (p. 218). It appears to us from the teacher's talk and action that she believes that she has resolved the problem by effecting a repair so that the children can return to and continue their educationally valuable play. According to Corsaro (1985), this is the usual practice of early childhood teachers.

The teacher's intervention is to provide a solution to the problem of a hurt child crying. Her role, to borrow a metaphor from Speier (1976), is that of a 'colonial administrator', whose duty is to successfully manage 'the native culture' (p. 99). As with colonization, there are two cultures (adults and children) in contact with each other in this classroom with one culture having the administrative management of the other (the teacher's involvement in solving the problem). The teacher's departure, with her version of the problem solved, leaves the children, the other culture, to do their own membership work using their own practices to restore their unsettled social order. The children do this in gendered ways.

Analysis of the transcripts show that after the teacher leaves, or in her absence, other forms of repair amongst the participants take place. Each episode results in a different type of repair, constructed by the participants through the local work of gendered membership. This is manifested by Portia and Amelia taking up the teacher's discourse of consolation and caring to effect their repair, which equals the teacher's. The older boys, particularly David, orchestrate their repair to discount the teacher's caring discourse by replacing it with the local hegemonic masculine version which is what they repair. For the girls, the repair restores their connection with each other; for the boys, their repair continues their celebration of masculinity. The analysis of the two episodes is presented to show three parallel phrases in each episode.

Phase 1: The Problem of a Crying Child

Typically, a child's cry quickly brings the teacher to the area. When children play within earshot of adults, it must always be a possibility to them that this type of interruption from the teacher will occur. In a preschool classroom, it is difficult to escape from the auditory vigilance of the teacher. Early childhood pedagogy expects the teacher to respond promptly to a distressed child (National Childcare Accreditation Council, 1993) and in conflict situations, it is usually the practice of early childhood teachers to step into the situation in order to quickly define the problem and resolve the dispute (Feeney, Christensen and Moravcik, 1991). Thus the problem of a crying child belongs to the teacher who needs to move swiftly to stop the crying and restore cooperative play.

In the first episode, the actual unsettling of the children's social order occurs when Portia physically restrains Elana (turn 4) and Elana begins to cry. In the video data collected for this study, this episode is the only example located so far where there is a direct physical confrontation among the girls whereas there are several episodes of aggravated talk and action among the boys. This finding is similar to that of Sheldon's (1992) study of preschool children engaged in conflict episodes. She points out that boys routinely engage in confrontational exchanges of aggravated talk and action whereas girls ordinarily do not.

Transcript 1

3	Elana	(1.0) ((Elana pushes open an imaginary door with a flourish of the right arm and walks out the home corner away from Portia. At this time, she is looking at Portia.)) the keys
4	Portia	No you can't (Portia, biting her lip, grabs Elana's right arm and vigorously tries to pull her back towards home corner)) the police [will get you]
5	Elana	((Elana resists while Portia continues to pull her arm.)) [NO:O], NO:O NO:O ((crying louder and looks at researcher. Elana grabs onto researcher.))

The pretend social order has been breached through this physical restraining; in other words, the conventions of the pretend play have been broken by Elana's spontaneous action of walking out the door. Elana's crying within hearing distance of the teacher effectively calls in the teacher. So too does a crying child call in the teacher in Transcript 2 (turn 26) when Connell finally begins to cry after David claps his hands close to Connell's face while making unintelligible vocal noises.

Transcript 2

```
25  David    Yeah, and then you'll ((points to Connell)) be
              going to jail. Rmmp Rmmp, [Rmmp ((David starts to
              make car noises, claps hands close to Connell's
              face, jumping up and down, making play sounds
              that are high and song-like.))]

26  Connell  ((starts to cry out)) [NO:O NO:O] ((to David)) I
              want to go home with mummy and my daddy. ((Connell
              crying, looks up briefly at the teacher when she
              arrives.))
```

Maynard (1985) proposes that children strategically call upon the teacher to defend particular positions that they have taken. He writes that children are 'political actors' from an early age, suggesting that they call on the teacher's intervention, not to end or settle disputes, but to 'solicit that participation to promote whatever position they have taken during the dispute process' (p. 216). This is an interesting point in light of the two episodes discussed in this chapter. It could be argued that both Elana's and Connell's cries were either cries for help because they could no longer stand the conflict or political moves resulting in the teacher responding in specific (and probably predictable) ways. Either way, the teacher entered into each of the scenes.

Phase 2: The Teacher Responds to the Problem of Hurt Feelings

In each episode, the teacher becomes involved by asking, 'what's the problem?'. This particular type of response when talking to children in conflict situations is encouraged in early childhood pedagogy. For instance, one possible response suggested by Stone (1990) is, 'Problem here?' (p. 38). Another recommendation by Feeney, Christensen and Moravcik (1991) has the teacher asking, 'What can we do to solve this problem so you can go back to building this tower?' (p. 272). So as the literature of early childhood pedagogy suggests, the teacher is responding typically to this type of conflict situation.

In this phase, the teacher moves quickly to define the problem as a hurt child's sad feelings. In doing this, she tries to make those whom she assumes responsible explain why the hurt child is crying. In the first transcript, the teacher from a distance initially and then close-up, first assigns Portia, and then Amelia, the responsibility for explaining what has just happened.

Transcript 1

→ 10 Teacher ((from a distance)) What's the problem Portia?
             (1.0) Amelia what's the problem Amelia why is
             Elana upset why is she sad? ((Portia, with a
             solemn expression, walks quietly towards home
             corner, turns around, gives a sideways glance
             to Amelia, and then walks away while giving a
             sideways glance at the teacher. At this point,
             Amelia joins her and they start to walk away
             together. Elana is silent.))

    11 Teacher ((Teacher is now at the scene.)) No Amelia Portia
             back here and you talk to Elana please ((Amelia
             and Portia turn around and come back. John is
             now standing as part of the group. Elana remains
             silent.)) What's the problem (1.0) why is she
             crying (1.0) why is she she crying? ((softer
             voice)) (1.0) Did you hurt her feeling

There is a similar pattern in the second transcript, although the teacher is in close proximity, actually touching David, when she assigns him the responsibility of answering.

Transcript 2

    26 Connell ((starts to cry out)) [NO:O NO:O] ((to David))
             I want to go home with mummy and my daddy.
             ((Connell crying, looks up briefly at the
             teacher when she arrives.))

→ 27 Teacher ((touching David)) David, what's the problem
             with Connell. ((Connell is still crying loudly,
             looks up briefly at the teacher and then John, who
             is still standing nearly and is now swinging a
             small plastic car towards Connell.))

Sacks (1974) discusses the restricted conversational rights of children when they engage in conversations with adults. Teachers, like parents (Speier, 1976), have the asymmetrical right to intervene. This is demonstrated in our data by the teacher's verbal interjections. The teacher claims her differential conversational right to regulate children's talk and action when she calls out from a distance, 'What's the problem Portia?' (turn 10) and when she touches David and asks, 'David, what's the problem with Connell' (turn 27). Here, the teacher is using her right to enforce a response from a child who is not crying.

'What's the problem' is a 'marked invitation' to speak (Psathas, 1995, p. 62). In Transcript 1, the teacher directs the question initially at Portia and then at Amelia (turn 10). The assumption may be that the one who responds to the question either has the problem or has created the problem; in either case they should implicitly know what it is. This may be why Amelia and Portia do not speak; if they talk, they acknowledge that there is a problem and that they may be assumed to have created it. Portia and Elana are made accountable by the teacher for their actions but they do not have a ready account of the event which will satisfy the teacher. After a number of requests for information (turns 10 and 11), Portia tentatively denies the teacher's accusation that she hurt Elana's feelings (turn 12). Amelia also denies any involvement in hurting Elana's feelings (turn 14).

Transcript 1

→ 10 Teacher ((from a distance)) What's the problem Portia? (1.0) Amelia what's the problem Amelia why is Elana upset why is she sad? ((Portia, with a solemn expression, walks quietly towards home corner, turns around, gives a sideways glance to Amelia, and then walks away while giving a sideways glance at the teacher. At this point, Amelia joins her and they start to walk away together. Elana is silent.))

11 Teacher ((Teacher is now at the scene.)) No Amelia Portia back here and you talk to Elana please ((Amelia and Portia turn around and come back. John is now standing as part of the group. Elana remains silent.)) what's the problem (1.0) why is she crying (1.0) why is she she crying? ((softer voice)) (1.0) Did you hurt her feeling

12 Portia No? ((Amelia looks at Portia.))

13 Teacher Who hurt her feelings then Amelia did you hurt Elana's feelings then

14 ((Amelia shakes her head and Portia looks at her.))

In the teacher's search for a confession, her adult-given control over speaking rights (Sacks, 1974) allows her to continue with this particular type of talk. The teacher's agenda is one of finding an account that satisfies her problem characterized as a child's hurt feelings. In turn 11, the teacher actually supplies one possible account when she asks, 'Did you hurt her feelings?'. As in murder interrogations, an invitation to tell the story of what happened, differing from a volunteered story, presupposes that the story requested is the one that the questioner wants to hear (Watson, 1990). The teacher may be setting guidelines for possible acceptable accounts when she proposes a storyline about feelings being hurt.

Finally, after the teacher repeatedly tries to elicit a response from Portia or Amelia, John informs the teacher of his account of the event (turns 15 and 17). John can do this as he is not 'marked' (Psathas, 1995), being only an observer of the conflict.

Transcript 1

    15 John   [She did] ((pointing to Portia))

    16 Teacher [Then why] is she sad Portia why is she sad?

    17 John   She did she she she pulled her hand ((pointing to Portia and then Elana))

    18 Teacher Did you pull her hand Portia but why is Elana crying yu'you have to tell me so we can solve the problem (2.0) Do you think you can talk to Elana and make her feel better? (1.0) Can you make her feel better? because she's feeling a bit sad at the moment. ((Elana remains silent.))

John's account finds a description which partly satisfies the teacher by naming the culprit. His response is not neutral; but like a referee's call, 'highly charged with effect' (Goodwin, 1995, p. 267) as his call credits one child (Portia) as creating the problem. Neither Portia nor Amelia challenge his account.

The teacher's response, 'Did you pull her hand Portia *but* why is Elana crying' (turn 18), with the emphasis on 'but', may signify that John's account does not fully satisfy the teacher. She wants more. It appears that she wants Portia to confess to the particular crime of having hurt another's feelings. It may be that the teacher wants to hear a version of the invited story that she had previously supplied (about hurt feelings in turn 11). To do this, Portia would have to account for her actions in ways prescribed by the teacher. While this would have Portia presenting a moral version of herself (Silverman, 1987) that would satisfy the teacher, this account does not take into account the breach of the pretend play. Portia does not provide the requested account at this time but later, in the repair process, we see this offered account by the teacher being taken up and used by Portia.

In Transcript 2, on the other hand, David responds quickly to the teacher's question. David, at this moment, is caught between the social order of the teacher and that of the boys. He must say something to the teacher that answers her question. At the same time, whatever he says must also work towards maintaining his membership within the social order of the boys. He tells the teacher, 'We're just talking to him' (turn 28). While the teacher had made David accountable and his response provides an account that the teacher appears to accept, his account also informs the other boys who are a silent overhearing audience (Heritage, 1985). His account here, shows the others (John, for example) what to say when the teacher comes.

Transcript 2

    27 Teacher ((touching David)) David, what's the problem with Connell. ((Connell is still crying loudly, looks up briefly at the teacher and then John, who is still standing nearby and is now swinging a small plastic car towards Connell.))

→ 28 David   ((turning away from Connell towards the teacher,
                  but looking at the block shelf and touching the
                  blocks))=We're just talking to him. ((John looks
                  on, standing a little away.))

In his account, David denies any injury or any attempt to injure Connell. His explanation attempts to exonerate himself from what happened; his response suggests he sees the problem not as his but as Connell's. David could be signalling that Connell is 'marked' (Psathas, 1995) because, through his crying, he did not fully understand threatening verbal exchanges are part of the masculine practices of the block area.

In each episode, the teacher does not ask either Elana or Connell, the crying children, why they are upset. By asking Portia and Amelia, and David, to talk for them, the teacher could assume that upset children cannot speak for themselves and so constitutes them as less than full members of the group (Payne and Ridge, 1985; Speier, 1982). She may suspect that she will receive a more immediate answer from a non-crying child than a crying child, thus hastening a possible resolution. Her willingness to seek the expedient option suggests to us that she may be unaware of or uninterested in finding the underlying cause of the children's unsettled order. Rather, her focus appears to be one of soothing hurt feelings. When the crying stops and her sense of the classroom social order is settled, her version of repairing classroom order is complete and her work is done. The disparity between the children's accomplishment of social order as described below and the teacher's serves to illustrate the difference of social orders between the teacher and children.

As the teacher talks about Elana and Connell in their presence, she refers to them as having 'hurt feelings' (Transcript 1: turns 11, 13) and being 'sad' (Transcript 1: turns 16, 18; Transcript 2: turn 29). The teacher has created a particular category for them, the category of 'the sad child.' This category appears designed to provide maximum consolation and caring by the teacher and at the same time, to put the instigators on the spot by having them take responsibility and making them accountable for their actions. Using Maynard's (1985) argument discussed in the previous phase, the cry for help from Elana and Connell could now be seen as specifically designed to promote these particular responses from the teacher. As subsequent data shows, this strategy appears particularly effective for Elana but not as effective for Connell. While both situations have participants seeking to mitigate interrupted relations, the data shows Amelia and Portia seeking to soothe over their previous actions towards Elana while David seeks to explain his to Connell. It could be argued that Elana was aware of the power of crying as a political move and its positive consequences for her, but Connell's cry for help was simply that, a cry for help. He could no longer stand the conflict and resorted to a disastrous political move in terms of his construction of a masculine identity in this male group.

In both episodes, the teacher requires a response from the suspected culprits. In Transcript 1, with Amelia and Portia, she insists that one of them speak while in Transcript 2, David is forthcoming with a response. The problem should be obvious — Elana and Connell are crying. But the problem to the teacher is not just that

Elana and Connell are crying. The crying is accountable because it involves the teacher's problem, which we have identified as that of having hurt feelings. The teacher imposes a moral charge, that hurt feelings are more important than hurt arms.

In Transcript 1, after a two second silence, the teacher changes her tactic to one of repair. Despite some attempts seeking to find the cause of the problems, she now moves to fix it without really determining the reason. The teacher's move from trying to solve the problem to repairing hurt feelings suggests that the teacher is not as concerned about the cause of Elana's crying as she is about soothing hurt feelings.

Transcript 1

→ 18 Teacher Did you pull her hand Portia but why is Elana
              crying yu' you have to tell me so we can solve the
              problem (2.0) Do you think you can talk to Elana
              and make her feel better? (1.0) Can you make her
              feel better? because she's feeling a bit sad at
              the moment. ((Elana remains silent.))

  19   ((Portia starts to walk away, turns, goes to
              Elana and gives her a hug; Elana looks down and
              remains silent; Amelia watches.))

In this silence looms the gap between children's social order and the teacher's. Portia's following action of giving a hug (turn 19) suggests that she now moves to operate within the teacher's discourse of care and consolation. This pragmatic move will enable the teacher to resolve the children's 'problem' as she had defined it for them so that her work is done.

Despite Elana crying, and John's account that Elana's hand had been pulled, the teacher does not ask Elana about a possible physical injury but continues to focus on Elana's hurt feelings. The understatements that Connell is 'very sad' (turn 29) when crying loudly, that Elana is 'upset' and 'sad' (turn 10) and 'crying' (turn 11) when in fact she is silent, suggest a stylized response by the teacher. This appears particularly so because the teacher's response in each situation is almost identical, yet the hurt children's responses are not. Connell cries (at varying intensity) all throughout the teacher's intervention (turns 26–42) and only stops after his nose is wiped. Elana cries briefly (turns 5–8) but stops before the teacher first calls out from afar (turn 10). Yet, the teacher uses the same strategy to deal with the problem. The accepted solution, a hug (turn 19), is one that is meant to address the hurt feelings, not the physical injury. The expectation that the hurt child needs to be made feel better becomes the vehicle for the teacher's moral lesson on care and consolation.

As we have noted, the teacher calling on Portia to help make Elana feel better (turn 18) is a typical response reflecting early childhood notions of pedagogy. The following example from an early childhood text demonstrates the importance given in early childhood pedagogy to making hurt feelings feel better:

> **Examples of ways of talking with children in conflict situations**:
> 'That hurt Althea's feelings and she's really sad now. Please stay with me —
> maybe we can help her feel better' (Feeney et al., 1991, p. 272 italics and
> bold type as in original).

This way of talking about the problem of hurt feelings is also found in the second
episode. The teacher attempts to resolve the conflict in ways that nurture Connell,
the distressed child. She asks David, 'Well, could you make him feel better please?'
(turn 29).

Transcript 2

→　29　Teacher　Well, he looks very sad. Look at his face.
　　　　　　　　　　((Connell appears to be crying more loudly with
　　　　　　　　　　his mouth wide open, almost a wail.)) (1.0) Does
　　　　　　　　　　he look happy? ((David looks up at the teacher.))
　　　　　　　　　　Well, can you make him feel better please?

　　　30　David　　((David is standing on the bottom shelf of the
　　　　　　　　　　block shelves, he starts to swing away from the
　　　　　　　　　　teacher and Connell; Connell is now crying more
　　　　　　　　　　loudly.))

In both episodes, the teacher uses a social problem solving strategy as a way of
inducing the 'culprits' to make the hurt child feel better. This in effect makes them
into culprits within the teacher's classroom order. At first glance, the teacher appears to be asking open-ended types of questions: What could you do to make the
hurt child feel better? It is possible to construct the belief that Portia and David
have the freedom to choose (Davies, 1993; Walkerdine and Lucey, 1989). At the
same time, however, the teacher is subjecting them to a set of values that will
restrict their choices (Davies, 1993). In fact, the teacher issues directives that they
must do something. Both Portia (turn 19) and David (turn 33) know the parameters
within which they can respond, and consequently they choose their responses to fall
within what is suggested and accepted by the teacher.

Transcript 1

　　　19　　　　　　　((Portia starts to walk away, turns, goes to
　　　　　　　　　　Elana and gives her a hug; Elana looks down and
　　　　　　　　　　remains silent; Amelia watches.))

Transcript 2

　　　33　Teacher　O-Okay, give him a cuddle. ((David leans across
　　　　　　　　　　for a fleeting moment to put an arm around
　　　　　　　　　　Connell)) (and) what else did you say could you
　　　　　　　　　　say make him feel better?

Portia and David each give the hurt child a hug. The teacher's moral lesson on providing care and consolation has been accomplished, at least for the teacher.

In both episodes, the teacher now encourages the hurt, but now soothed, children to return to their play. The children's hurt feelings are presumed by the teacher to vanish quickly upon the giving of the hugs. This is despite the hugs, particularly David's hug to Connell, being at best fleeting. The teacher's comment to Elana, 'Go and play again?' (turn 22) and to Connell, 'Are you going to build with the blocks now?' (turn 42), suggest that she sees the job or duty of children is to play. This fits within a commonsense notion that play is a natural function of childhood. Under this version of 'natural life' (Atkinson, 1980), a child who is crying (and thus not playing in a proper way) implies a defective version of childhood and consequently a defective child. By returning children to their play, the teacher restores the presumed natural order of childhood. The teacher's departure may suggest that she sees this work of hers as finished, as her problem of a crying child with hurt feelings and a disrupted classroom are solved. It is now the children's turn to repair what has happened to them. This occurs in the third phase, which explores what the children do in the wake of the teacher's intervention to restore their own unsettled order.

Phase 3: The Problem of Restoring Social Order Among the Participants

While the teacher's leaving suggests that she sees the conflict as resolved so that play can continue as before, this phase shows that the hug (Transcript 1; turn 19) or the cuddle (Transcript 2; turn 33) does not conclude or repair the children's problem of unsettled social order. There is more work needed, it seems.

In Transcript 1, this is achieved through an intricate choreography of care and condolence orchestrated among Amelia, Portia, and Elana. This non-verbal weaving of bodies across the spaces of the classroom only became visible on repeated viewing of the video data and certainly was not visible to either the teacher or researcher when it took place. But before the non-verbal choreography of care is begun, Portia and Amelia have unfinished business. They walk to book corner and have the following conversation.

Transcript 1

```
    24  Portia  ((to Amelia)) (    ) Go and make Elana feel better
                 (1.0) go and make her ((nodding towards Elana))
                 [feel better]

    25  Amelia  [II didn't] do (anything)

→   26  Portia  Yes you did

    27  Amelia  No:o ((shaking her head))
```

```
28              (5.0) ((Amelia and Portia look at each other;
                Portia looks away and back again.))

29  Portia  (    ) ((in a very quiet voice))
```

The realignment of power and social identities is at stake here and opposition is effective in accomplishing this (Goodwin and Goodwin, 1987). Goodwin and Goodwin discuss how children seek opportunities to 'test or realign the current arrangement of social positions among their peers' (*ibid.*, p. 205). Portia is the one who grabbed Elana's arm but Portia wants Amelia to do the repair. It could be argued that Portia chose to take action, realigning her current position from that of being seen as the cause of the problem to that of helping Elana feel better. Portia engages Amelia in a 'character contest' (Goffman, in Goodwin and Goodwin, *ibid.*). Portia, by her blaming of Amelia, and then her fierce opposition to Amelia's claims of innocence, tries to realign herself as a different 'character.'

Turn 26, the partial repetition of talk from the previous turn, locates the 'trouble source' (Goodwin and Goodwin, 1987, p. 207) in the other's talk. After Amelia asserts that she 'didn't do anything' (turn 25), Portia's emphatic 'yes you did' (turn 26) highlights her opposition. As 'yes' begins Portia's turn, it does not disguise, but indeed emphasizes, opposition (*ibid.*) to Amelia's assertion. So too does Amelia's single oppositional utterance, 'No:o' (turn 27). Goodwin and Goodwin write that children do not disguise their opposition in conversations, unlike adults who will hedge and use delaying tactics to mitigate the disagreement.

While neither Portia nor Amelia admit to the problem of causing Elana's hurt feelings, their conversation suggests that they agree that this is a problem still. As evidenced in the segment below, Portia reproduces the very words used by the teacher when she tells Amelia to 'Go and make Elana feel better' (turn 24).

Transcript 1

```
18  Teacher  Did you pull her hand Portia but why is Elana
             crying yu' you have to tell me so we can solve the
             problem (2.0) Do you think you can talk to Elana
             and make her feel better? (1.0) Can you make her
             feel better? because she's feeling a bit sad at
             the moment. ((Elana remains silent.))

and:

24  Portia   ((to Amelia)) (    ) Go and make Elana feel better
             (1.0) go and make her ((nodding towards Elana))
             [feel better]
```

The echoing of the same words and sentiments is manifested as some acknowledgment of the guilt and responsibility assigned by the teacher and taken up by Portia. Portia's use of the imperative form or directive ('Go and make Elana feel better') is not a typical linguistic feature of girls' talk (Sachs, 1987). It may be that Portia, in appropriating the teacher's discourse of care and consolation, has also appropriated the directing nature of the teacher's question, signalling to us Portia's immersion in and acceptance of the teacher's version of social order.

It is the duty of consolation, assigned first by the teacher and then by Portia, which propels Amelia, despite her assertion of innocence, to leave book corner and approach Elana at the puzzle table. This is when the choreography of care and consolation occurs:

Transcript 1

30	((Amelia immediately walks over to the puzzle table, the other side of the room, where Elana is standing with a book. Amelia sits down and glances briefly as Elana walks away.))
31	((Elana walks away looking at the book until she stands in front of book corner, but facing away from Portia, looks up, and swings arms and book from side to side, looks briefly at researcher.))
32	((Portia walks out of book corner, past Elana on her way to her locker, and pulls out something from her locker and then replaces it.))
33	((Amelia leaves the puzzle table and brushes past Elana towards the preparation room.)) whe whe whe (in a rhythmic fashion)
34	((John brushes past Elana)) ( ) ((says something to Amelia))
35	((Portia brushes past Elana, giving her a brief glance, and goes to the preparation room, meeting the teacher as she comes out)) ( )
36	((Teacher acknowledges Portia by a look and weaves around her as she keeps walking; Portia stops and holds her dress.))
37	((Amelia and Elana talk briefly to each other. Amelia then walks into home corner and Elana follows.))
38	((Portia goes to sit beside the teacher assistant in manipulative area.))

Bodies weave close to each other and brush against each other. They show a knowledge of an 'art of walking' (Ryave and Schenkein, 1974) finely tuned to the physical and relational circumstances of this preschool space. Finally, in turn 37, Amelia and Elana talk briefly to each other, Amelia returns to home corner and Elana follows. This suggests that the repair work on the relationship, at least between Amelia and Elana, is accomplished. Portia and Amelia, and to a lesser extent

John, enacted their repair by brushing past Elana. In turn 37, Elana and Amelia
finally reconnect through words, but the major repair work was already done through
the physical membership work of approaching Elana. This non-verbal repair finally
results in Elana being able to talk to Amelia again. Elana and Amelia are together
again in home corner but Portia is alone.

The repair sought by the girls featured qualities of talking to each other and
togetherness, which Nilan (1991) describes as the moral order of girls' friendships.
Care is built through a web of connection and relationships (Gilligan, 1982). While
Elana and Amelia reconnect their relationship, Portia does not. After her attempted
unsuccessful reconnection with Elana, Portia endeavours a repair with the teacher
but the teacher sidesteps her (turn 36). Portia then moves to another part of the room,
where the manipulative materials are, and sits near the teacher assistant (turn 38).
Portia's isolation from Amelia and Elana suggests to us that her initial transgression
of the moral order of togetherness and friendship (Nilan, 1991) (by physically
breaching the pretend play) excludes her now from the relationship with Amelia
and Elana despite Portia's earlier efforts to repair the social order with them. In this
way, Elana's and Amelia's exclusion of Portia further affirms their belonging to a
moral order of togetherness and care (*ibid.*) while demonstrating what happens to
those who rupture it.

The social order of the girls' episode is in sharp contrast to that in the boys'
episode. There, David, a central player, does not accept the feminized discursive
position offered by the teacher. He is not concerned with making Connell, the hurt
child, feel better. Instead, when the teacher goes to get a tissue, he puts his finger
under Connell's chin and tells him that 'it was a joke'. While the teacher's attention
is diverted as she gets a tissue, he uses the first opportunity that he can to assert
his other version of events to Connell.

Transcript 2

	35	Teacher	Is that are you feeling okay now Connell? ((Connell shakes his head and continues crying.)) We get you a tissue? Wipe the tears away? ((Teacher leaves for a tissue.))
	36	John	((steps closer and swings the plastic car close to Connell's body))
→	37	David	((Connell is still crying quietly; David looks at the teacher leaving and then puts his finger gently under Connell's chin, talking in a cajoling tone. Andrew, who has been playing nearby, stands beside Connell and looks at David.)) ( ) it was a joke ((turns towards John)) ( ) a joke
	38	Teacher	((Teacher returns; Connell starts crying more loudly; teacher wipes Connell's nose.)) Wipe the tissues away?

In the teacher's absence, David discounts the teacher's caring discourse by replacing it with his own local male version. There appears to be no damage to his inner self here; he, unlike Portia, does not try to implicate someone else or even be seen to accept any guilt or responsibility for Connell's crying. Unlike the girls, he does not accept a relationship requiring care and consolation. In his version of the event, no relationship or person is mentioned, and so his actions typify what Gilligan (1982) describes as males operating independently of relationships but within a hierarchy of order (for example, ability, height) which serves to distance males, one from another.

Davies (1989) suggests that boys generally find ways to circumvent adult power and construct their sense of maleness independently of the female teacher. This episode is an encapsulation of this. By redefining the situation when the teacher leaves to get a tissue, he effectively undermines her while appearing to agree to the hug and to the discourse of consolation and care. This shows the distance between the worlds of teachers and children. It also shows children operating in the worlds of adults as well as in their own worlds, a sophisticated achievement not reciprocated by adults (Payne and Ridge, 1985).

David treats the teacher's discourse of consolation as an interruption to more important things (the boys immediately return to talk about size). In this way, David makes immediate use of the teacher's intervention as more material around which to organize masculinity. In effect he makes the teacher's version of social order a foil for his own. David even goes so far as to dispute the feminized discourse of care that has been demonstrated by the teacher. Positioned powerfully, he turns his back to her and contradicts her stated views (and consequently her authority) by openly disagreeing with her about whether the younger boys should be allowed to play in the block area.

Transcript 2

43	David	Bpp, bpp, bpp ((a play sound rising in tone)) they should(n't) even be (here) ((David is leaning against the block shelf, facing away from the teacher.))
44	Teacher	Well Dave, if you can't co-operate with the little ones in the group, you'll have to find something for you to play with away from them=((David walks away with his back towards the teacher as she talks.))
45	John	((standing nearby then starts to play with blocks))
46	David	((jumps over blocks, makes a play sound))=They're not even four.

The teacher responds to David by calling him 'Dave' (turn 44). This could be heard as her appeal for his cooperation. Walkerdine (1986) argues that the teacher cannot insist on compliance as this could be seen as 'a dangerous voice from the past, the spectre of authoritarianism, of the old ways, of overt power and regulation' (p. 60). This reluctance further strengthens David's position of assertive masculinity while diminishing the power of the teacher's nurturing and feminizing discourse. It also serves as a notice for Connell in highlighting the power of the masculine discourse within' which David is operating.

The third phase signals the conclusion of each episode that began with a crying child. The children used the intervention of the teacher to pursue and restore their respective social orders and as we described, our analysis reveals the gendered work of the participants in this restoration of order. We found, as Gilligan (1982) did, girls weaving a web of care through their relationships while the boys focused on the hierarchy of power and ability and distanced themselves from the caring they were meant by the teacher to do.

Conclusion: Three Definitions of 'What's the Problem?'

When the teacher asked, 'What's the problem?' the problem initially appears to be that of an upset child. This initial defining of 'problem' however is only one of three ways that we have identified that the 'problem' can be defined. Each of the three interpretations depends upon particular viewpoints of participants. The first way, as we initially suggested, saw the problem as a crying child in the classroom. This was the teacher's problem, as there is an expectation of harmony and co-operation existing in early childhood classrooms. The teacher therefore needed to resolve this situation. This way of viewing the problem is probably the one that is most often proposed and accepted in early childhood pedagogy.

The second way of viewing 'the problem' is closely aligned to the first. This view saw the problem as one child or children having hurt another child's feelings. This was also seen as the teacher's problem as she needed to make the hurt child feel better. But in order to do this, the teacher first had to make responsible for their actions those who did the hurting and then direct them towards consoling the hurt child. This involved the teacher relaying her problem, that of making a hurt child feel better, onto those whom she perceived made the hurt child cry. This second view encompasses, as part of the problem, the individual child whose feelings are hurt and who will have to overcome these sad feelings.

The third perspective saw 'the problem' as situated within the children's social orders. This perspective recognized that the children perceive that there is a problem which needed to be repaired, but their problem is different and is not resolved until the teacher departs. The teacher did not really attempt to resolve this problem of the children's unsettled social order; in fact, she appeared either unaware of or uninterested in it. The third problem is the one that the children themselves actively sought to restore upon the teacher's departure. It is the third definition of problem that most strongly suggests the disjunction between the children's social order and that of the teacher. It also most strongly suggests the competence of children in constructing and maintaining their social worlds. 'The problem' for Daniel and the boys seems to be: (i) Connell's attracting the teacher's attention through Connell's own incompetence; and (ii) the teacher's interruption to the more important work of constructing masculinity. 'The problem' for the girls who accept part of the teacher's version of social order appears to be the insufficiency of the hug. Their repair — of their own 'characters' and of their relationships — involves more work than the superficial hug. They appear to need to reconnect in other ways.

In early childhood pedagogy, strategies are suggested to help teachers to deal with conflict in their classrooms. The teacher is expected to respond immediately to the distressed child and to help the participants find a solution to the problem of conflict so that they can then return to their educationally valuable play. While these strategies may result in an appearance of classroom order being reestablished, this chapter has highlighted that this may in fact be an illusion. The children's work of restoring their own social orders occurs outside the audible and visual scrutiny of the teacher. The traditional approach to dealing with conflict in early childhood classrooms ignores the power of this work of restoring social order that is operating all the while the teacher is effecting her notion of repair. The children's gendered social order exists outside the teacher's known and sanctioned versions of play in the preschool classroom. Our identification of three perspectives of 'the problem' illustrates this complex and dynamic nature of children's social orders and the power of children working to restore their own social orders.

Appendix 1: Note on Transcription

Data are transcribed using a system created by Jefferson and described in Psathas (1995). The following are the features used in these transcripts.

( )	word(s) spoken but not audible
(was)	best guess for word(s) spoken
(( ))	transcriber's description
voice	normal speaking voice
but	emphasis
BUT	greater emphasis
[no]	two speakers' turns overlap at this point
=	no interval between turns
do::n't	sound extended
(2.0)	pause timed in seconds

Punctuation marks describe characteristics of speech production. They do not refer to grammatical units.

him-	a dash indicates a cut-off of the prior word
four.	a period indicates a stopping fall in tone
please?	a question mark indicates a rising intonation
away!	an exclamation mark indicates an animated tone

References

ATKINSON, M.A. (1980) 'Some practical uses of "a natural lifetime"', *Human Studies*, **3**, pp. 33–46.

ATKINSON, P. (1981) 'Inspecting classroom talk', in ADELMAN, C. (ed.) *Uttering, Muttering*, London: Grant McIntyre.

BAKER, C. (1997) 'Transcription and representation in literacy research', in FLOOD, J., HEATH, S.B. and LAPP, D. (eds) *A Handbook for Literacy Educators: Research on Teaching the Communicative and Visual Arts*, New York: Macmillan.

BREDEKAMP, S. (1987) *Developmentally Appropriate Practice in Early Childhood Programs Serving Children from Birth through Age 8* (expanded edn). Washington, DC: National Association for the Education of Young Children.

CORSARO, W.A. (1985) *Friendship and Peer Culture in the Early Years*, Norwood, NJ: Ablex.

CORSARO, W.A. (1997) *The Sociology of Childhood*, Thousand Oaks, CA: Pine Forge Press.

CORSARO, W.A. and STREECK, J. (1986) 'Studying children's worlds: Methodological issues', in COOK-GUMPERZ, J., CORSARO, W. and STREECK, J. (eds) *Children's Worlds and Children's Language*, Berlin: Mouton de Gruyter.

DANBY, S. (1996) 'Constituting social membership: Two readings of talk in an early childhood classroom', *Language and Education*, **10**, pp. 151–70.

DAVIES, B. (1982) *Life in the Classroom and Playground: The Accounts of Primary School Children*, London: Routledge and Kegan Paul.

DAVIES, B. (1989) *Frogs and Snails and Feminist Tales: Preschool Children and Gender*, Sydney: Allen and Unwin.

DAVIES, B. (1993) *Shards of Glass*, St Leonards, NSW: Allen and Unwin.

DENZIN, N.K. (1982) 'The work of little children', in JENKS, C. (ed.) *The Sociology of Childhood: Essential Readings*, Aldershot: Gregg Revivals.

DENZIN, N.K. (1989) *The Research Act: A Theoretical Introduction to Sociological Methods*, (3rd edn), Englewood Cliffs, NJ: Prentice Hall.

EVALDSSON, A.-C. (1993) *Play Disputes and Social Order: Everyday Life in Two Swedish After-school Centers*, Linkoping: Linkoping University.

FEENEY, S., CHRISTENSEN, D. and MORAVCIK, E. (1991) *Who am I in the Lives of Children?* Englewood Cliffs, NJ: Prentice Hall.

GARFINKEL, H. (1967) *Studies in Ethnomethodology*, Englewood Cliffs, NJ: Prentice-Hall.

GILLIGAN, C. (1982) *In a Different Voice: Psychological Theory and Women's Development*, Cambridge, MA: Harvard University Press.

GOODE, D. (1994) *A World Without Words: The Social Construction of Children Born Deaf and Blind*, Philadelphia, PA: Temple University Press.

GOODWIN, M.H. (1985) 'The serious side of jump rope: Conversational practices and social organization in the frame of play', *Journal of American Folklore*, **98**, pp. 315–30.

GOODWIN, M.H. (1990) *He-said-she-said: Talk as Social Organization Among Black Children*, Bloomington, IN: Indiana University Press.

GOODWIN, M.H. (1995) 'Co-construction in girls' hopscotch', *Research on Language and Social Interaction*, **28**, pp. 261–81.

GOODWIN, M.H. and GOODWIN, C. (1987) 'Children's arguing', in PHILIPS, S.U., STEELE, S. and TANZ, C. (eds) *Language, Gender and Sex in Comparative Perspective*, Cambridge: Cambridge University Press.

HERITAGE, J. (1984) *Garfinkel and Ethnomethodology*, Oxford: Polity Press.

HERITAGE, J. (1985) 'Analysing news interviews: Aspects of the production of talk for an overhearing audience', in VAN DIJK, T.A. (ed.) *Handbook of Discourse Analysis, Volume 3*, London: Academic Press.

JACOB, E. (1987) 'Qualitative research traditions: A review', *Review of Educational Research*, **57**, pp. 1–50.

JENKS, C. (1989) 'Social theorizing and the child', DOXIADIS S. (ed.) *Early Influences Shaping the Individual: NATO Advanced Study Workshop*, London: Plemum Press.

KAMLER, B., MACLEAN, R., REID, J.-A. and SIMPSON, A. (1994) 'Shaping up nicely: The formation of schoolgirls and schoolboys in the first month of school', Report to the Gender Equity and Curriculum Reform Project, Department of Employment, Education and Training, Canberra, Australian Government Printing Service.

KANTOR, R., ELGAS, P.M. and FERNIE, D. (1993) 'Cultural knowledge and social competence within a preschool peer culture group', *Early Childhood Research Quarterly*, **8**: pp. 125–47.

MACKAY, R.W. (1991) 'Conceptions of children and models of socialization', in WAKSLER, F.C. (ed.) *Studying the Social Worlds of Children: Sociological Readings*, London: Falmer Press.

MAYNARD, D.W. (1985) 'On the functions of social conflict among children', *American Sociological Review*, **50**, pp. 207–23.

MEHAN, H. (1979) *Learning Lesson: Social Organisation in the Classroom*, Cambridge, MA: Harvard University Press.

MEHAN, H. (1993) 'Why I like to look: On the use of videotape as an instrument in educational research', in SCHRATZ, M. (ed.) *Qualitative Voices in Educational Research*, London: Falmer Press.

NATIONAL CHILDCARE ACCREDITATION COUNCIL (1993) *Putting Children First: Quality Improvement and Accreditation System Handbook*, Sydney: National Childcare Accreditation Council.

NILAN, P. (1991) 'Exclusion, inclusion and moral ordering in two girls' friendship groups', *Gender and Education*, **3**, pp. 163–82.

PALEY, V.G. (1984) *Boys and Girls: Superheroes in the Doll Corner*, Chicago, IL: University of Chicago Press.

PAYNE, G. and RIDGE, E. (1985) ' "Let then talk" — An alternative approach to language development in the infant school', in CUFF, E.C. and PAYNE, G.C.F. (eds) *Crisis in the Curriculum*, London: Croom Helm.

PSATHAS, G. (1995) *Conversation Analysis: The Study of Talk-in-interaction*, Thousand Oaks, CA: Sage.

REID, J.-A., KAMLER, B., SIMPSON, A. and MACLEAN, R. (1996) ' "Do you see what I see?" Reading a different classroom scene', *International Journal of Qualitative Studies in Education*, **9**, pp. 87–108.

RYAVE, L. and SCHENKEIN, J.N. (1974) 'Notes on the art of walking', in TURNER, R. (ed.) *Ethnomethodology: Selected Readings*, Harmondsworth: Penguin Education.

SACHS, J. (1987) 'Preschool boys' and girls' language use in pretend play', in PHILIPS, S.U., STEELE, S. and TANZ, C. (eds) *Language, Gender, and Sex in Comparative Perspective*, Cambridge: Cambridge University Press.

SACKS, H. (1974) 'On the analysability of stories by children', in Turner, R. (ed.) *Ethnomethodology: Selected Readings*, Harmondsworth: Penguin Education.

SACKS, H. (1984a) 'Notes on methodology', in ATKINSON, J.M. and HERITAGE, J. (eds) *Structures of Social Action: Studies in Conversation Analysis*, Cambridge: Cambridge University Press.

SACKS, H. (1984b) 'On doing "being ordinary"', in ATKINSON, J.M. and HERITAGE, J. (eds) *Structures of Social Action: Studies in Conversation Analysis*, Cambridge: Cambridge University Press.

SACKS, H. (1992). *Lectures on Conversation*, (2 volumes, edited by G. Jefferson.), Oxford: Blackwell.

SHELDON, A. (1990) 'Pickle fights: Gendered talk in preschool disputes', *Discourse Processes*, **13**, pp. 5–31.

SHELDON, A. (1992) 'Preschool girls' discourse competence: Managing conflict', in HALL, K., BUCHOLTZ, M. and MOONWOMON, B. (eds) *Locating Power: Proceedings of the Second Berkeley Women and Language Conference*, Berkeley, CA: University of California, Berkeley Linguistics Group.

SHELDON, A. (1996) 'You can be the baby brother, but you aren't born yet: Preschool girls' negotiation for power and access in pretend play', *Research on Language and Social Interaction*, **29**, pp. 57–80.

SILVERMAN, D. (1987) *Communication and Medical Practice*, London: Sage.

SILVERMAN, D. (1993) *Interpreting Qualitative Data: Methods for Analysing Talk, Text and Interaction*, London: Sage.

SILVERMAN, D. (1994) 'Competing strategies for analysing the contexts of social interaction', *Sociological Inquiry*, **64**, pp. 179–98.

SPEIER, M. (1976) 'The child as conversationalist: Some culture contact features of conversational interactions between adults and children', in HAMMERSLEY, M. and WOODS, P. (eds) *The Process of Schooling: A Sociological Reader*, London: Routledge and Kegan Paul.

SPEIER, M. (1982) 'The everyday world of the child', in JENKS, C. (ed.) *The Sociology of Childhood: Essential Readings*, Aldershot: Gregg Revivals.

STONE, J.G. (1990) *Teaching Preschoolers: It Looks Like This . . . in Pictures*, Washington, DC: National Association for the Education of Young Children.

THORNE, B. (1993) *Gender Play*, Buckingham: Open University Press.

WAKSLER, F.C. (1991) 'Dancing when the music is over: A study of deviance in a kindergarten classroom', in WAKSLER, F.C. (ed.) *Studying the Social Worlds of Children: Sociological Readings*, London: Falmer Press.

WALKERDINE, V. (1986) 'Post-structuralist theory and everyday social practices: The family and the school', in WILKINSON, S. (ed.) *Feminist Social Psychology: Developing Theory and Practice*, Milton Keynes: Open University Press.

WALKERDINE, V. and LUCEY, H. (1989) *Democracy in the Kitchen: Regulating Mothers and Socialising Daughters*, London: Virago.

WATSON, D.R. (1990) 'Some features of the elicitation of confessions in murder interrogations', in PSATHAS, G. (ed.) *Interaction Competence*, Washington, DC: University Press of America.

Chapter 9

Difference and Similarity: How Children's Competence is Constituted in Illness and Its Treatment

Pia Haudrup Christensen

Visibility and Social Representation

Traditional perspectives in the study of childhood health and illness emphasize the child as a subject 'acted upon by others'.[1] Most research interests have primarily considered adults' perspectives (such as mothers' and professionals'), perhaps including observable assessments of child health or focusing on different external factors and conditions of children's lives. Such perspectives leave more or less unaddressed the understanding of the child as a social person with their own experiences, perceptions and actions in the social and cultural world.

This chapter is based on an ethnographic study of children's experiences and agency in health care conducted in a local district of Copenhagen, Denmark. The study shows that children's specific contributions provide important understandings of the dynamics of family based health care in particular as well as the health care system as a whole. I use a 'vertical' view (Nader, 1981) to reveal the complex relationship between children and the formal and informal hierarchies that influence their lives. In doing so I suggest that the hierarchical relationships of biomedicine can be seen as reaching into the family. Children's position within these formal hierarchies is constrained and dependent because children's status is constituted as inferior to adults in general and health professionals in particular. This point is convincingly demonstrated in studies of Strong (1979) and Davis (1982) who through careful observations revealed the processes by which children became muted actors in clinical consultations. Whilst doctors and parents specifically encouraged the enrolment and collaboration of babies and infants in clinical examinations, in the case of older children, who might be expected to have gained more competence, adults would paradoxically seek to constrain the active and independent participation of the child.

Ethnographic work more specifically investigating children's agency in illness confirms that children can no longer be comprehended as passive recipients but must be understood as active participants. Two pioneering studies focused on the role of children in everyday social negotiations of sickness with mothers and teachers (Prout, 1988) and with parents and health professionals in hospital (Bluebond-Langner, 1978 and 1991). Prout's study of school sickness absence in a small community in England showed how children, without having any formal power in decision-making, had important influence through informal interaction such as persistent claims of illness or by feigning symptoms. Myra Bluebond-Langner's study of leukemic children addressed the different sources that children used in making sense of their illness (1978, p. 181). This study made evident how children involved each other in conceptualizing their illness. Children read clues off pharmaceuticals, adults' behaviour and treatments in order to make sense of their illness. Then they exchanged and discussed this information with their peers in the hospital ward.

The problems that these studies attempt to tackle are not solely located within childhood health research. In recent years claims have been made for the 'lack of visibility' of children within the academic disciplines (Hardman, 1978; Alanen, 1988; James and Prout, 1990; Qvortrup, 1991). These claims may seem superfluous in view of the apparent centrality of children in European and North American cultures, exhibited in the highly staged material and symbolic worlds of modern childhood. The aim, however, has been to contest some traditional perspectives that have neglected or only left children little influence over their own social representation, the importance of which is emphasized by Dyer's (1993) statement that, 'How we are seen determines in part how we are treated, how we treat others is based on how we see them; such seeing comes from representation' (p. 1).

The Cultural Constitution of Difference and Similarity

Within the social and cultural sciences various efforts have been made to re-examine the conceptual frameworks that influence the ways that children are represented. For the purpose of this chapter I will take departure from Jenks' investigation (1982) of the ways children are constituted in social and cultural theory. Jenks revealed what could be seen as a ceaseless paradox. He writes:

> The child is familiar to us and yet strange, she/he inhabits our world and yet seems
> to answer to another, she/he is essentially of ourselves and yet appears to display
> a different order of being. (p. 9)

The child cannot be imagined in the absence of an idea about what an adult is just as it is impossible to picture an adult and his/her society without positing the child. The ambiguity in the relationship between the child and the adult is encapsulated in the notion of 'difference'. This perception of 'difference', Jenks suggests, may be attributed to a theoretical focus on the social processes of overcoming it — that is, socialization. It is an underlying Western cultural premise that 'people are made, not born' (Riesman, 1990). In this view people are made what they become through the influence of their parents and education which is seen as essential for their successful development and future life. The emphasis is therefore put on understanding children in terms of 'becoming' rather than 'being' a social person. Thus at the same time as child and adult are seen to form a continuum, there is an implication of a socially and culturally constituted opposition, an opposition which designates not only difference but also hierarchy. Crawford's (1994) suggestion that 'stigmatizing images of the other are founded in a social self which needs this other' may, in regard to children, suggest that to establish the norm of the adult as an independent, responsible and competent person necessarily constitutes its opposite which at the same time is its complement through notions of vulnerability, dependency and incompetence in children.

But, as is implied in the notion of becoming, the relationship between the categories of child and adult, whilst depending on the construction of difference cannot be simply characterized by this alone. For difference is only one side of the processes through which social and cultural relations are made, maintained, reproduced and transformed. As Douglas (1975), in a large body of work on cultural theory has persistently argued, cultures can be understood by what they do and do not allow to be brought together. There is always, therefore, the possibility that cultural categories are enmeshed in relations of sameness as well as difference. This point can be taken further when the possibility that social relations might be constituted precisely through 'partial connections' (Strathern, 1992): a formulation that allows for more fluid, mobile and heterogeneous sets of difference and similarity than Douglas's more static conceptualization. In this sense social and cultural relations might be thought to involve both bringing items in its repertoire together and keeping them separate. The contradiction is only apparent. Sameness and difference (i.e. the work of making connection and disconnection) might go on in different times and spaces, at different points in a process — or, as also seems likely, held in tension through moment by moment interaction.

It might be noted that in the above discussion, an implicit shift has been made from culture as the moving force (that does something) towards culture as a less solid phenomenon that is constructed through the situated activities, practices both discursive and non-discursive, of connection and disconnection. Latour (1993) refers to one side of this equation as the work of purification — by which he means the work that goes into keeping things apart — for it is not reified culture that does this but social actors. On the other side we might speak of the labour of connection by which things or persons (such as children and adults) are brought into proximity, made to interact and through which, it might be suggested, they are made to be more similar (or at least less different).

This chapter draws on a Danish ethnographic study in order to examine the various practices through which children's and adults' competence are made similar or different. In a cultural approach 'competence' is understood not as a psychological property of an individual but as a relational constitution or attribution that is socially constructed and negotiated. In everyday child illness these constitutions centre around practices of therapy and are particularly illustrated in the use of pharmaceuticals. Through these practices children learn not only the instrumental and other contingencies of how to perform sickness in a particular, Danish, context but also how to enter into broad social relations concerned with age hierarchies. This engagement is, however, not constituted as a simple hierarchy in which children are always and to the same scale in a subordinated position. Rather child-adult relations are constituted in more varied and mobile ways on a continuum of difference and similarity. This is partly because there is a divergence between cultural categories and real actors' everyday experience and practice. Children and adults do not belong to a fixed category of child or adult. Eventually children are going to grow into the category of adult, a transition which is not fixed in time or place. Furthermore, in everyday interactions both children and adults observe situations and contexts where adults exhibit incompetence and children act competently and skilfully. This again leaves scope for interactions and negotiations which may obliterate or demarcate the accepted categorical positions.

The Study

The study took place in a local district of Copenhagen in Denmark with fourteen months of ethnographic fieldwork over two years. The focus was 6–11-year-old children's experiences and (inter)actions during everyday episodes of illness and minor accidents. It was carried out among children, their families and professionals in different situations and contexts of children's everyday life at home, school and after-school centres. The study used participant observation, ethnographic interviews and more purposeful data production methods such as children's essays, drawings and drama and adults' diaries.

Children as the Incompetent 'Speaker of Fact'

Therapies, therapeutic actions and particular medical examinations during illness constitute a field which engages both children and adults in producing difference and similarity of competence. In children's accounts, therapies had central importance for their understanding of illness and illness processes. As suggested in an earlier published paper based on Cohen's analytic conception of symbolic boundary markers (1985), practises such as specific medical examinations and therapies act as symbolic boundary markers in illness for children (Prout and Christensen, 1996). In our cross-cultural comparison of material produced with children in Denmark and in England [2] it was revealed how therapies helped children identify graduations of illness. Therapies acted as boundary markers distinguishing for children transitional stages in illness simultaneously enabling them to classify therapies and gain ideas about hierarchies of medicine. In general the start of a therapy marks the child's shift from health to illness and its cessation marks the move from illness to being well. Particular therapies such as the use of pharmaceuticals mark different degrees of illness.

Everyday interactions about illness and therapy constitute competence among adults and children. In general adults constitute themselves as competent by drawing on 'rational' knowledges and mediating devices (such as a thermometer) to classify children's mental and bodily experiences as 'real' illness. This simultaneously entails that children's competence becomes suspended; their subjective experiences of their own bodies do not qualify them as 'speakers of fact'. Adults accomplish this in a number of ways. First is the significance of temporal aspects such as 'duration' in adults' definition and classification of a condition and its severity. Both in the accounts of mothers, teachers and staff in the after-school centres and in my own observations of child-adult interactions, duration was an important referential point for adults in deciding whether a child was 'really ill' and whether his/her complaints were to be taken seriously (Christensen, 1997). A general theme in adults' accounts revealed for example that children 'might have a high temperature, 39°C or 40°C without being really ill'. This normalization of children's symptoms, adults related to what they perceived as rapid changes in children (*ibid.*). In adults' experiences a child could seem to be very ill with fever during a couple of hours at night and the next morning wake up fever free, refreshed and well again. Duration thus acted as an important boundary marker between a well or an ill child. A common adult response, (both at home and in the institutional settings) when a child said they were ill or felt unwell was: 'Go and sit down for twenty minutes and let's see if you'll feel better'. From adults' point of view time would reveal whether the child's claim was dependable and the child was 'really ill'. 'Duration of symptoms' constituted a point of comparison with adults' illness. If the child's symptoms endured over a period it validated for adults that the child was ill. However, if symptoms did not endure the child's claim was proven wrong and consequently they were not ill. From adults' perspectives the child's claim signified the unreliable and contestable aspects of children's illnesses and ultimately of children themselves.

This adults understood to be the result of one or a combination of the following factors. First, children may, in order to gain adult attention or be let off a demand, deliberately fake illness. However, the expectation was that children were not able to persevere in such pretended performances for a long time, thus 'time' and 'passive waiting' seemed an appropriate test of the child. Second was a psychosomatic explanation. If children felt neglected or lacked adult attention and care they would tend to express their psychological and social needs through claiming illness. Third, children forwarded 'false' claims of illness because of their inexperience and incompetence in interpretation and classification of mental and bodily experiences. In this situation the child expressed momentary bodily sensation because they could not, yet, distinguish between common experiences of healthy bodily processes and illness. Accordingly temporal contradictions in the subjective experiences of the 'natural course' of child illness epitomized the differences between children and adults in illness transitions and in social negotiations between them (Christensen, 1993). For adults, children's expressions of subjective experiences, 'I don't feel well', were translated into the task of defining 'Is there a disease?': a question for which they sought objective evidence in the child's body rather than engaging with the child's expressive statement in itself. In this way, the performance of the child-adult relationship mirrors what Kirmayer (1988) identified as important values of biomedical practice, that is, to keep rational control over and distance to bodily and emotional experiences.

Another important symbolic marker in the classification of an illness is temperature taking. A general understanding among 6–7- and 10–11-year-old children interviewed for this purpose was that they were the first person to recognize when they were ill. However there was also differences in the accounts of the children in the two different age groups. 6–7-year-old children would generally describe being ill as 'natural' and rather unspecific. One frequent phrase was, 'It does not feel very nice' or 'I did not feel well'. The youngest children would rarely attempt to label their condition specifically and the illness process would appear as almost instinctive. For example as Tina, 7 years old, described her last illness episode:

> I was lying in bed for three days reading Donald Duck, then I got well again and went back to school.

Even though none of the children in either age group expressed doubt in their ability to recognize that they were ill, 10–11-year-olds acknowledged that having fever was a determining factor in being accepted as ill by parents or teachers. Anna, 10 years old, told this story about her last illness. Anna said:

> I felt ill, then my dad took my temperature and he said, Yes you are ill.

Anna's father thus confirmed and validated Anna's own experience. Children also recognized that practices such as having one's temperature checked acted as the explicit confirmation of being well again. For example as Charlotte, 10 years old, wrote in an essay:

> 'I yawned and got out of bed. I took a glass of water because I was thirsty. Mummy shouted to me that I should go back to bed, but I said, I feel well now. Mummy looked at me and said, "We must take your temperature". It showed 37.2°C. Mummy exclaimed: "But, you are well!! Run out and play with the others, but wrap up well".'

Accounts such as these suggest that, on the one hand, children recognize that they have to go through the 'tests' but on the other hand they express no doubt in their own judgment. However, children also learn that their own views are less 'true' until confirmed by higher status adult action. A child cannot make this judgment on their own and their claim does not constitute a priori evidence. As evidence, it is neither necessary nor sufficient.

The above examples demonstrate that the examination of the child's body temperature was an important marker of 'illness' and 'well being' for children and for adults. When illness or health was established it facilitated other steps in the process of illness or recovery. For Charlotte, for example, her mother's recognition that Charlotte was well again meant that she was allowed to play outside. It seems that adults subject themselves to the 'rational' measures that objectify children's condition. However, as the following example shows, this was not only of significance in parental practice at home but was also important in the interactions and negotiations of children's everyday illness at school. The example shows that the overall importance of establishing children's status as well or ill lies in the fact that illness literally places children outside the domain of the school: to be ill is not to be at school but at home. In Prout's (1986) ethnography of an English primary school he pointed to the powerful role of the school secretary as gatekeeper in children's illness episodes. When confronted with a child's complaints of illness the school secretary took their temperature to conclude whether they were 'really' ill and consequently unable to stay at school — a procedure she conducted more or less detached from the accounts of their illness given by the children. Thus the school secretary established what she perceived as a reliable diagnosis. A child's vague bodily sensations were given a name: 'fever'. The typical practice of taking the child's temperature in the course of illness thus reveals itself as not only an instrumental act accomplishing a practical objective but at the same time an expressive symbol of the location of competence in adults (parents or professionals).

Situations such as the ones described above illustrate important elements of difference in the social relationships between child and adult. Illness classification indicates the position of the child as incompetent (as well as dependent, passive and subordinate) while the adult is seen as competent, active and in charge. These typifications are embodied and encoded in practices of surveillance and regulation. When a mother, or a staff member at school or an after-school institution check a child's temperature, there is the underlying notion that the adult acts as a competent and responsible carer. For example if a professional does not 'discover' that a child is ill they may in the eyes of parents (and sometimes even from an official or organizational perspective) appear irresponsible and neglectful. Likewise if a mother/parent does not carry out tasks such as taking the child's temperature (at the doctor's request) or giving a child their medication it questions the adult's ability and competencies and ultimately their status as a 'good mother' or 'good parent'. On the other hand the successful handling of the means and practices which served to determine children's health and illness demonstrate adult skills and competencies over and above those of the child. Through persistence and authority adults conduct procedures that inevitably exhibit particular competencies: keeping time, taking the temperature and reading the thermometer, opening the bottle of medicine (indeed the specially secured screwcap lids for 'child protection' mean that they cannot be opened by a child), determining the dose of medicine and making the child comply with taking the medicine (even when it tastes disgusting).

Many of these procedures, however, may also be acknowledged as practices that cannot be carried out by the adult single-handedly. They may involve a number of persons and at the very least involve the cooperation of the child for their successful completion. This was recognized by children in their accounts of their own active participation in taking medicines. Most children emphasized that they took medicines by themselves when they referred to incidents; for instance the following description by Lasse, 7 years old:

First my mum pours the medicine into a small glass and then I drink it.

In addition, children would often stress the unpleasant taste of medicine but they were at the same time able to describe how they explored different food items and techniques they used to cover the taste of medicine and make it easier to swallow. These accounts emphasize the interactional aspect of therapy and the importance of children's active participation in conducting therapies. However in adults' accounts children's cooperation would often appear as taken for granted. It was children's different attempts to control or their objections to adults' practices that, although regarded as common experiences, were acknowledged for their significant and even provocative challenge of adults' sole competence and authority. An infant or a young child might scream, cry or fight to avoid an unexpected, unpleasant or even possibly painful procedure (in Denmark children's temperature is still generally measured rectally). As Nina, 7 years old, said giggling:

> I don't like to have my temperature taken. I scream.

Parents who wish to persist in conducting the test or give a medication therefore have to hold the young child firmly, or try to persuade or negotiate with the child to obtain his/her collaboration. In and through these potentially conflictual situations, that may occur in the home between children and parents and at school (for example in the chaotic turmoil following an accident in the playground), adults exhibit their competence in keeping control and order and taking calm strategic action. Thus a child's illness episode acts as a medium for adults to express and confirm their competence and position in relation to children. A school nurse echoed the views expressed by some of the other teachers and staff in the after-school centres. She said:

> When I help them (the children) they know I am a nurse. And I'm quite pleased when they are grateful (she laughs and continues thoughtfully). I like children to know that they can always come to me for help. Because if they can come with a minor problem they'll also know to come back when they've got a bigger problem.

On the other hand, any doubt about a child's health and welfare could potentially challenge the status and position of the adults charged with protecting and being responsible for them. Of course the adults did genuinely want to safeguard the health and well being of children. But in the institutional settings adults also had to protect their own competence through their everyday routine advice to children. This was:

> If you need help remember to go and find an adult.

Although teachers and other staff expressed the plea in general terms they meant specifically those situations when a child got involved in a conflict, a fight or an accident (i.e., those situations where children were seen as particularly vulnerable). Despite its open and helpful tone this advice communicated to children a view of their incompetence in personally handling these sort of situations and undermined the idea that they may be able to help each other without adult intervention. This was underlined when children were told off if they failed to call an adult. This occurred whether or not their own actions had led to a successful management of the situation — a fact which was easily dismissed as incidental by the adults. In such ways illness and accidents become strong symbolic events for the display and confirmation of the child-adult relationship. One important element of this relationship is that togetherness is intertwined in the constitution of difference between them.

The Competent Affectionate Child

The above shows that children are generally constituted as incompetent in speaking the 'facts' of their own body — that is of translating a bodily experience into a disease state or condition. I have also shown how the processes of everyday life emphasize the importance for adults in constituting their competencies in opposition to or through children's constitution as incompetent and dependent. It would be a mistake, however, to interpret this as meaning that children in the study were constituted as incompetent in all respects. The incapacity of children to understand or judge the facticity of illness can be contrasted to the special capacity children were seen to have in the sphere of emotions, especially the giving and receiving of affection.

Let me first return to the situations where the meaning of therapeutic and similar practices was not shared by children and adults. These are powerfully exhibited in a battle between parents' (and by implication also doctors') and children's views which may lead to a child being 'forced' into collaboration, for example to make the child take an unpleasant but necessary medicine or pursue an examination through holding him or her firmly. These incidents would most likely be resolved in the parent's gentle comfort of the child and this forms part of children's experiences of illness. The love, affection and care, however, which formed part of adults' interactions with children does not alter the basic hierarchy of the relationship.

The reason for this is that, as Kirmayer (1988) notes, in the Western world view rationality has precedence over affect. Both children and their parents emphasized that children's illness episodes and time off from school represented an opportunity for child and parent to spend time together. This aspect was regarded by adults as having increased in importance because of the large proportion of mothers in the labour market in Denmark. In the context of a hectic and pressurized everyday work life a child's illness episode may thus provide families with an opportunity to express and maintain the affective bonds between child and adults.

This was reflected in the type of therapies used in children's illness episodes. The families used a wide range of home remedies and other means of self-care as well as pharmaceuticals. Home remedies and therapeutic practices such as clothing, baths, specific drinks or food, temperature regulation therapies, massage and relaxation usually involved several persons. Parents and staff in the after-school centres related the use of home remedies to their knowledge of traditional self-care practices and to their personal and familial experiences. Although parents, teachers and other staff may be recommended to use a simple home remedy by the school nurse or their general practitioner, these remedies were generally used independently of any involvement by health professionals. Home remedies were seen as time consuming in the families both in preparation and conduct and their effect may be slow or diffuse. However their appeal was in concordance with the general (perhaps Danish) principle of using noninvasive therapies on children.

According to this view intrusive medical practices such as medicines, injections and radiotherapy are to be avoided or at least monitored carefully with children to prevent inflicting unnecessary harm or pain. An ideal image of child health is characterized by elements such as purity, naturalness and simplicity. Basic essentials such as food, drink, sleep and activity further supported by adults' sensitivity to the psycho-social aspects of child health fed in to the very same model of the importance of adult attention and care. Most importantly these therapeutic practices offer ways of expressing the affective bonds between child and adult which together with their engagement in sociable activities such as playing games, aloud reading and watching television together emphasized reciprocity in their relationship.

However, the emotional expressiveness of children had a double edged quality. In my conversations with children and their parents I asked what children did when somebody was ill in the family. In conversations with the children they pointed very specifically to some exclusive action or they would more generally list the various activities they engaged in to help and comfort a parent or a sibling. Such as for example to fetch things for the ill person, make tea, get sweets or ice creams, pick flowers, comfort them and playing or loud reading for a sibling but it also included going shopping, helping with domestic work and assisting parents in looking after a younger sister or brother. Gitte, 6 years old, told how she had helped her mum by staying at home and looking after her 2-year-old brother when he was ill while her mother 'nipped out' to do some shopping.

In contrast to the precision of children's replies, the most frequent response from their parents to this question was hesitation eventually followed by a statement of the child's affectionate personality or character. For example Lene, mother to 6-year-old Gitte, said:

> Gitte, she is a very caring and helpful child.

For most parents it was difficult to point out the actual actions the child engaged in to help and comfort a family member. In this way the competence of children to give and receive affection rendered invisible their capacity to give practical therapy and help. This was possibly underlined by the important value of everyday childhood illness as providing parents with an occasion to express key parental values such as affection, protection, care and responsibility which ultimately leave children at the passive and receiving end.

The Negotiabilty of Children's Competence Through Pharmaceutical Practices

These understandings are associated with cultural conceptions of children as particularly vulnerable beings (Christensen, 1997) which support the idea of keeping children apart from pharmaceutical use. In this final section I will suggest that pharmaceuticals are embedded in a biomedical hierarchy. When they are used in the household this hierarchy is 'imported' in a way that delegates authority in medicine use to parents and constitutes children as less competent. At the same time, however, the grounds are created for children to negotiate access to and use medicine which may shift ideas of their competence and status.

From a societal viewpoint pharmaceutical use is subject to both market structures, such as the range of available pharmaceutical products, and official regulations about their distribution and cost. The pharmaceutical market is also a domain of powerful societal gatekeeping. It is the doctor's prescription that forms the essential access to a pharmaceutical thus detaching it from any subjective experiences and judgments on the part of the patient. The decision by which medicine can be bought over the counter is conditioned by ministerial legislations but pharmaceuticals are further supervised or may even be subjected to the control of a pharmacist. In the family and household the use of pharmaceuticals again forms part of a set of social relations and interactions including parental gatekeeping.

In their encounters with medicines, children came to understand their special character. Children from 6 to 11 years old could map in more or less detail the quest for pharmaceuticals. Their accounts emphasized the social organization in which pharmaceuticals are embedded. They told me about how the doctor was consulted to prescribe the medicine, the pharmacy where they subsequently bought the medicine, and the persons involved in the transactions. They explained where pharmaceuticals were kept in the house and by whom, how and when they were used within the family. They also acknowledged how medicines in particular were kept away from children in the household.

However, the children did not distinguish between a therapy and the social interaction surrounding its use. In particular children described therapies as inseparable from the person who provided care, for example their mother, a general practitioner or a teacher. They described different therapeutic actions simultaneously identifying the roles and positions of the persons involved in the illness episode. A general practitioner was most commonly referred to by saying:

The *doctor* prescribes *medicine*. (my emphasis)

On the other hand mothers were identified with home remedies. Many children's descriptions were similar to that of Marian (7 years old):

When I am ill, my *mother* always puts *a cloth with cold water* on my forehead. (my emphasis)

In this way children sketched out the social organization of everyday illness through an understanding that a therapeutic action defines the status of the person involved.

That children were not systematically told about the use of pharmaceuticals did not hinder the way that pharmaceutical use implicitly communicated cultural conceptions of hierarchy to children. In dispensing pharmaceuticals both the formal hierarchy of competence and negotiating status on this ground were made possible. This was illustrated by Alice, 10 years old, who explained:

> Usually I get those headache pills for adults — it says do not take under 16 (years old), but I only get a half. Then once I was ill, my mum went to buy some for children. I could not swallow one, then I got sick. Oh, it was disgusting.

Most 10-year-old children described Panodil[3] in terms of 'adult pills' adding, 'you know, prohibited for children under 12' (years old) or 'under 16 years old'. However, in everyday experience children found that tablets restricted to adults were divided and given to them in a smaller dose. Through dividing a tablet into smaller pieces the once prohibited was made accessible and thence the idea that therapy is negotiable. At the same time the division of the tablet confirmed the child's position in relation to adults in its symbolic portrayal of the child as metaphorically half the size of an adult.

Access to medicine and the ability to use it independently is suggested as one of the 'charms' of pharmaceuticals (Van der Geest and Whyte, 1989). The flexibility of pharmaceuticals makes it possible to act privately or to engage socially in different exchanges within families and other social relations. This contributes to the process of deconstructing and distributing medical power and status from the doctor and pharmacy to the level of family and peers. The use of pharmaceuticals is thus embedded in a set of hierarchical relationships which may, for children, indicate the achievement of independence and personal control. Most importantly pharmaceutical use may represent to children the scope for independent action within or towards the constraints of different social relationships.

These elements of control, privacy and independence, here exemplified in the use of pharmaceutical therapy, have been suggested as cultural values at the core of European and American understandings of personal health (Crawford, 1989 and 1994). If an important aspect of growing up for children is to achieve the competencies and be recognized as having the controls of adult life then pharmaceutical use may symbolize important relations of power and hierarchy in children's everyday life. My data suggest that as well as communicating their general position as subordinate to parental and professional adults, for children getting access to medicine or using medicines independently could also contribute to their sense of an improvement of social status. For example, a mother related this story to me about her two sons, Thomas and David. David who is 14 years old had been suffering from asthma since he was very young and had to use an asthma inhaler daily. However, when Thomas, who is 9 years old, was ill recently he was given a nasal spray to relieve his cold. During his illness he said to her, 'I am just as big as David now'. She was bewildered and had asked him what he meant. Thomas explained, that now he used an inhaler just like his older brother, David.

Parents, teachers and staff in the after-school centres saw themselves as competent and in charge of care and treatment. Responsibility and protection of the child was seen as an adult domain. Even though this approach emphasized the dependent and more passive role of the child, there were in fact differences in the degree to which they permitted the child's active involvement. Adults tended to take responsibility and to take action over acute conditions. This limited in some ways the scope for children's competence. However a child suffering from a chronic condition or one who was in need of a treatment for a longer period was often taught how to conduct the treatment (more) independently. Thus control and responsibility were actually delegated from adult to the child. In regard to long-term conditions such as eczema, warts or blisters, children said that they would apply the cream themselves. This was also the case of children with asthma. They kept the asthma inhaler in their school bags and used it without consulting an adult. Linda, 10 years old explained:

> When I have a big attack (asthma) I have difficulties in getting my breath, that is mostly, when I get breathless. Then I am not going to school, then I am at the doctor's. But if I take the 'turbohaler' over here (at school) then I just continue to play.

Linda used the turbohaler when she felt it was necessary and at the same time she was able to continue her activities without any unwanted interruption.

However, the actual competence and control that children with chronic illness achieved would confirm their status as different from other children rather than exemplifying the potential capacity of children to administer and use pharmaceuticals independently. This means that in 'bracketing off' these children as different from other children, their competence was discounted as being part of childhood itself.

Conclusion

In everyday child illness, this chapter has suggested, the idea of children as incompetent is relationally constituted. It cannot be separated from the ways in which adults render themselves as competent. This depends not only upon general cultural assumptions of adult competence and child incompetence but is accomplished in everyday social interactions — in this case, those specifically dealing with children's everyday illnesses. Here we see the points at which differences and similarities between children and adults are made more or less visible and stable. In everyday child illness, interactions at home and school between children and adults draw on the traditional hierarchies and values of biomedicine in various ways: parents and teachers are delegated responsibility, competence and intervention rights; 'rational' methods are employed in preference to children's subjective experiences; children's ability in giving and receiving affection (as part of health care) is both valued as part of the reciprocity of human relationships but remains subordinate to other competencies; and children's actual contribution to practical care is often rendered invisible to adults. In relation to pharmaceutical use, which children saw as embedded in societal hierarchies, I showed how children within these 'rigid' relationships found scope for negotiating independent social status and competence. However, I finally suggested that even in the case of chronic illness, where children are seen as capable of medicine use, their competence becomes constituted not only as different from adults but also as different from their peers which again distance them from 'ordinary' childhood.

Notes

1   I wish to thank Allison James and Alan Prout for their valuable comments on an earlier draft of this chapter. I also wish to acknowledge the Health Insurance Foundation (Sygekassernes Helsefond) and the Danish Research Council for the Humanities who funded the research project on which this chapter is based.
2   The general ethnographic study presented in this chapter included a smaller part particularly focused on investigating 6- and 10-year-old children's perceptions and use of pharmaceuticals (Christensen, 1996). This part of the study was the Danish component of a nine nation cross-cultural study of young children and medicine use: (EEC) COMAC/HSR 'Childhood and Medicines' project. The paper cited here was a comparative analysis of data from the children in Denmark and from the study carried out in England.
3   In Denmark, Panodil is a brand name for paracetamol (an analgesic). Panodil can be obtained as over-the-counter medicine from the pharmacy in two forms. One, the most commonly used, is intended for adults; the other is provided in a weaker dosage for children.

References

ALANEN, L. (1988) 'Rethinking childhood', *Acta Sociologica*, **31**, pp. 53–67.

BLUEBOND-LANGNER, M. (1978) *The Private Worlds of Dying Children*, Princeton, NJ: Princeton University Press.

BLUEBOND-LANGNER, M. (1991) 'Paediatric cancer patients' peer relationships: The impact of an oncology camp experience', *Journal of Psychosocial Oncology*, **19**, pp. 67–80.

CHRISTENSEN, P. (1993) 'The social construction of help among Danish children', *Sociology of Health and Illness*, **15**, pp. 488–502.

CHRISTENSEN, P. (1996) 'The Danish participation in the COMAC medicines and childhood project', in TRAKAS, D. and SANZ, E. (eds) *Childhood and Medicine Use in a Cross Cultural Perspective: A European Concerted Action*, Luxembourg: Report EUR 16646 EN, European Commision.

CHRISTENSEN, P. (1997) 'Vulnerable bodies: Cultural meanings of child, body and illness', in PROUT, A. (ed.) *Childhood and the Body*, London: Macmillan.

COHEN, A. (1985) *The Symbolic Construction of Community*, London: Routledge.

CRAWFORD, R. (1989) 'A cultural account of "health": Control, release, and the social body', in McKINLAY, J. (ed.) *Issues in the Political Economy of Health Care*, London and New York: Tavistock.

CRAWFORD, R. (1994) 'The boundaries of the self and the unhealthy other: Reflections on health, culture and AIDS', *Social Science and Medicine*, **38**, pp. 1347–65.

DAVIS, A. (1982) *Children in Clinics*, London: Tavistock.

DOUGLAS, M. (1975) *Implicit Meanings: Essays in Anthropology*, London: Routledge.

DYER, R. (1993) *The Matter of Images: Essays on Representations*, London: Routledge.

HARDMAN, C. (1978) 'Can there be an anthropology of children ?', *Journal of the Anthropology Society Oxford*, **4**, pp. 85–99.

JAMES, A. and PROUT, A. (1990) *Constructing and Reconstructing Childhood: Contemporary issues in the Sociological Study of Childhood*, London: Falmer Press.

JENKS, C. (1982) *The Sociology of Childhood: Essential Reading*, London: Batsford.

KIRMAYER, L. (1988) 'Mind and body as metaphors: Hidden values in biomedicine', in LOCK, M. and GORDON, D. (eds) *Biomedicine Examined*, Dordrecht: Kluwer Academic Publishers.

LATOUR, B. (1993) *We Have Never Been Modern*, Hemel Hempstead: Harvester Wheatsheaf.

NADER, L. (1981) 'The vertical slice: Hierarchies and children', in BRITAIN, G. and COHEN, R. (eds) *Hierarchy and Society: Anthropological Perspectives on Bureaucracy*, Philadelphia, PA: Ishi.

PROUT, A. (1986) 'Wet children and little actresses: Going sick in primary school', *Sociology of Health and* Illness, **8**, pp. 111–36.

PROUT, A. (1988) 'Off school sick: Mothers accounts of school sickness absence', *Sociological Review*, **36**, p. 4.

PROUT, A. and CHRISTENSEN, P. (1996) 'Hierarchies, boundaries and symbols: Medicine use and the cultural performance of childhood sickness', in BUSH, P. et al. (eds) *Children, Medicines and Culture*, New York: Hayworth Press.

QVORTRUP, J. (1991) *Childhood as a Social Phenomenon: An Introduction to a Series of National Reports*, Eurosocial Reports vol. 36, Vienna: European Centre.

RIESMAN, P. (1990) 'The formation of personality in fulani ethnopsychology', in JACKSON, M. and KARP, I. (eds) *Personhood and Agency: The Experiences of Self and Other in African Cultures*, Uppsala Studies in Cultural Anthropology 14, Stockholm: Almquist and Wiksell International.

STRATHERN, M. (1992) *Partial Connections*, Savage, MD: Rowman and Littlefield.

STRONG, P. (1979) *The Ceremonial Order of the Clinic*, London: Routledge and Kegan Paul.

VAN DER GEEST, S. and WHYTE, S. (1989) 'The charm of medicines: Metaphors and metonyms', *Medical Anthropology Quarterly*, **3**, pp. 345–66.

Chapter 10

In the Company of Strangers:
Being a Child in Care

Gerald de Montigny

The Local/Extra Local

Ellen is a 16-year-old ward of the state who lives in a group home with four other young women.[1] On Tuesday she received a telephone call from Peggy, her Children's Aid Society (CAS)[2] social worker, who said that they had to meet. Ellen returned to her group-home after school to see Peggy sitting at the kitchen table. The social worker directed Ellen to the living room. Ellen certainly knew something was in the air for why else would the social worker have made such a big fuss about getting together. Struggling to control her anxiety Ellen settled herself uncomfortably into the overstuffed couch and waited for the social worker to deliver the news. Once the preliminaries were dispatched the social worker informed Ellen that she would have to move at the end of the month to a privatized 'Outside Placement Resource' (OPR). The home where Ellen had lived for the past five years was going to be closed as part of the agency's efforts to reduce costs.

From the couch in the living room Ellen could not see the background web of accounting, managerial, and administrative practices that produced this decision that so dramatically affected her life. The butterflies in Ellen's stomach, the tears on her face, and her worries and fears are rooted in a series of bifurcated social relationships marked by divisions between insiders and outsiders, adults and children, informal and formal powers, and face to face contacts — i.e., as between children and front-line workers — and impersonal directives — i.e., as between children in care and organizational managers. Yet, for Ellen and other children in care[3] day-to-day emotional survival demands an attempt to penetrate, question, analyse and understand the extra-local institutional apparatus that regulates their daily lives.

From their location, 'the extra-local organisation of an administrative apparatus remains opaque' (G. Smith, 1990). However, although outside organizational and administrative sites of power, youth in care nevertheless struggle to make some sense of the puzzles that appear to surround agency decision-making. Sorting out these puzzles requires that the youth employ various strategies including sharing information with other youth; questioning group home staff and social workers; becoming involved in youth in care groups; and attending special fora, workshops and symposia organized by the agency. Despite their efforts to penetrate or go inside the organizational apparatus children and youth in care can gain only a proximity to power but somehow, never the power to make agency policy itself. Thus even those children who might imagine themselves to be insiders are, when considering the power to make decisions and policies for the agency, fundamentally outsiders.

Whilst CAS managers may toss and turn at night trying to figure out how to balance the agency budget in the face of 6 per cent cuts in funds from the province, and further cuts from the municipality, Ellen and other youth will toss and turn in strange beds in yet other strangers' homes. Whilst the CAS managers may struggle to reform budget lines, projected costs, and unit prices, Ellen and other youth in care struggle to make sense of living in these strange homes, attending a strange school, making new friends, and coping with the loss of old friends, places, and routines. Whilst CAS managers work to justify their actions and their choices, Ellen and other youth in care seek answers to the questions, 'why did they do this to me?', 'why don't I count?', 'why has my life been turned upside down?'

Until very recently the Children's Aid Society of Ottawa Carleton directly operated over twenty group homes and residential services. As a result of budget cuts the majority of these homes have been closed. In 1996 the agency responded to further cuts from funders by closing the remaining seven residential services and group homes. It has moved to replace these services with privatized 'Outside Placement Resources' (OPRs). The closure of the agency run homes resulted in laying off unionized staff and the displacement and relocation of dozens of children living in these homes (CAS, 1995). The pain of relocation and personal disruption has created a sense of betrayal, anxiety, and vulnerability not only among the children directly affected but among a wider group of children and youth in care who could see the plight of their friends. Concern about the group-home closure preoccupied the members of the Children's Aid Society Teens (CAST) and dominated discussions during their weekly meetings.

Indeed the general topic of cutbacks that frames the background to this chapter was suggested to me by members of the CAST group whom I had come to know through my participation in their weekly meetings. I had been attending the CAST meetings as part of a research project to explore the experiences of children coming into and being in care. The CAST members decided to deal with the issue of the cuts by organizing a 'Cutbacks Forum' for youth in care in early February 1996, and fortunately they granted me permission to attend and to tape-record the event. Although the turnout was less than the CAST planning team had hoped there were nevertheless about fifteen youth present. Much of the information addressed in this chapter is derived from this forum.

The forum brought youth in care together to discuss the effects of the cutbacks on their lives, whilst at the same time enabling them to share information, and to develop strategies to respond to the cuts. The decision of agency managers to pursue cutbacks through elimination of residential services for children in care created real dislocation and hardship in the lives of many children and youth in care. The challenge facing the youth was multiform as it included understanding the organizational background against which the decision was made, identifying the major decision makers, and developing some strategy for coping with or resisting the effects of cut-backs on their lives. Through their discussions we can begin to grasp the complex skills that children and youth bring to sense making inside organizational contexts. The conversations of the children and youth underscore their sense that if the Children's Aid Society is their 'parent' then this parent needs to listen to them, and needs to count their voices among those responsible for decision-making. As this chapter hopes to make clear the voices of children in care provide a substantial challenge to the actions of CAS board members, administrators, and staff.

The analysis of the CAST forum developed in this chapter is informed by an ethnomethodological sensitivity to the artfulness of every-day practices. This sensitivity to the every-day unfolds the elegant complexity of the communicative practices that the youth employed not only to express their views and understandings, but to produce the relational coordination of activities of the forum as such. The youth had to navigate through the difficult waters of communicative ambiguity, disagreement and difference. By attending to the coordinated production of the occasion as a forum the notion of children's competencies is transformed from a rhetorical assertion to that which is demonstrably present at hand. The explication of how these children and youth produced or communicated for each other an accountable sense of both their situations as children in care and as participants in a forum on cutbacks reveals the artful execution of complex moral, ethical, relational, reasoning and sense making practices. Beyond the words, understandings, and opinions, is the rhythm of the talk, the turn-taking, the attention to the talk of the other, the resolution of demands for the floor, and the management of trouble both potential and real.

Whilst this chapter shares the concerns of ethnomethodology and conversation analysis, the talk is understood to be rooted in socially organized practices. Thus, the sensibility of the talk emerges and is recoverable only by recourse to the lived histories, relations, and socially grounded (Bologh, 1979) lives of the participants. The talk of the youth in care is woven into determinate sites, relations, and discourses of power and control. This chapter seeks to demonstrate that for children and youth in care contact with the organization is profoundly problematic, as it is carried out on a terrain and inside spaces that are marked by profound disparities between participants' status, authority, and power. The agency context relies upon practices for producing centralized and hierarchically organized forms of power that descend outward and downward from agency managers, to team directors, to front-line social workers to children in care.

The paradox that children in care face is that to assert their powers or to contest organizational decisions, policies, and practices, they need to learn how to think organizationally, hence to absorb organizational and professional discourses. Yet this absorption necessarily results in the displacement and subordination of their everyday language and localized understandings in favour of formalized professional and organizational discourses. By taking up the formal language of professional and organizational discourses children in care simultaneously learn to devalue situated and locally sensible relevances and accounts. In this sense their life–worlds become colonized by the system, and their localizable experiences are articulated in instrumental and rationalized language (Habermas, 1987, p. 333). One effect of the colonization of everyday worlds or life–worlds by the system, as Habermas observed, is that, 'Everyday consciousness is robbed of its power to synthesise; it becomes fragmented' (*ibid.*, p. 355). To state the problem slightly differently, the articulation of everyday realities that constitute 'children's culture' (Fine and Sandstrom, 1988) are ideologically reformed and deformed such that contingent and practical rationalities are subordinated to the singular authority of an extra-local and universalized rationality.

As children in care become participants in agency functions — for example, through the Children's Aid Society Teen, or the Youth Advisory Committee — their lives, activities, and relations are inscribed with the language, understandings, and moral organizations of the agency. Their lived standpoints become inserted and thereby absorbed by the horizons of organizationally sanctioned discourses. The processes of coming to understand how the organization works necessarily obliges youth to enter into a dialogue with the practitioners of the organization — i.e., group home workers, social workers, and managers. Through this dialogue youth internalize the logic, the judgments, the ethic, and the order of reality produced inside an organizational horizon. The search for understanding through absorption of organizational discourses while providing a basis for opposition, simultaneously seduces children and youth in care with its chimera of power and authority.

Methodology and Politics: The Obligation to Political Action

Considerations of relative power, control, and authority are important for recovering a full sense of meaning from the talk of children in care. When considering children's talk about being in care, it is necessary to attend to or examine not only the talk but the socially organized contexts and the relationships of power in which those utterances were produced (de Montigny, 1996; Smith, G., 1990). Thus the talk of children must be understood not only as contextual, located, and performative, but as inherently political and transformative.

Perhaps equally important we must ask, who is the enquirer who would listen to children's talk, analyse children's talk, and report on that talk to yet other 'enquirers'. Furthermore what is it that the enquirer seeks to do with children's talk? A considered examination of these questions leads to a recognition of the fundamental question, why do we care about what children in care have to say about being in care? What do we do if we discover that children experience cutbacks as adversely affecting their lives? Are we obliged to pursue correctives? Need we become involved as advocates in a political process?

This research project, and the present author's work, are located inside the profession of social work, and accordingly are oriented towards interventions and correctives in the lives of others. This location is hardly inconsequential, for social work as with other helping professions whether medicine, nursing, psychology, physiotherapy, and so forth, is irremediably about remedial action and correctives. As social workers our task, to paraphrase Marx in his *Theses on Feuerbach*, is not just to interpret the world but to change it.

The task is not just to understand children's talk, nor to merely report on children's 'experiences' but to judge and to act on those experiences, particularly, when they are negative, to pursue correctives. The possibility of what has been called 'ethnomethodological indifference' (Garfinkel and Sacks, 1986, p. 166)[4] is not sustainable personally or professionally.[5] As George Smith (1995) argued, 'In beginning from the local historical setting of people's experiences, the ethnographer must start in a reflexive fashion from inside the social organization of not only his/her own world, but by extension the social world he/she intends to investigate' (p. 26). Attention to the reflexivity of analysis directs us to appreciate that analytic practices are thoroughly implicated in the local settings and the life–worlds of those whose lives are being examined. Analysis is always embedded in the tensions between life–worlds and the system, and as such, all analysis is irremediably situated and accordingly political.

The primary challenge for social workers is to develop strategies that defend the professional values of empowerment, client involvement, and particularly in children protection work, to provide services that actually operate in the best interests of the child. The secondary challenge is to resist the unfortunate tendency to rationalize, justify, and support the destruction of social services as necessary, inevitable, or as somehow correcting social services. Not just social workers, but researchers must be prepared to take a side. They cannot pretend that their work is neutral and that it is somehow above the hard choices presented by daily life and political action. By addressing the voices of children in care this chapter takes a side. It makes a choice to present an analysis of children's competencies as actors and enquirers in their everyday worlds. By developing an analysis of children's competencies this chapter affirms the importance not only of listening to children, but of respecting children by involving them in decision-making that affects their lives.

The Intrusive Mystery

For children who are permanent wards or crown wards the Children's Aid Society is in law their parent. Yet, what a peculiar parent the society is. This parent is a corporate entity not a human entity. This is a parent who becomes present for the children only through the work of paid employees. This is a parent whose modes of everyday conduct are legal, documentary, and textual (de Montigny, 1995). For a child in care the agency that is responsible for being their 'parent' is a vast external force often housed in steel and glass corporate offices, regulated with security guards at the door, bound to codes of confidentiality, and peopled by a cadre of hierarchically organized professionals. Yet, children in care struggle to create a workable sense of this dense maze of people, rituals, and organizational relations. To create an accountable sense of their everyday lives children draw on readily available analytic, moral, and rhetorical tools. Yet, whilst such tools may be the stuff of everyday life, the commonality of their currency belies the skill and complexity required to effect their execution. Indeed attention to the talk of children in care about their parent reveals tremendously complex background understandings, stores of knowledge, and analytic practices.

All the youth that I encountered recognize that the Children's Aid Society is a major site of power in their lives and as such the agency, its front-line workers, executives, history, policies, and legislative mandate comprise ongoing topics of everyday conversation. The CAS evaluates their families and their own behaviours, places them in foster homes, group homes, residences, or treatment facilities, provides them with the necessities, and with many of their small pleasures, whether in the form of allowances, trips to restaurants and shopping malls, or small gifts on important occasions. It is equally true that whilst the agency and its forms of operation may be a constant topic of conversation, often its rituals, patterns, trajectories, and directions remain indecipherable. Of course, the indecipherability of the agency is not a surprise given that the agency and accordingly their parent is a corporate entity whose forms of operation are woven into institutional structures of government — federal, provincial and municipal — the professions, and discursively organized knowledge (Smith, D.E. 1987).

Although for children in care the state is their parent, and in a curious sense this makes them child members of a corporate family, decision-making processes in the corporation exclude them. Access to, and participation in, decision-making is constructed along very narrow corporately defined lines of hierarchical position, rank, and mandated authority. Children in care are denied a formal place on corporate decision-making bodies, whether the Board of Directors, or the Executive Offices. Their place in decision-making is strictly limited as they have been allowed to play only an advisory and at best advocacy role.

The only formal avenue for the expression of the collective will of children in care is through the CAST group which has existed since the early 1970s. Although the agency has allocated the services of one social worker to act as a guide and coordinator for the youth, CAST can operate only as an advisory and advocacy body for the youth. The advisory function of the CAST group is largely expressed through the appointment of eight members to sit on the Children's Aid Society Youth Advisory Committee (YAC).[6] YAC meetings are organized to communicate information between the agency and youth in care rather than to engage in policy formation or decision-making.

The exchange of information between children in care and the CAS through YAC, whilst commendable, gives voice only to a select few and as a result excludes the vast majority of children in care from an opportunity to make their voices heard. The majority of children are outside the loops of power. As we will see below a dilemma faced by YAC participants is that their involvement in this structure places them in the position of a cognoscenti who can claim special insiders' knowledge against the majority of other youth in care. Once YAC participants encounter and are made to understand the arguments, rationales, and decision-making processes of the agency their ability to articulate their own interests is vitiated. As they embrace the universalized professional and organizational discourses children in care not only lose their ability to articulate their life experiences in everyday language, but they lose their ability to undercut and to slice through authoritative structures that warrant organizational knowledge. Simply put they become coopted.

Accounting for Organizational Action

The following exchange occurred near the beginning of the forum organized by CAST to talk about the closure of agency run group homes and residences.

```
A:  Like ah, can we ask, can I ask you why are they closing?
B:  Because, like they think that by putting kids on OPR that
    it'll save money like fer instance, uhm, for a kid in care to
    live in a home, it costs two hundred dollars a day, but in an
    OPR it costs . . . only costs them a hundred dollars there, so
    they save a hundred dollars there. To put them all
    onto . . . or into OPR or back home or foster homes, they'll
    save money
A:  Okay, I got something to say. Instead of buying those brand
    new ah, Ford Escorts downstairs, those ah cars like fer
    agencies, they coulda saved a house fer the kids instead of
    buying those new cars.
C:  Okay, yah, nnh (direction from someone). Okay, here's what,
    ah:h. What we need to do is find a.a solution that is not only
    one time, because to keep a house going you need money every
    year. Right?
A:  Yah
C:  Right. So they can maybe save it fer a year, but after that
    they can't save . . . because money's not coming in from the
    government right, so if ah, if the money's not coming in from
    the government they hafta say, 'What're we gonna do with less
    money?', and they look where they spend the most money, on
    ho . . . at homes, right, on residential care, so that's where
    they cut the money. I.I think our . . . my concern, my concern
    is is that the government doesn't uhm, respect us, and give
    us enough money, ah to to . . . so that we have to close the
    homes. . . . (extended address continues)
```

Youth A opens the discussion by inviting one of the forum organizers — B — to respond to his question, 'Like ah, can we ask, can I ask you why are they closing?' A's opening operates inside an implicit background of differentials in positions, roles, and status among the forum participants. The form of A's question relies upon that which everybody at the forum knows, that there is a group of insiders, such as B and C, who have organized the forum, and another group of outsiders such as himself who have merely been invited to attend. A's question makes explicit that which was implicit. First it makes visible the differential location between himself and B, and second it interpellates B into the position of standing in for the agency. In this sense A's opening generates a script through which B, by accepting A's invitation to respond, provides an explanation of group home closures that can be treated as authoritative or quasi-official.

B's response signifies her acceptance of A's implicit categorization of her as an insider who can provide an authoritative explanation for group home closings. What enables B to presume that she can provide an answer to A's question? A detailed examination of the opening structure of her response provides some clues. B observes, 'Because, like they think that by putting kids on OPR that it'll save money.' First, B makes the connection between the closure of the group homes and the thoughts and actions of others signified through the pronoun 'they'. It is worth noting that B, by using the plural 'they' rather than the singular 'he' or 'she', refers to a group of actors rather than an individual actor who thinks. Now this in itself is an intriguing assertion, for we must ask, how is it that this young woman can presuppose to know what a group of other persons think and believe? How is it that she can with undisputed certainty attribute thoughts, motivations, goals, and actions to this other group? How can she assert that this group thinks x, y, and z, in unison, together, without apparent disagreement or conflict? Yet, B's assertion is not treated as problematic by the others present at the forum. Why is this? It would seem that B's assertion is constituted in the bedrock of common-sense formulations about how life in organizations works. It is precisely in organizations, through the medium of directives, policy statements, operational protocols, and so forth, that corporately uniform sets of thought and action are accomplished day-by-day. Indeed, this sense of uniform thought and action constitutes the common-sense fabric of understandings about bureaucrats, functionaries, and paper pushers. The second intriguing facet of B's utterance, is not only that she identifies a group of actors whose thinking is consequential for the agency, but that she herself 'knows' how they think and what they think. She is able to speak with some authority about what it is that 'they think'.

We cannot answer the question of how B can presume to know that there is a connection between a group of people, their thinking and goals, and the closure of the group homes, by looking solely at the talk, though the talk does indicate that there is a missing piece. The missing piece is that B has had a lengthy background of involvement in CAST and the Youth Advisory Committee (YAC). This background enables her to develop an apparently authoritative discussion of agency priorities, 'it'll save them money'. B relies on background information gained through CAST and YAC, first as enabling her to presume that she has an 'answer', and second, as providing a repository of background knowledge about how actors, decision-making, and priorities are developed in the agency. B relies on this background knowledge to speak of relative cost differentials between different forms of care. B's argument ties organizational decision-making to financial or accounting matters. She sketches an argument outlining comparative costs, to conclude 'they'll save money somehow'.

B's specification of the goal 'it'll save them money' functions as an explanation of the closure of the group homes. B asserts that the goal of saving money shapes decision-making and choices, by structuring a preference for options that cost less, hence OPRs rather than agency run group homes. Although, she may not be privy to, or remember if she was told, the exact cost of running specific group homes she 'knows' that the cost of the new OPRs is considerably less than the old agency run residences. This assertion that the OPRs cost less than the agency run residences remained uncontested throughout the forum. In this sense her assertion functioned as common-sense, or as that which everybody knows. By invoking her knowledge of differential costs for agency and private residential services, against what she understands to be agency priorities, B advances strong explanatory claims for the closure of the group homes.

B's response, when viewed in light of A's next turn, appears to have been orchestrated by A as it provides him with an argument that can stand in for an official version, and against which he can launch a moral challenge. A in his recovery of the next turn does not direct his response to B's answer, but to making a statement that charges the agency — identified as 'they' — with purchasing new cars instead of keeping group homes open: 'Okay, I got something to say. Instead of buying those brand new ah, Ford Escorts downstairs, those ah cars like fer agencies, they coulda saved a house fer the kids instead of buying those new cars.' For A the new cars in the parking lot become a readily identified target for his dissatisfaction and anger.

Moral Aesthetics and Action

A's argument is fundamentally moral as it juxtaposes expenditure on 'brand new cars' to expenditure on children. In a culture where millions of dollars are spent on advertising new vehicles each year, where newspaper stands are stacked with myriad magazines about new vehicles, where billions are invested in the purchase of new vehicles, and where new vehicles are deeply interwoven into the structures of desire as status symbols and signs of wealth, 'brand new cars' represent a visible sign of materialism, consumerism, individualism, and greed. Clearly, for this young man the presence of 'brand new cars' in the parking lot occurring at the same time that group homes are being closed stands as a moral affront.

A's argument relies on the understanding that the ultimate force determining whether a group home is opened or closed is money. Additionally, it follows from the trajectory of his argument that he recognizes that there is a finite supply or command of money at the disposal of the agency. Because money is finite, agency administrators must make choices about how money is to be spent. He understands that these choices are fundamentally rooted in a moral universe. He understands that one can make good or bad choices, wise or foolish choices, helpful or harmful choices. To his mind the agency executives have made the wrong choices. Yet what makes this young man believe that these are the wrong choices?

As A observes 'they coulda saved a house fer the kids instead of buying those new cars'. What informs A's preference? He does not say, 'they coulda saved a house fer me'. Instead, A formulates a challenge that demonstrates a concern and caring for 'the kids'. This manner of expressing his argument allows A to communicate through his talk in action his orientation to others, and thereby his claim to a moral high ground against his opponents. By focusing on the needs of other kids, A can be seen to perform an attitude of compassion and caring for others. His words demonstrate that he is not preoccupied with his own loss and pain, but that he can consider the loss and pain of others. Against his own embodied and active, demonstrable orientation is the orientation of those unspecified and generalized others that he opposes.

A's arguments are built on the assumption that the world of concrete and actual choices is rooted in a moral universe that is not merely out-there but present in the immediacy of everyday actions. His utterances are oriented to a moral demonstration of the good as he understands it. It does not seem too extravagant to claim that this young man develops a moral argument that is rooted in a repudiation of material things and the elevation of human qualities and human caring. By producing his argument in a form which demonstrates a concern for others rather than an egocentric focus on his situation and sufferings, A establishes moral grounds for the criticism of the actions of agency managers who by his definition do not care for or consider the needs of others.

Moving now to the subsequent talk, it is possible to say that C believes that A's utterance is incompetent or naive, as is suggested by his rejoinder, 'What we need to do is find a.a solution that is not only one time, because to keep a house going you need money every year. Right?' Yet C refrains from a direct contradiction of A. Instead, he begins by signifying a general agreement with A, and then proceeds to formulate an objective with which he imagines A will agree:

```
C:  Okay, yah, nnh (direction from someone). Okay, here's what,
    ah:h. What we need to do is find a.a solution that is not only
    one time, because to keep a house going you need money every
    year. Right?
A:  Yah
C:  Right. So they can maybe save it fer a year, but after that
    they can't save . . .
```

Although C relies on an extensive background knowledge about the agency, he uses this knowledge in a way that does not attack or belittle A. His exercise of the power that the information gives him, while marked by a confident authority, is also marked by a dialogic humility, that enjoins A to enter into the logic of his argument, — 'Right?' — to which A responds affirmatively — 'Yah'. Once C has orchestrated A's agreement with his objectives, and hence implicated A in the logic of his argument, C proceeds to provide an elaborate explanation of the belief systems, priorities, and prejudices of government funders. It should be noted that C, by framing the problem as the incommensurability of the costs for automobiles with those of keeping a group home open, effectively bypasses the problem of engaging in a moral disagreement with A. Unfortunately, by reframing the argument pragmatically rather than morally, the full import of A's challenge is also bypassed. By reframing the problem of cutbacks within the pragmatic orientation of agency financial accounting practices and priorities, C undercuts the radical challenge posed by A's argument.

C, who is a long standing CAST member as well as formerly a participant in YAC, is oriented to the pragmatics of running the agency. His observation, 'What we need to do is find a solution that is not only one time' signifies an orientation informed by the logic of agency decision-making. As with B, C develops his argument by relying on complex background information about how financing of group homes actually works. Both B and C develop arguments that are predicated on insider's knowledge of agency structures and decision-making. Although A opened this sequence, he is not an ongoing member of the CAST group whilst both B and C are. Clearly, B and C by virtue of their past involvement with CAST and YAC and accordingly with the agency can lay claim to insider knowledge about how the agency actually works. As insiders they have absorbed and accepted the agency organization of knowledge that posits significant connections between financial costs and policy and program decisions. They rely on background knowledge about relative costs that enables them to recognize that the expense for two or three $12,000 automobiles is not commensurate with the $250,000 cost of keeping a group home open for a year — paying five or six employee salaries, heating, light, cable, building maintenance, taxes, and so forth. Thus, through their contact with the agency, youth in care learn how to employ organizationally conditioned rhetorics of justification.

The radical critique of agency policy launched by 'outsiders' through the conjunction of morality, aesthetics, and choice was clearly revealed in another sequence that occurred later in the same forum.

```
M:   Okay, uhm, I gotta. I gotta a question. Actually, why did
     Children's Aid move to this beautiful building=
G:   it's not beautiful
M:   to, ah from Clark Street, there wasn't nothing wrong with
     the building on Clark.
A:   ah.it was ah.
J:   space wise//
M:   it was tal.taller than here//
N:   I heard that that building was not so good though, like the
     walls weren't doing good to them=
J:   =No, it wasn't that good//
N:   it wasn't pure room, the walls, it was just wrecked, it was
     ready to wreck. It wasn't good, it wasn't safe.
B:   Rennovations, there coulda been rennovations.
D:   like yah, the old (id) why move here.
SW:  Brief . . . briefly what happened the building was too small
     and we were spread out, and at the time, ah, it was quite
     overcrowded. It wasn't efficient, and it belonged to somebody
     else, and the lease was comin up for renewal, and it wasn't
     just that one building, it was the other building across the
     street which was very old, building A, building A, B, and C.
     Building A was very old too, and needed lots of major work
     done on it and the opportunity presented itself, that in the
     long run its cheaper for the children's aid society to own
```

```
this building then it would have been to maintain, to
maintain and upgrade the oldest building and continue to pay
rent at the building C. So in the long run the children's
aid actually saves money by owning this building.
```

As with the previous exchange a youth from 'outside' locates his criticism of agency decision-making by pointing to the visible manifestations of the agency, that is, the building. The youth's argument relies on the familiar device of invoking a dichotomy between proper or modest expense against improper and excessive expense. Interestingly the youth's implicit evaluative aesthetics of modesty and excess are immediately challenged by the next participant, G, who asserts, 'no it's not beautiful'. M recognizes that his first line of attack is disputed, and that his aesthetic judgment of beauty is not shared by all present. Rather than pursuing the difficult road of establishing that the building is 'beautiful' he shifts his argument to the opposite element of the dichotomy to argue that the old building was adequate. Once again he is immediately challenged. Sensing the direction of the challenge, as signified through J's utterance 'space wise', A attempts a recovery, by claiming, 'It was taller than here'.

The more experienced CAST members take over the floor, to share their understandings of the agency decision to move to new accommodations. Their strategy is to translate stories and fragments overheard into some sort of account for why the move was necessary. Finally, the social worker intervenes with an 'authoritative' account, rich in details and specifics, that undermines M's argument by claiming both necessity and cost benefit over remaining in the old building. The social worker's account effectively brings discussion of the building to a close, and moves the youth back to a discussion of the importance of telling 'the government how the cuts are affecting us'.

Dilemmas of Privilege

We can see, then, that access to agency information is always a two-edged sword, as the information is never neutral, but carries with it the logic and assumptions of its producers. Youth take up this information at the peril of losing their own position and capacity for resistance. The problem of access to agency information and the dilemmas it poses for youth in care were expressed rather dramatically at the forum in the following segment.

```
B:  Okay, I'm gonna move onto the next question, it says here,
    Have you been consulted before changes have taken place? What
    it means is uhm if you are in a home, were you told that you
    were gonna be moved, that the house is gonna be closed, like
    way before it happened or jist like three or four weeks
    before, like how are your feelings on that?
C:  How . . . how did you find out?
```

```
F:  I . . . I found out, because ah, like one of the staff I was
    talking to, they were hiding it//[they didn tell me
B:                                  [Can you talk up a
    little bit?
F:  They didn't, they didn't tell me anything. They didn't say
    anything. It, it was jist like one of the staff told me, and
    ah, like I couldn't tell anybody else ya know. It was jist
    the staff, they were hiding it from the kids, so ah//
B:  What do you mean hiding it from the kids?
F:  They wouldn't say anything, and knew what was happening.
C:  They wouldn't tell anybody, an ah, did they, did they tell
    you what was gonna happen, where you were gonna go, didja
    know that?
F:  I knew that I was eventually gonna go to Salmon House, cause
    like you know. I . . . I graduated, you know, like I didn't
    need that. That's what they said, you know.
C:  What about the other kids, where did they go?
F   They're still there. They just run and stuff, they're just
    kids.
C:  So what's gonna happen to them, when they, do ya know?
F:  I'm not sure, like they . . . they say that there'll be homes
    and stuff
C:  They say that . . . an, ah . . .
F:  I . . . I don't think that they're just gonna kick them out on
    the street.
C:  Well I hope not, heh. . . .
```

As with the previous two segments the utterances are imbued with a deep moral sense of right and wrong. Speaker B, who we met above, begins by reading from a list of questions and concerns that the CAST group had developed prior to the forum. The question asks participants to address the issue of consultation, thereby implicitly indicating both a preference for consultation, information disclosure and a problematization of dictated decisions and secrecy. C takes up B's cue to elicit information from one of the 'outsiders', inviting F to respond.

F's answer, and the dialogue that follows demonstrate the contradictions, hard choices, conflicting loyalties and bitterness that selective disclosure of information by social workers or staff can create for children and youth in care. F, speaking very softly, answers C's question, by revealing, 'I . . . I found out, because ah, like one of the staff I was talking to, they were hiding it they didn tell me.' As he suggests in his next turn, this created problems for him, as 'like I couldn't tell anybody else ya know'. The implication is clear, that whilst he might have wanted to tell others, because he knew that the information was secret — 'It was jist the staff, they were hiding it from the kids' — he felt unable to do so. In this way, his loyalty to 'the kids', his fellow housemates and friends conflicted with his sense of having been given secret and privileged information.

Youth C's access to secret and privileged information operates to create deep moral difficulties for him. As with B and C in the first segment, where access to information provides a source of power and authority, so too does F find himself ensnared in positions of power and authority. Indeed, F in this segment continuously differentiates himself from 'the kids', whom he suggests cannot cope with the information in as mature and responsible manner as himself: 'They just run and stuff, they're just kids.' In a direct way, F reveals his sense that access to information becomes a sign of adult status, responsibility, and power. Yet, although a participant in adult power by virtue of access to secret information, he remained a child among children in a group home. In this sense he was torn between the agency and its codes and the codes of loyalty that obtain in daily life.

For the youth at the forum there was a shared sense that social workers and group home staff were responsible for honest, open, and clear communication with them. However, the youth clearly felt that such moral and philosophical preferences for practice were consistently violated. Instead of these values children in care felt that decisions were made in secret and that information was hidden from them. Yet, when they were party to secret and hidden information, this conferred on them some privilege, and accordingly a complicity in its further concealment. In this sense children and youth are seduced into the acceptance of the rationales developed by group home staff, social workers, and others in positions of authority to legitimize secrecy. Yet, while seduced into acquiescence, they simultaneously sensed that such rationales conflicted with other deeply held moral and value orientations. In truth the youth were torn between their sense of respect for group home staff and social workers and their loyalty towards friends and housemates.

It should be clear that secrecy of information results in a jealous hoarding of both information and the power that information brings to its recipients. Information in the agency becomes a currency. As currency information purchases enhanced status, a sense of authority, and a sense of being inside and in the know. Yet, the cost of these enhancements is a profound compromise, if not an antagonism, that invades not only relationships between youth, but the core sense of integrity and being of the youth themselves. In the segment outlined above, the youth in his expression of pain, tacitly acknowledged the compromised position that he had been put in. His pain arose from an attention to the moral landscape of action. This youth, along with other youth at the forum had a keen sense of the moral integrity of action that extended not just to others but to themselves.

Organizational Competence

All of these segments from the forum reveal a series of themes that bear further investigation. First, the segments underscore the difficulty that all children in care face when attempting to make sense of the organization that manages their daily lives. Although I have distinguished between youth in care as insiders and outsiders with regard to involvement in, or exclusion from the formally constituted bodies for youth in the agency, with regard to the dimensions of power and decision-making they are all outsiders. The operations of management in the agency remain not only closeted and secret from the youth, but often from the agency staff as well.

Children in care are denied access to accounting documents produced by organizations such as routine printouts of salaries, benefits, property rentals, taxes, mortgage rates, work orders, and so forth. In the absence of access to such information and the skills to 'read' these documents the best that children in care can do is to repeat what they have overheard or have been told by staff, who themselves may only grasp the generalities of organizational decision-making and action. Those youth who have access to staff accounts about the organization can at least claim some greater sense of authority over other youth in care.

The contributions of youth to the discussion during the forum are conditioned by their differential locations and relationships to the Children's Aid Society. Children who are outsiders draw on the stock in trade of common-sense everyday moral argument, rhetorical devices, and indisputable 'fact' — for example, the 'brand new cars, ah, Ford Escorts downstairs'. On the other hand, children who have a history of involvement in CAST and YAC are able to draw on complex background knowledge about the agency to develop, assess, and make sense of proposed strategies and responses to cut-backs. They employ this knowledge as an essential stock in trade for assessing what is possible, realistic, productive, desirable, and so forth. For a youth cognoscenti their vision, and their grasp of the possible is conditioned by their place inside the organization, and accordingly expresses organizational regulation of action as proper, warrantable, and sanctioned. Unfortunately, their appreciation of this knowledge provides them with such a strong sense of confidence and truth that they often failed to fully engage with the profound nature of challenges initiated by outsider participants. Thus, in the exchanges reviewed above it would seem that a youth cognoscenti are too quick to dismiss the claims and arguments made by the outsiders. Because they believe that they know the true story about agency operations they are too quick to respond to other's accounts as naive or wrong. As a result they unwittingly confine themselves to the inner logic and structure of the agency whose policies and decision-making they in fact seek to oppose.

All this raises the question not only of whether involvement in agency consultative processes coopts youth members, but how such cooption structures the range of actions youth might take in their own defence. Does involvement in the workings of the agency through CAST and YAC teach children and youth to recast their needs, projects, and goals into the forms provided by organizational and professional language, values, and orientations? Certainly, through involvement in CAST and YAC, some youth become a cognoscenti that can claim privileged knowledge about how things 'really are' against other youth whose moral stances are judged to be naive. The dilemma for youth involved with CAST and YAC is that their knowledge of agency discourses results in the generation of understandings that place them on the side of the agency against other youth in care.

Whilst the issues identified above would not be problematic if the interests of the agency and children and youth in care were identical, in a situation of cut-backs and elimination of services it becomes increasingly important that those affected by the cuts are able to develop and articulate strategies from the standpoint of their everyday lived experiences that are in fundamental opposition to the warranted logic, morality, and knowledge of the agency. Just as a child who is being abused in a family is encouraged to speak out and to expose his or her parent's acts to a CAS, children in care whose lives are being disrupted by the CAS must be able to not only speak out, but to act out against the agency that is in law and practice their parent. The development of effective resistance to agency cut-backs may very well require pursuit of courses of action that embarrass agency executives, oppose agency policies, and violate agency routines. The question is whether such actions can be developed inside the spaces and under the auspices of a formally constituted body such as CAST? It follows that youth in care need to recognize their own competencies, strengths, and compelling moral orientations when determining courses of action to protect their interests.

Conclusion

Perhaps children and youth in care are no different from other children and youth, however, what cannot be denied is that many have suffered extreme and recurrent losses over the brief courses of their lives. Many have lost parents to death, mental illness, disease, alcohol or drug addictions. Many are the victims of abuse whether physical, sexual, or emotional. Many children bear a strong sense of stigma and shame due to their victimization, due to their association with parents and family who were highly stigmatized, and due to their own experience of rejection. Despite such personal trauma youth in care demonstrate an enormous capacity to care for others, whether other children in care or group home staff and social workers. Throughout the forum youth were able not only to talk about this caring but to demonstrate their concern for others, through the consistent attention to turn taking, listening to others, and a genuine effort to respond to and understand each other.

This foundation of caring expresses deeply held moral orientations. Despite the allure of commodities in a consumer society, the power of money, and the seemingly inevitable drive to cut government costs, some children and youth in care are able to articulate a counter position which values people — the kids — over commodities — brand new cars. Unfortunately, although the youth believed in the priority of people over things, they generally expressed the belief that 'the society' and 'the government' cared more about saving money than about them. The youth felt that they were highly stigmatized, stereotyped as bad, and generally regarded as not worth any expense. Yet, even in this regard the youth struggle against the tension posed by stigmatization by engaging in a practice that recognizes that even if 'society' does not care for them, they must demonstrate their care for each other.

Notes

1   This account has been generated from stories told by youth participants in the Children's Aid Society Teen (CAST) group.

2   In the province of Ontario mandated child protection services are provided through a network of Children's Aid Societies. Children's Aid Societies are responsible for investigating reports of children in need of protection, apprehension, and placement, as well as a range of other family support services.

3   The phrase 'children in care' designates an extremely broad range of people. Children in care includes people of various ages and abilities, ranging from infants who cannot use language to express their understandings about being in care, to developmentally handicapped children who may have considerable difficulty speaking of their experiences in a manner that others might understand, to young adults of various natures and character who would speak of widely divergent experiences. Although throughout this chapter I will refer to children in care, all of the children who were interviewed, participated in the CAST group, or the forum were teenagers. I will use the term children and youth as substitutes. Second, the notion of being in care itself designates an extremely wide range of arrangements that includes everything from permanent adoption homes, foster homes, group homes, and a range of treatment facilities. Clearly if the decision of an agency is to close group homes to save money, children in those group homes will be more affected than children who are in long-term stable foster homes. Third, how are we to determine whether or not children are affected? Do we speak to social workers? Do we speak to the children themselves? Who is going to do the work of speaking to these people? How are the investigators located relative to the child welfare agency?

4   Garfinkel and Sacks (1988) outline that ethnomethodological studies when addressing 'formal structures' seek to describe members' accounts, 'wherever and by whomever they are done while abstaining from all judgments of their adequacy, value, importance, necessity, practicality, success or consequentiality. We refer to this procedural policy as ethnomethodological indifference' (p. 166). The argument this chapter makes is that there are substantial socially organized differences in location that structure and condition membership, and accordingly what are produced and become warrantable as adequate accounts. The point of difference appears to originate in the peculiar way that Garfinkel and Sacks define membership, as for them it does not refer to a person, but 'refers instead to mastery of natural language' (*ibid.*, p. 163). Yet, as I have argued, the language of professional and organizational discourses can hardly be characterized as a natural language (D. Smith, 1987 and 1990), as it is embedded in the extra-local, formalized, and objectified forms of power, authority, and regulation of an institutional apparatus, which is set over and against the forms of language and understanding produced in local and everyday situations.

5   Ethnomethodologists and conversation analysts generally understand that their work is 'not directed to formulating or arguing correctives' (Garfinkel, 1967, p. viii); or to 'solving problems as "constructively" specified' (Button, 1991, p. 7). Similarly, conversation analysts such as Psathas (1995) urge the adoption of a method he calls 'unmotivated looking' (p. 45). Of course, there has been considerable debate about what such terms and orientations might mean for sociology, with a resulting problematization of issues of the timing of indifference, the place of unmotivated looking as an initial strategy, and a critique of the narrow definition of ethnomethodological interest (Sharrock and Anderson, 1991, p. 62; Jayyusi, 1991, p. 247). Clearly the ability to provide an adequate review of this debate is outside the scope of this chapter; however, it remains necessary nevertheless to flag the tension and the debate, as conditioning the analysis and the topical choices that follow.

6   In addition to the eight youth on the Youth Advisory Committee there are an equal number of agency executives and supervisors of various departments. The YAC meets

once a month, and provides youth with an opportunity to express their views, understandings, and proposals to CAS managers, whilst allowing the agency to inform youth
of recent developments and policy changes.

References

Bologh, R.W. (1979) *Dialectical Phenomenology: Marx's Method*, London: Routledge and
Kegan Paul.
Button, G. (1991) 'Introduction: Ethnomethodology and the foundational respecification of
the human sciences', in Button, G. (ed.) *Ethnomethodology and the Human Sciences*,
Cambridge: Cambridge University Press.
Children's Aid Society of Ottawa Carleton (1995) *Annual Report/Rapport Annual*,
Ottawa, Ontario: CAS.
de Montigny, G. (1995) *Social Working: An Ethnography of Front-line Practice*, Toronto,
Ontario: University of Toronto Press.
de Montigny, G. (1996) 'Children's experiences of being in care: Writing and erasing
children's accounts', paper presented to the 13th Qualitative Analysis Conference: Study-
ing Social Life Ethnographically, McMaster University, Hamilton, Ontario, May.
Fine, G. and Sandstrom, K. (1988) *Knowing Children: Participant Observation with Minors*,
Newbury Park, CA: Sage Publications.
Garfinkel, H. (1967) *Studies in Ethnomethodology*, Englewood Cliffs, NJ: Prentice Hall.
Garfinkel, H. and Sacks, H. (1988) 'On formal structures of practical actions', in
Garfinkel, H. (ed.) *Ethnomethodological Studies of Work*, London: Routledge and
Kegan Paul.
Habermas, J. (1987) *The Theory of Communicative Action: Life World and System*, Boston,
MA: Beacon Press.
Jayyusi, L. (1991) 'Values and moral judgement: Communicative praxis as moral order', in
Button, G. (ed.) *Ethnomethodology and the Human Sciences*, Cambridge: Cambridge
University Press.
Psathas, G. (1995) *Conversation Analysis: The Study of Talk-in-Interaction*, Thousand
Oaks, CA: Sage.
Sharrock, W. and Anderson, B. (1991) 'Epistemology: Professional scepticism', in
Button, G. (ed.) *Ethnomethodology and the Human Sciences*, Cambridge: Cambridge
University Press.
Smith, D.E. (1987) *The Everyday World as Problematic: A Feminist Sociology*, Toronto,
Ontario: University of Toronto Press.
Smith, D.E. (1990) *Texts, Facts, and Femininity: Exploring the Relations of Ruling*, London:
Routledge.
Smith, G. (1990) 'Political activist as ethnographer', *Social Problems*, **37** pp. 629–48.
Smith, G. (1995) 'Assessing treatments: Managing the AIDS epidemic in Ontario', in
Campbell, M. and Manicom, A. (eds) *Knowledge, Experience, and Ruling Relations:
Studies in the Social Organization of Knowledge*, Toronto, Ontario: University of Toronto
Press.

Chapter 11

The Case of the Silent Child: Advice-giving and Advice-reception in Parent–Teacher Interviews

David Silverman, Carolyn Baker and Jayne Keogh

In this chapter, we are interested in children's common silence in parent–teacher interviews. As we show, this silence often occurs even when they are expressly nominated to take next-turn (for instance by a question aimed at them).

Instead of treating this silence as indicating some deficiency on the part of the child, we argue that, faced with the ambivalence built into such questions and comments by teachers (and parents), silence can be treated as a display of inter-actional competence. This is because silence (or at least lack of verbal response) allows children to avoid implication in the collaboratively accomplished adult moral universe and thus, as is shown in other chapters in this book, enables them to resist the way in which an institutional discourse serves to frame and constrain their social competencies.

As we later show, children's silence often follows adult turns which have a strong 'advice' component. To put our data into context, we begin, therefore, by reviewing the literature on institutional advice-giving and reception.

Advice-giving and Advice-reception

In a service encounter, Jefferson and Lee (1981) argue, 'an advice-seeker properly receives and accepts advice' (p. 421). However, what counts as 'proper' reception and acceptance of advice has been shown to vary. For instance, Heritage and Sefi (1992) find that much advice given by health visitors to first-time mothers receives only lukewarm unmarked acknowledgments, indicating no preparedness to follow the advice. Moreover, Silverman (1996) shows that advice from AIDS counsellors can, in certain environments, be actively resisted. But both studies find that clients routinely attend to the need to preserve social solidarity, by marking their pre-ference for agreement and consistently offering some sort of response (if only a continuer).

The most striking feature of a number of our teacher-parent interviews is that advice is routinely and non-problematically *non-receipted by its target*. The follow-ing examples involve Donna (S), her parents (F and M) and her teacher (T). In

Extracts 1 and 2 there are no audible responses from Donna or Donna's parents to a piece of advice from the teacher (arrows indicate turn-slots where it seems receipts are absent):

Extract 1
```
T:  that's the only way I can really (1.0) really help at the
    moment and (.) for Donna herself to um do a little bit more
    in class and not chat so much down the back with Nicky and
    (.) Joanne?
->  (1.0)
T:  um (2.0)
```

Extract 2
```
T:  Or we maybe, if- our next unit of work, Donna? if it's (.)
    another group do you think you- you'd perform better not
    working with the same girls?
->  (1.0)
T:  work with a different, with someone different in the class?
->  (2.0)
T:  you'd prefer to work with the same girls
```

In Extract 3 below, Donna's father eventually responds after a pause in a turn-slot in which Donna might have spoken:

Extract 3
```
T:  I- don't- know it's really the three of you got to pull up
    your socks sort of thing or (.) or you sit somewhere
    different but
->                (2.0)
T:  [(    )
F:  [I think you should sit somewhere different
```

Finally, in Extract 4, Donna does not respond to her father's advice:

Extract 4
```
F:  I think you should sit somewhere different
M:  Mm?
F:  well think of your marks it's just (4.0) it's pretty
    rubbishy
```

The absence of (spoken) responses by students to their teacher's or parents' advice in Extracts 1–4 gives us the puzzle with which this chapter will be concerned. Not only does it appear to be out of line with what we know about professional-client interaction but it does not fit with what we know about 'ordinary' conversation where the absence of a response by someone selected for next turn is remarkable and accountable (Sacks, Schegloff and Jefferson, 1974). To try to solve this puzzle, we have searched other data for comparable findings.

In over 60 advice sequences in pre-HIV test counselling, we have only one example of such a silent response to advice. This is shown below [C=counsellor, P=patient]:

Extract 5 [Silverman 1996:118]
```
C:  this is why we say hh if you don't know the person that
    you're with (0.6) and you're going to have sex with them hh
    it's important that you tell them to (0.3) use a condom
->  (0.8)
C:  or to practice safe sex that's what using a condom means.
->  (1.5)
C:  okay?
    (0.3)
P:  uhum
    (0.4)
C:  has your pa:rtner ever used a condom with you?
```

Notice the 1.5 second pause. Since this follows a possible turn-completion point as C concludes her advice, the pause can be heard as P's pause. Moreover, C demonstrates that she monitors it this way by going in pursuit of some response-token ('okay?') to indicate that, at least, P is listening. When, after a further pause, she obtains the continuer 'uhum', C can now continue.

However, it is also worth noting C's explanation (or gloss) on her phrase 'use a condom'. Since that phrase could also have been heard as terminating C's advice, she seems to have inspected the 0.8 second pause that follows as representing an absent continuer and, therefore, a possible lack of understanding. So she provides her gloss in order, unsuccessfully as it turns out, to create a stronger environment in which to get a continuer.

Extract 5 shares one further similarity with the teacher–pupil advice sequences. Here the patient is a 16-year-old person — by far the youngest of all the clients in our HIV counselling extracts.

On a non-analytic level, what we seem to be dealing with here is the social problem well-known to both professionals and parents — namely, the common non-response of adolescents when told what to do by adults (or even when asked questions).

This social problem is seen massively in hospital clinics run for adolescents and evokes continual, unsuccessful attempts to get the child to speak (see Silverman, 1987). In Extracts 6–8 below, taken from such clinics, we also find non-response to advice [D=doctor, P=patient and M=mother]:

Extract 6 [Diabetic clinic 1 (NH:17.7)]
```
D:  What should we do about your diabetes? Because you've not
    been doing your testing
    (untimed pause)
D:  I know at the moment you're feeling sod all this altogether
P:  Don't know
```

D: Would it help if we got off your back?
    (untimed pause)

Extract 7 [Diabetic clinic 2 (S:12.2)]
D: The blood sugar is really too high
    (untimed pause) [P is looking miserable]
M: We have to fight this all the way
D: One or two units, does this really upset you?
    (untimed pause) [P is looking down and fiddling with her
    coat]

Extract 8 [Cleft-palate clinic (14.32-3)]
D: Um (2.0) but you're satisfied with your lip, are you, we
    don't want anything done to that?
M: She doesn't (1.0) it doesn't seem to worry her
D: Heh heh don't want anything done about any[thing?
M: [heh heh
D: Not your nose?
    (3.0)

Throughout Extracts 5–8, adolescents fail to respond in the next-turn position to advice and questions. In Extracts 5 and 6, they eventually offer a minimal response after a second prompt. By contrast, in Extracts 7 and 8, when these young patients fail to take a turn when nominated as next speaker, their mothers speak for them, offering a commentary on their child's behaviour or feelings. Finally, in Extract 8, when D once more renominates the patient as next speaker, nothing is heard.

Explaining Children's Silence

If this chapter were simply to stop at the observation of a congruence between professional-client encounters involving young people in both medical and educational settings, it would only be restating a social problem well known to parents and professionals dealing with young people.

We work on the assumption that the skills of social scientists arise precisely in their ability to look at the world afresh and hence hold out the possibility of offering insights to practitioners. The question is, then, how can we move from our commonplace observation to a social science analysis?

One familiar solution is to look *behind* our data in order to find explanations for our observation. To this end, we might note various features of the apparent contexts in which communication is taking place here. For instance, we might expect that advice-giving is more problematic in those service encounters, like health visiting, HIV-test counselling and diabetic and cleft-palate clinics where the professional's advice is not necessarily sought by the client and where the professional's role is mainly that of gate-keeping (offering a blood test, supplies of insulin or cosmetic surgery).

By contrast, when parents attend interviews with teachers, they may be expected to be advice-seekers and any gate-keeping aspect of the encounter is difficult
to detect. However, there is nothing to suggest that the students at such interviews
are there because they are themselves seeking advice or even information. Therefore if the student rather than the parent is treated as the client, then these school
interviews fall into line with the other settings where reluctant advice-recipients are
common. If the student is constituted as the client, parent–teacher interviews are
like health visiting, HIV counselling and consultations with adolescent diabetics
where advice has not been sought by the client. Indeed, like the adolescent diabetic
and the first-time mother, the student may hear a disciplinary intent behind the
'advice'.

This suggests another explanation of advice non-recipiency. A common feature of both teacher–parent and paediatric interviews, although not found in most
pre-test counselling, is that there are potentially multiple clients.[1] Therefore, we
might speculate that one party (namely, a parent) might non-problematically claim
the right to speak on behalf of another party (the student or patient). This allows
parents to talk instead of the child and children to remain silent (after all, their
parents can respond, as in Extracts 7 and 8). In this way, by working as a hearable
'team' (Goffman, 1961), the rules of turn-taking are maintained.

However, the danger is that we become so obsessed with finding an *explana-*
tion of some phenomenon that we fail to investigate adequately whether there is,
indeed, such a phenomenon and, if so, how it is locally 'put together'. This danger
has been characterized as the problem of 'relevance' and 'procedural consequentiality' by Schegloff (1991) and as the 'explanatory orthodoxy' by Silverman (1996,
pp. 23–6).

Our initial response is to shift the focus away from explaining our observation
towards locating its interactional achievement. Thus we ask: how is advice-giving
and advice-reception interactionally managed, turn by turn, where the ostensible
advice-recipient is apparently non-responsive? Rather than this being an obscure
question of purely analytic interest, we will demonstrate how it can feed directly
into policy debates through closer analysis of the turn-by-turn organization through
which advice-uptake can be maximized in apparently unfavourable environments.[2]

In the analysis that follows, we focus on three relevant issues:

(i) How is the potential advice-recipient actually constructed? Multi-client
settings are seen less as a constraint on interaction and more as something all parties can play with.

(ii) How is the format of the advice actually constructed? Are there forms
of advice-giving which make non-recipiency less problematic to stable
communication?

(iii) How is advice-giving and advice-reception organized in such a way as
to display particular identities of the participants? As we shall see, the
moral adequacy and special knowledgeability of the (adult) parties are
matters to which they collaboratively attend.

Constructing the Advice Recipient

In multi-party professional-client settings, the recipient of a particular turn is not given by some institutional rule but is actively 'worked at' by the participants. Extract 8 is a very nice example of this:

```
Extract 8 [Cleft-palate clinic (14.32-3)]
D:  Um (2.0) but you're satisfied with your lip, are you, we
    don't want anything done to that?
M:  She doesn't (1.0) it doesn't seem to worry her
D:  Heh heh don't want anything done about any[thing?
M:                                           [heh heh
D:  Not your nose?
    (3.0)
```

As we have already remarked, notice that, in the first turn here, D appears to nominate as next speaker someone who might appropriately make an assessment about their 'lip'. However, although next speaker orients to this nomination (talking about 'she' and 'her' rather than 'I' and 'me'), she is not the next speaker so nominated. Moreover, when D appears to renominate M's daughter as next speaker in the following turns, although she is silent, M claims recipiency via her laughter at line 5.

Extract 8 shows that recipiency is constructed on a turn-by-turn basis. Moreover, even within a single turn, the recipient may be redefined. Notice, for instance, how D switches from the voice of 'you' to 'we' within line 1.

We would argue that such a switch is interactionally ambiguous. First, 'we' may be heard as no more than the patronizing way of referring to organizational clients quite common in England (and, sometimes, the object of a sarcastic response, for example, 'me and who else?'). Second, in this local context, it creates the possibility that D's question about 'lip-satisfaction' is addressed to both or either mother and daughter. Indeed, it may be this very possibility that allows a parent to respond without a pause (in line 3) in a slot in which the child might have been expected to answer a question.

Extract 8, from a cleft-palate clinic, shows how the parties play with the ambiguity about who is the recipient of a particular question. Such ambiguity also arises in Extract 9, taken from the beginning of a parent–teacher interview:

```
Extract 9
T:  hh right um Donna um I just took over Mister Jay's class um
    four weeks ago so, I don't really know a lot about Donna's
    work I've had a quick look at her work in her folder, and
    from her marks she um, you seem to have, passed in the
    first part of the year
```

In the first line, T's 'right um Donna' is ambiguous. It could be either a Summons–Answer (S–A) device (Schegloff, 1968) or a statement of first topic. If the first, there is no verbal response from Donna, although there could be a shift in Donna's gaze towards T. However, the ambiguity is removed at lines 2–3: 'I don't really know a lot about Donna's work', where the reference in the third person constitutes Donna as the topic rather than as the addressee. Yet later, T's repair (line 4) 'and from her marks she um, you seem to have, passed' reinstates the ambiguity (from 'her' to 'she' to 'you').

Normative theories of communication may treat such ambiguity as a 'problem'. Our response is quite different. We focus on the interactional skills of participants and ask instead: what are the *functions* of how parties organize their talk?[3] How is such ambiguity usable by participants as an interactional resource?

We start to see these functions by looking at a later extract where the addressee is quite unambiguous. In Extract 10 below, T firmly names her pupil as Donna or 'her' in the course of a question:

Extract 10

```
T:  do you work with Donna at home with her schoolwork at all?
    do you see it at all or?
F:  Not really no=
```

By naming her pupil, T makes clear that her question is aimed at her parents rather than Donna (and it is heard as such). We could follow this up by making a mental experiment where we imagine that the whole teacher–parent interview followed this pattern. The problem that this might create could be that, while the ostensible goal of such interviews is to deliver information to parents, it may be problematic to ignore the presence of the student as an overhearing audience. Indeed, we are familiar with criticism of people being spoken about in their presence (hence the attack on what is sometimes called the 'third person absent' voice).

We see the power of this popular criticism in the way in which, in the context of family quarrels, parties may be heard to be 'deliberately' using this 'third person absent' voice. Ambiguity of addressee may thus have the function precisely of attending to the overhearing audiences. In this way, ambiguity may be seen as an interactional resource rather than necessarily a 'problem' for participants.

As in Extract 9, the same issue of the audience recurs later. Although Extract 11 below begins with a question not addressed to Donna, T immediately reconstitutes Donna as the addressee:

Extract 11

```
M:  Maybe (if she was in a different group) they might push
    her harder [(and that)
T:               [Or we maybe if- (.) um our next unit of work-
    Donna? if it's (.) another group do you think you- you'd
    perform better not working with the same girls?
    (1.0)
T:  work with a different, with someone different in the class?
    (2.0)
T:  you'd prefer to work with the same girls.
F:  Yeah but will you work with them or will you just play up
    or what?
```

```
S:  (      )
T:  Mm
M:  (What if they didn't work, like if they were just talking)
S:  (      )
```

Notice how both T and F and M reconstitute Donna as the addressee. For T, this shift from responding to M's suggestion, to asking a question aimed at Donna, is a nice way of reasserting T's control over the turn-taking. However, F and M show that parents can play the same game by following it up with their own questions aimed at Donna.

Remember that the professional–client exchanges in these settings are occurring in the context of an 'overhearing audience' (Heritage, 1985). Who this audience is and who is instead the recipient (and, more generally, the client) is something that all parties work at.

Another clear instance of one of the participants claiming a client position is found in Extract 12 below. This extract is at the beginning of a teacher–parent interview involving the student Barry, who is present:

Extract 12
```
T:  Right now Barry (2.0) how did you go can I have a look at
    that?
M:  Not real good actually [we're not really happy with it
T:                         [NO
    (3.0)
T:  I think Barry he's had a lot of activity
M:  Mm
T:  With his um, er rap dance
```

The teacher's opening, 'right now Barry', is again ambiguous as to whether Barry is addressee or topic. 'Right now Barry', as in other professional encounters, constructs Barry as one of a series of students the teacher is talking about that evening. The teacher's 'how did you go' (line 1) appears on the surface to nominate Barry as the recipient of the question. However, Mother answers, and further states her interests in being the client with the statement 'we're not really happy with it' (line 3). This 'we' might involve Barry, or might refer to Mother and (absent) Father. In any case, Barry remains silent.

Later in the interview, throughout which the Mother has spoken for and about Barry, the teacher readdresses Barry about the need to keep up his school grades regardless of his outside school activities:

Extract 13
```
T:  Um Barry (1.0) er to build up your grades (1.0) because er
    you'll find it a lot (.) a lot easier to, just, to get
    auditions [as you say
M:            [Yeah
T:  That's that's what you gotta do first=
```

```
M:  =Yeah
T:  er that that's er the next er thing in line (.) if you
    haven't got the grades you won't even make the auditions
    stage at this (.) at this stage
    (2.0)
T:  I suppose although I I'm not talking about outside things,
    you don't [need school
M:            [No
T:  But if you want to do it [in this class
M:                           [Within a class situation, yeah
```

In this sequence, Mother both receives the advice on Barry's behalf and backs up the teacher's advice given to Barry. One upshot of this is that she is filtering the teacher's advice to Barry such that Barry does not (need to) acknowledge receipt of it himself.

Through this work of claiming and/or deciding recipiency of advice, particular functions are obtained. These include the following achievements in the talk:

- the location of a client who has wishes which take priority over the wishes of other interested parties;
- the location of the rights of such interested parties to be heard;
- the recognition that parties who are constituted as an overhearing audience nonetheless are not ignored, nor are they spoken about as 'third person absent'; in these cases, they are 'third person present'; and
- the maintenance of a moral order in which all parties' wishes, rights and moral probity are continuously reaffirmed.

How the Format of Advice-giving Provides for Non-recipiency

So far we have been looking at how advice-reception is organized in the kind of multi-party settings that are typical of professional-client interaction targeted at children. However, advice-giving can be fraught with interactional difficulties whatever the setting (Silverman, 1996, pp. 134–81).

First, advice-giving is particularly sensitive to the categories and descriptions employed in any turn at talk. For instance, if an HIV counsellor advises me 'to be sure to have safer sex in future', the implication may be that I have not been having safer sex in the past.

The second problem, which is peculiar to advice-giving, is that it requires strong uptake from its recipient if the advice-giving is going to persist over many turns. For instance, imagine this sequence:

```
A:  You really must change your life
B:  hmm
```

In this invented example, we take it that A will hear B's 'hmm' as indicating possible resistance to the advice. The absence of clear uptake markers (like 'oh really' or 'I think you're right' or 'how do you mean?') implies that A will now have to search for more uptake from B or abandon the advice. Although we cannot know whether B will actually follow the advice afterwards, the talk itself is strongly implicative of B's resistance to the advice offered (see Heritage and Sefi, 1992).

Earlier research suggests that advice-reception is strongly tied to how the advice is organized. As Jefferson and Lee (1981) argue:

> acceptance or rejection may be in great part an interactional matter, produced by reference to the current talk, more or less independent of intention to use it, or actual subsequent use. (p. 408)

With Jefferson and Lee's argument in mind let us now inspect a rather long extract from a teacher-parent interview.

Extract 14 (Extract 1 extended)
```
1  T: This novel in another form (6.0) I don't know (1.0) I
2     think (.) the only way I can really (.) what I can really
3     suggest at this stage is that (.) she does do, um (1.0)
4     draft copies and give them to me, and if I think (.)
5     obviously her- her standard of english is okay because she
6     isn't (.) corrected everywhere but the ideas if they need
7     improvement I can help her in that way, and say look this
8     isn't really uh you're not really getting you're not really
9     understanding it here? and try and look at it again,
10    that's, that's the only way I can really (1.0) really help
11    at the moment and (.) for Donna herself to um do a little
12    bit more in class and not chat so much down the back with
13    Nicky and Joanne?
14    (1.0)
15 T: um (2.0) just showing you the work that has to be done(.)
      for the rest of the ye:ar
```

As in Extracts 1–4, the lack of uptake of T's advice (seen here at line 14) is remarkable. Equally remarkable is that this non-uptake does not cause a break down in communication; T simply resumes her turn, remodelling her advice towards what Donna's parents can do.

Our earlier discussion suggests one possible explanation for the non-accounted absence of uptake. First, as suggested in the previous section, ambiguity in the audience for the advice may allow non-uptake to be heard as lack of clarity about who should properly respond and hence to indicate uncertainty rather than non-recipiency. In Extract 14, however, at first glance, no such ambiguity seems to exist. T stays in the third person mode when referring to Donna herself, moving between 'she', 'her' and 'Donna'.

However, at line 11, T's advice terminates with a reference to Donna's own actions for which she as well as her parents are responsible. In this way, a nice ambiguity has been established about the appropriate recipient of the advice. Even though Donna has not earlier been framed as the addressee of T's turn, it will be Donna, after all, who can properly respond to any advice to 'not chat so much down at the back with Nicky and Joanne?'.[4]

In a sense, then, for different reasons, *both* Donna and her parents may be heard as the appropriate recipients of T's advice. Given this ambiguity about recipiency, the absence of response at line 14 is hearable simply as uncertainty about who is the appropriate recipient. Hence T can recommence her turn without any apparent difficulty.

If the audience is ambiguous, the absence of response can be heard as related to confusion about who should reply rather than to non-uptake of the advice. Hence ambiguity about the audience, just like ambiguity over the format (advice or information) handles otherwise problematic (non-) responses. Teachers and other professionals can play with the ambiguity about audience and addressee and thus protect themselves against non-response from any one of the possible clients in the setting. This kind of ambiguity is unavailable where there is only a single client. We can see this if we return to Extract 5, taken from HIV-test pre-counselling:

Extract 5 [Silverman 1996:118]
```
C:    this is why we say hh if you don't know the person that
      you're with (0.6) and you're going to have sex with them hh
      it's important that you tell them to (0.3) use a condom
->    (0.8)
C:    or to practice safe sex that's what using a condom means.
->    (1.5)
C:    okay?
      (0.3)
P:    uhum
      (0.4)
C:    has your pa:rtner ever used a condom with you?
```

We noted earlier the two slots where P might have acknowledged C's advice about condoms (both marked ->). We also pointed out that C seems to monitor this absence as implying something remarkable, eventually going in search of a response ('okay?'). In the absence of other clients (for example, P's parents), C appears to have no alternative but to take P's non-response as indicating non-recipiency.

However, even in the absence of an overhearing audience, advice-givers can play with other potential ambiguities about how their advice is to be heard. In Extract 5, notice how C prefaces her advice (line 4) by 'this is why we say'. Silverman (1996) has suggested that this way of formatting advice creates ambiguity about whether what follows is indeed 'advice' or information about the kind of advice given in this clinic (pp. 154–81). This ambiguity allows Cs to cope with mere response tokens (unmarked acknowledgments) from Ps to advice. The evident problems for C here arise because, as we have noted, P fails even to produce such a response token.

So far, we have identified two ambiguities in how advice may be constructed. One involves the assumed recipient of the advice. The other concerns the status of the advice. However, it would be wrong to assume that each ambiguity is specific to a particular environment, like the presence or absence of an overhearing audience.

First, in a sense, the ambiguity (information or advice) identified in Extract 5 is also ambiguity about the audience/addressee. For information can be heard as for anyone, while advice in face-to-face communication is heard as personalized. The ambiguity surrounding 'information as advice' or 'advice as information' can be used by any of the parties to acknowledge impersonal information rather than personalized advice.

Second, if we return to Extract 14, we may note other ambiguities than the advice-recipient. We can identify these if we just return to the first few lines of this extract:

Extract 14
```
1 T: This novel in another form (6.0) I don't know (1.0) I
2    think the only way I can really (.) what I can really
3    suggest at this stage
```

Note how T produces her advice in an environment of hesitancy through pauses, repairs and a preface of 'I don't know' (line 1) At the very least, this serves to downgrade what she is saying from 'advice' to a set of provisional suggestions. But additionally, her hesitancy makes it possible for her clients to interpret T's later pauses not as turn-transition points but as further hesitancy prior to a recommencement of T's turn. Hence her clients' non-response need not indicate non-recipiency but its opposite — carefully waiting until present speaker has completed her turn.

Moreover, T's 'what I can really suggest' (lines 2–3) may be hearable as a kind of memo for T's future action and hence able to be eventually receipted (via response-tokens) simply as information (but not advice) about what can be done. Thus I may be heard as working to the defensive advice-as-information sequence that is clearly employed in Extract 5.

Later on, T returns to the same kind of defensive strategies. Extract 15 below arises after a discussion about the 'groups' that Donna is working with. It is followed by an eight second pause immediately before the extract begins. This pause allows T to change both topic and format to general observations about 'happiness' and group work.

Extract 15
```
1  T: Ye:s, yes well, you've gotta be happy °haven't you° if you
2     do it with some one you don't want to then you'll feel um
3     (1.0) resentful and don't put an effort in (2.0) well, yes,
4     all I can suggest is, um (2.0) I don't know what to do
5     about, I mean it really depends how (1.0) um see everyone
6     has to do it and how she she copes in front of a situ-,
7     unless you act at home (hh) get up in front of the family
8     (hh) and do some heh
9  S: No but I [(    )
10 T:          [(hh) and do some practice
11 F: Yeah, we can give her some lessons
```

Note how T's two 'yous' in the first line are ambiguous — are they addressed to people in general or just Donna? Eventually T appears to reach a piece of advice (lines 7–10) but note how, as in Extract 14, this advice is considerably downgraded ('all I can suggest' 'I don't know what to do' and 'unless') and that the audience for the advice is ambiguous, moving from 'you' to 'she' followed by 'you' (lines 6–7).

This ambiguity is reflected in the fact that *both* Donna and F respond in turn. In this local environment, Donna's 'no but I (   )' (line 9) is itself ambiguous (is it resistance to advice or resistance to the premise upon which the advice is being given?). In any event, as T completes her advice, F comes in with a marked acknowledgment ('Yeah, we can give her some lessons' line 11) based on a claim to be the addressee of the advice.

F's turn is followed by a four second pause. Extract 15 continues below with T reconstituting Donna as her addressee (the 'you' of line 1). T now gives a piece of advice (lines 1–2) which receives absolutely no uptake during the two second slot (line 2):

Extract 16 [continuation of Extract 15]
```
1 T: No, but if you, if you're doing it in front of the family
2    maybe picture it, picture the class (2.0) and if you've
3    done it a few times, then when you're getting up in front
4    of the class, it's more familiar
5 M: (When is it)?
6 T: It's um (2.0) the twenty-fifth of August
7 F: And if you're sure of your subject you won't be nervous
     anyway because you know you've got more confidence
```

Despite the absence of verbal uptake, as in earlier similar extracts from parent–teacher interviews, the talk proceeds unproblematically. Once again, this non-uptake is made to appear less remarkable by T's downgrades on her advice ('maybe', line 2). We saw similar downgrades by the teacher earlier in this interview 'all I can suggest' 'I don't know what to do' and 'unless' (Extract 15).

T now elaborates her advice (lines 2–4) and Donna's parents now pile in, first with M's question (line 5) and then with F's own elaboration of T's advice (lines 7–8). As in Extracts 7–8, a mother claims the right to constitute herself as the advice-recipient and maintain the advice-format by a marked acknowledgment (the question 'when is it?'). This acknowledgment produces a topic shift, a side-sequence that could derail the advice-giving. But now, in lines 7–8, F elaborates T's advice and thus retargets Donna as its recipient.

As we shall see in the next section, both parents are engaged in important moral work which establishes them as the teacher's potential ally in the context of their special access to (and responsibility for) the object of T's advice (who is not just a 'student' but also a 'daughter').

Extract 16 shows a parent elaborating a teacher's advice. But, in these interviews, parents are sometimes even more proactive, with the teacher becoming overhearing audience to a display of parental advice. Extract 17, below, begins with F offering his own piece of advice to D:

Extract 17 [Extract 4 extended]
```
1 F: I think you should sit somewhere different
2 M: Mm?
3    (2.0)
4 F: Well, think of your marks it's just (4.0) it's pretty
5    rubbishy
6 T: mm so: (2.0) mm I, er, yeah, is there any? is there any
7    other way I can help you at all?
```

Notice how M offers a response-token (line 2) to F's advice to Donna despite not being the addressee. It as if M is marking her co-presence as a member of the parent 'team' and also underlining F's advice as a team production.[5]

Despite this jointly produced advice-sequence, there is no turn by Donna in the two second slot on line 3. It seems that parents are no more successful than professionals in obtaining even minimal receipts of advice.

Now F retrieves the hiatus created by the noticeable absence of response, offering grounds for the advice given by both teacher and parents. But note that, since Donna is being advised to 'think' about something (line 4), the absence of a turn from her now is no longer accountable. Instead, T simply takes next turn to do agreement and then switch topic. So the whole thing has worked despite the absence of any advice-uptake from the ostensible advice recipient.

In this section, we have reviewed the various strategies that participants use to cope with both potential and real non-recipiency to advice. Moreover, in the face of a challenge to the normal expectations about turn-taking and advice-reception, we have demonstrated how social solidarity is reasserted by the cooperative work of parents and teachers.

Moral Work

The analysis so far has largely focused on how parents and professionals collaborate to ensure that advice-sequences work non-problematically (that is, that they are produced and completed) despite children's recurrent non-response. We now want to address directly a topic so far only touched upon. Namely, how both sides establish a shared moral universe in which each party has special knowledgeability and responsibility and does the markedly 'right' thing within each area.

Extracts already used from paediatric clinics show mothers engage in such moral work. For instance:

Extract 7 abbreviated (Diabetic clinic 2]
```
D:  The blood sugar is really too high
    (untimed pause) [P is looking miserable]
M:  We have to fight this all the way
```

As we observed, when this young patient fails to take a turn after what is hearable as a piece of information addressed to her, her mother takes a turn. M's comment serves two functions:

- showing that D's information is something that she should monitor; and
- rebutting a possible charge against her mothering skills (see Silverman, 1987, Chapter 10), i.e. that she didn't advise her daughter to take the actions which might have stopped this problem with blood sugar — thus constituting herself as the doctor's ally in this matter.

In the cleft-palate clinic example, a mother claims the right to voice her daughter's wishes:

Extract 8 abbreviated [Cleft-palate clinic]
```
D:  Um (2.0) but you're satisfied with your lip, are you, we
    don't want anything done to that?
M:  She doesn't (1.0) it doesn't seem to worry her
D:  Heh heh don't want anything done about any[thing?
M:                                            [heh heh
```

Here M shows her special knowledgeability (line 3) and, through her overlapping laughter (line 5) constitutes herself as the doctor's ally in a world in which adults might be surprised that someone turned down an offer that is designed to 'improve' their appearance.

In interviews with teachers, parents, as well as doctors, also receipt information and advice actively in ways that display their moral adequacy and special knowledgeability. As we saw in Extract 15, parents can establish themselves as the teacher's ally.

Extract 15 [abbreviated]
```
T:  unless you act at home
    (hh) get up in front of the family (hh) and do some heh
S:  No but I [(    )
T:           [hh and do some practice
F:  Yeah, we can give her some lessons
```

F's marked acknowledgment ('Yeah, we can give her some lessons') is based on a claim to be a part of the family 'team' and hence situates F as just as much an addressee of T's advice as S. Once he is in, F collaborates with T's version of the moral universe in which parents do these sorts of things for their children.

In Extract 18 below, F also figures centrally. T is in the middle of a long piece of information aimed at Donna's parents. Compared to Donna's earlier silence, notice the active and cooperative character of F's turns:

Extract 18
```
1  T: we're going to write a front page story (.) and what will
2     happen is Mister Kay the Principal comes into the
```

```
3      classroom, he gives a talk, and then the students have to
4      write it up as a news article=
5  F: =Oh I see
6  T: All right? a- um, so we in the next week (1.0) are going
7      to practice writing front page stories, now, um (1.0) if
8      you want to check you know her, what she's doing at home
9      (.) with that? and you could read it through? And um, and
10     I'll (.) have a look at how she's going but when it comes
11     down to it it's an exam it's not a, an assignment (.) so
12     really it's um (.)
13 F: uh hu it's important that she does it right
14 T: Yes that's right, she gets the, she has to have um some
      short sentences, um all the information in the first
      paragraph,
```

In Extract 18, F provides a newsworthiness token ('oh I see') at line 5, a marker of very active recipiency (Heritage and Sefi, 1992). Now T continues with a turn (lines 6–12) which establishes the adult parties as partners in a joint project to improve Donna's schoolwork.

Later, F completes T's proposal by 'uh hu it's important that she does it right' (line 13) which orients to T's reference to 'an exam' (on line 11). Hence F is establishing his credentials as a concerned parent. Notice, however, that T, in her next turn ('Yes um that's right'), warrants the content of F's utterance thereby reestablishing the claims of the professional to do an evaluation (Mehan, 1979).

Extract 18 shows how the adult parties establish themselves as partners in a joint enterprise based on a division of labour where each side defers to the other's competence and knowledge even as they assert their own.

The work of displaying moral adequacy/knowledgeability and of managing advice-reception is thus cooperatively done. Together, parents and professionals produce a world of no charges/no blame. Part of this activity involves both professionals and parents in routinely abstaining from utterances that might seem to make a moral charge against the other.

Thus, in the settings discussed here, professionals display expressive caution in delivering advice, providing information or even asking questions which might imply that parents were anything other than morally adequate and knowledgeable in relation to family matters. As Strong (1979) remarked, in a study of Scottish paediatric clinics, 'politeness is all' is the rule when doctors communicate with parents. In an extreme example, Strong notes how one mother who evidently was grossly over-feeding her baby was nonetheless not overtly criticized (in her presence).

However, information can be just as delicate a matter as advice. Using our data on teacher–parent interviews, Baker and Keogh (1995) have shown how teachers attend to the 'delicacy' of delivering bad news or results to parents. In the parent–teacher interviews, almost anything said could be made out to be morally implicative, since parenting practices are by implication part of the connection teachers make between home and school. Parents are present because they are there to hear how their child is doing, how problems could have arisen, and how any problems can be solved. If their presence is meant to be part of any problem-solution, then their presence conveys the possibility that home practices (for which they claim to be/are made responsible) could be part of any problem.

For example:

Extract 19 [Extract 12 extended]

```
1  T: Right now Barry (2.0) how did you go can I have a look at
2     that?
3  M: Not real good actually [we're not really happy with it
4  T:                        [No
5     (3.0)
6  T: I think Barry he's had a lot of activity
7  M: Mm
8  T: With his um, er rap dance=
9  M: =Yeah, yeah
10 T: The rock eisteddfod
11 M: He's had the rock eisteddfod and he's had ((theatre
12    company)), yeah I know, that's all finished now
13 T: Yeah, but that's good, I mean I don't think there's
14    anything wrong with that and I think it might um perhaps,
15    had something to do, perhaps, with his results
16 M: Yeah
```

In this opening exchange of the interview, the bad news on Barry's report card is made the first accountable matter. It is the mother who announces it as bad news, and after a three-second pause (line 5), it is the teacher who first nominates a reason.

Now the teacher begins a list of Barry's out of school activities, a list whose production the mother stops with 'that's all finished now' (line 12). This is heard by the teacher as the mother's recognition that this has indeed been Barry's problem. But notice the extreme delicacy with which the teacher restores the mother to competent parenthood and the tentativeness of her attribution of Barry's schoolwork problems to his activities (lines 13–15).

This expressive caution extends to delivering advice. As we have already seen, Donna's teacher offers her advice in a very hesitating manner. Extract 20, which follows information on Donna's recent poor run of marks, is an interesting case in point:

Extract 20

```
T: would you like to- do you work with Donna at home with
   her schoolwork at all? do you see it at all or?
```

Notice here how T seems about to offer some (downgraded) advice to Donna's parents ('Would you like to') but then repairs into some questions. From these questions, we might guess that the aborted advice had something to do with checking

Donna's schoolwork. However, such advice might imply that Donna's parents do not already do this. Hence it is more cautious to inquire first.

However, any conversational gambit inevitably has a debit, as well as a credit, side. T's first question might imply a moral charge ('do you work with Donna at home with her homework'). Without giving the family a chance to answer, T continues with another question which gives them an excuse should they have to answer in the negative ('do you see it at all or').

This cautiousness of professionals is shown nicely in Extract 21 below taken from a diabetic clinic. In this clinic, patients are given 'testing books' to keep the results of their urine and blood tests and D is looking at such a book as the extract starts:

Extract 21 (Diabetic clinic 1)
```
D:  Alan these (figures) look too good to be true. Is that
    right, Alan?
P:  No
F:  What he means is have you been making them up?
    (long pause, followed by further turn from D)
```

When the family is not present, the physician and health visitor who run this clinic openly speak about the likelihood that many of their patients lie about their testing figures. D's utterance here is the closest that he comes to making such a charge in the presence of the patient and his family. But note that, even here, D does not directly charge Alan with lying.

It is left to Alan's father to make the charge explicit. By doing so, he reaffirms the adult moral universe. First, he shows that, as a parent, he knows what his son might not understand. Second, he exhibits his responsibility to make sure that the family 'team' is telling the 'true' story. Third, in doing so, he casts himself as the physician's ally in the task of maintaining Alan's health.

So, in Extract 21, Alan's father exemplifies the metaphor 'sometimes it is necessary to be cruel to be kind'. In doing so, he shows that he is a responsible parent, willing to ask awkward questions of his son when his son's health is at stake.

Conclusion: Settings, Speakers and Silences

Differences Between Settings

In contrast to our paediatric clinics where both professional and parent orient towards the child as the client, in our school interviews, parents routinely are constructed or construct themselves as the client (addressee). In addition, while visits to the paediatric clinics take place because there actually is a problem, parent–teacher interviews take place because they are part of the school's programme. That is, some of the attending students will be doing very well, and the interviews are essentially courtesy visits. In these no-problem cases, parents and teachers may agree to agree that all is well, although no student is ever perfect, and improvement is always possible (Baker and Keogh, 1995).

Here, unlike the diabetic clinics, the professional (a teacher not a doctor) puts considerable work into displaying her moral adequacy/knowledgeability. In the case of the interview with Donna's parents, one of T's apparent concerns is to deflect an available charge that she doesn't seem to know much about Donna's work. (This may also be found in public health clinics where doctors are interchangeable.)

Unlike the clinical visits, the parent–teacher interviews are conducted by teachers and parents each of whom has continuing knowledge about the student. While the possibility of a parent knowing much about clinical practice is slim, parents can know a great deal second-hand about what teachers do in class. Thus the possibility exists that parents can question school practices as much as teachers can question home practices. In some of our parent–teacher interviews, this happens (*ibid.*).

In these interviews, parents and teachers model their utterances to defer to the special competencies that each presumably possesses (as knowledgeable about, respectively, the home and the educational requirements of the school). This adds a little to the expectations of preference organization (Pomerantz, 1984): not only are 'agreements' generally preferred, they are particularly preferred when all parties have special claims to knowledgeability. Hence the expressive caution in delivering anything that could turn out to be criticism.

The Work of Keeping Quiet

In the case of the school interviews, the student is witness to the work of both parents and teachers in describing their and each other's competence and moral adequacy as parents and teachers. In witnessing the agreement of the parents and teachers regarding what can be done to improve performance, the student is deemed to be a theoretic actor (McHugh, 1970) who is ultimately responsible for carrying out whatever the agreed course of action is. This means that the student's silences (unlike the silence of, say, an infant) are heard as theoretic choices.

This implies that it is possible also to consider the non-responses of young people in these settings as accomplishments in their own right. To the extent that speaking at all is potentially morally implicative, as we have shown it to be where parents talk with clinicians and teachers, not speaking is an interactive possibility for the young person (perhaps more than it is for any of the other participants).

Further, in that agreement is preferred, and agreement is mostly about what the young person should do more of or do differently, by not saying anything the young person is not necessarily agreeing to resolutions either. One cannot be held accountable for what one did not say more than one can be held accountable for what one was supposed to hear. To enter into the problem-definition or resolution in an active way would align the young person with his or her elders possibly against other young people.[6]

The young person's silence, then, can be seen as a form of interactive work in relation to the design of the talk between parent and professional. By no means is the silent child not a competent child.

Notes

1 An exception is where AIDS counsellors, often using methods derived from 'Family Therapy', encourage clients to attend with their partners (see Peräkylä, 1995).

2 This is discussed, in the context of the delivery of advice after a problem has been elicited from a patient, by Heritage and Sefi (1992) and Silverman (1996, pp. 115–8).

3 Of course, every interactional gambit has both a credit and debit side. This means that we should attempt to identify the interactional *dysfunctions*, as well as functions, of gambits like 'ambiguity'.

4 Our assertion relates to McHugh's (1970) account of 'theoreticity'. As a teenager, we may assume that Donna is framed as a 'theoretic' actor able to make her own choices. Consequently, in regard to the kind of practical actions that T is recommending here, Donna's parents would only be given the right to support (or oppose) what T is advising. It will be up to Donna herself to *implement* the advice — if she chooses. Hence Donna is, implicitly, the addressee of the advice.

5 This has strong parallels with how non-addressees in family therapy respond to talk by others about their own experience by claiming ownership through response-tokens and the organization of gaze (see Peräkylä, 1995, pp. 103–43).

6 To show how speaking can implicate the student, consider the contrasting case of one student, Christa (C), who, in a parent-teacher interview, entered into conversation and advice-giving herself:

(Segment 9.1: Ellen/Christa/Mother)
```
T:  So anyway you're going to have to, maybe practice a little
    at home or something and you're going to have to steel
    yourself for this one (1.0) so that's, out of this semester
    you've got two orals so you've got that, that's an SA
    already, that's, if can get a high on tha:t, try not just
    to say I'm going to get an SA for this, you might surprise
    yourself you know?
C:  I have to get into a different group of people (    )
    maybe=
M:  Maybe yes
T:  Why not? Is there someone [else you like?
M:                           [What about some of those other
    girls you did the radio play with [(   ) them
C:                                     [No hh
T:  Yeah, 'cos that really affects you too, if they've got no
    enthusiasm and you do all the work again, you've had all
    the ideas you're exhausted you've run out of steam when it
    comes to performing. Is there anyone else that you get on
    with in that class?
C   Daniel? (hh)
T   Well at least Daniel's got a little bit of get up and go
    he may act all right
C   Yeah, he'll do stuff=
T   =Yeah
```

C: and um like, Julie and Melissa and Katie they're all sort
of fairly rough but (1.0) at least they do things (hh)

References

BAKER, C. and KEOGH, J. (1995) 'Accounting for achievement in parent–teacher interviews', *Human Studies*, **18**, pp. 263–300.

GOFFMAN, E. (1961) *Asylums*, New York: Doubleday.

HERITAGE, J. (1985) 'Analyzing news interviews: Aspects of the production of talk for an overhearing audience', in VAN DIJK, T.A. (ed.) *Handbook of Discourse Analysis, Vol. 3*, London: Academic Press.

HERITAGE, J. and SEFI, S. (1992) 'Dilemmas of advice: Aspects of the delivery and reception of advice in interactions between health visitors and first-time mothers', in DREW, P. and HERITAGE, J. (eds) *Talk at Work: Interaction in Institutional Settings*, Cambridge: Cambridge University Press.

JEFFERSON, G. and LEE, J.R.E. (1981) 'The rejection of advice: Managing the problematic convergence of a "troubles-telling" and a "service encounter" ', *Journal of Pragmatics*, **5**, pp. 399–412.

McHUGH, P. (1970) 'A common-sense perception of deviance', in DREITZEL, H.P. (ed.) *Recent Sociology No 2: Patterns of Communicative Behaviour*, London: Macmillan.

MEHAN, H. (1979) *Learning Lessons: Social Organisation in the Classroom*, Cambridge, MA: Harvard University Press.

PERÄKYLÄ, A. (1995) *AIDS Counselling*, Cambridge: Cambridge University Press.

POMERANTZ, A. (1984) 'Agreeing and disagreeing with assessments', in ATKINSON, J.M. and HERITAGE, J. (eds) *Structures of Social Action: Studies in Conversation Analysis*, Cambridge: Cambridge University Press.

SACKS, H., SCHEGLOFF, E.A. and JEFFERSON, G. (1974) 'A simplest systematics for the organization of turn-taking for conversation', *Language*, **50**, pp. 696–735.

SCHEGLOFF, E.A. (1968) 'Sequencing in conversational openings', *American Anthropologist*, **70**, pp. 1075–95.

SCHEGLOFF, E.A. (1991) 'Reflections on talk and social structure', in BODER, D. and ZIMMERMAN, D.H. (eds) *Talk and Social Structure: Studies in Ethnomethodology and Conversation Analysis*, Cambridge: Polity Press.

SILVERMAN, D. (1987) *Communication and Medical Practice: Social Relations in the Clinic*, London: Sage.

SILVERMAN, D. (1994) 'Analyzing naturally-occurring data on AIDS counselling: Some methodological and practical issues', in BOULTON, M. (ed.) *Challenge and Innovation: Methodological Advances in Social Research on HIV/AIDS*, London: Falmer Press.

SILVERMAN, D. (1996) *Discourses of Counselling: HIV Counselling as Social Interaction*, London: Sage.

STRONG, P.M. (1979) *The Ceremonial Order of the Clinic: Parents, Doctors and Medical Bureaucracies*, London: Routledge and Kegan Paul.

List of Contributors

Leena Alanen is a Lecturer in the Department of Education, University of Jyväskayä, Finland.

Carolyn Baker is an Associate Professor in the Graduate School of Education, University of Queensland, Brisbane, Australia.

Rachel Baker is a Lecturer in the Department of Anthropology, University of Durham, UK.

Helen Barrett is a Lecturer in the Department of Psychology, Birkbeck College, University of London, UK.

Pia Haudrup Christensen is a Research Fellow in the Department of Sociology and Anthropology, University of Hull, UK.

Susan Danby is a Lecturer in the School of Early Childhood, Queensland University of Technology, Brisbane, Australia.

Gerald de Montigny is an Associate Professor of Social Work, Carleton University, Ottawa, Canada.

Kurt E. Freeman is a Doctoral Student in the Department of Communication, University at Albany, SUNY, USA.

Hilary Gardner received her Doctorate in Linguistics from the University of York, UK.

Ian Hutchby is a Lecturer in the Department of Human Sciences, Brunel University, UK.

Allison James is a Senior Lecturer in the Department of Sociology and Anthropology, University of Hull, UK.

Jayne Keogh is a Doctoral Student in the Faculty of Education, Griffith University, Brisbane, Australia.

Jo Moran-Ellis is a Lecturer in the Department of Sociology, University of Surrey, Guildford, UK.

Robert E. Sanders is Professor of Communication, University at Albany, SUNY, USA.

David Silverman is Professor of Sociology, Goldsmiths College, University of London, UK.

Joanna Thornborrow is a Senior Lecturer in the Programme in English Language and Linguistics, Roehampton Institute, London, UK.

Index

Schieffelin, B., 46, 135
School settings, 20–1, 60, 157–83, 187–8, 190–5, 220–39
Sheldon, A., 18, 169
Silence, 220–39
Smith, D., 32
Smith, G., 206
Socialization, 8–10, 46–7, 51, 135, 188–9
Sociolinguistics, 19–20, 134–6
Standpoint, 30–5 (*see also* Feminism)
Strange Situation procedure, 74–5
Street children, 46–62
Strong, P.M., 235
Structuration, 30, 31

Tarplee, C., 121, 122
Teachers
    and interventions, 157–83
    in teacher-parent interviews, 220–39
Therborn, G., 30–2
Thompson, J.B., 23n
Thorne, B., 9
Tripp, D., 137, 152n

Vormbrock, J., 73

Walkerdine, V., 18, 181, 182
Weiss, R., 37
Why Don't You?, 138, 149–51